THE ART
OF GEORGE ELIOT

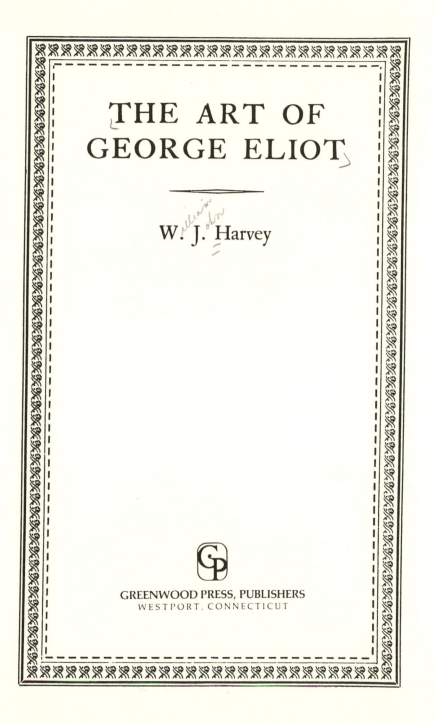

THE ART OF
GEORGE ELIOT

W. J. Harvey

GREENWOOD PRESS, PUBLISHERS
WESTPORT, CONNECTICUT

Library of Congress Cataloging in Publication Data

Harvey, William John, 1925-1967.
    The art of George Eliot.

    Reprint of the 1969 ed. published by Chatto & Windus,
London.
    Bibliography: p.
    Includes index.
    1. Eliot, George, pseud., i.e. Marian Evans, after-
wards Cross, 1819-1880--Criticism and interpretation.
I. Title.
[PR4688.H28 1978]   823'.8   78-786
ISBN 0-313-20267-2

Reprinted with the permission of Chatto & Windus Ltd.

Reprinted in 1978 by Greenwood Press, Inc.
51 Riverside Avenue, Westport, CT. 06880

Printed in the United States of America

10 9 8 7 6 5 4 3 2 1

To my Wife

Contents

✳

Acknowledgments

Grateful thanks for permission to quote extracts are due to the following:

Messrs Methuen & Co. Ltd. for *The Wheel of Fire* by Wilson Knight; Messrs Rupert Hart-Davis Ltd. for *The Psychological Novel* by Leon Edel; the Syndics of the University Press Cambridge for *George Eliot* by Joan Bennett; The Athlone Press for *The Novels of George Eliot* by Barbara Hardy; Messrs Chatto & Windus Ltd. for *D. H. Lawrence, The Common Pursuit* and *The Great Tradition* by F. R. Leavis; John Farquharson Ltd. on behalf of the Estate of the late Henry James for quotations from the works of Henry James; the Editors of *Essays on Criticism* for 'The New and the Newer Critics' (Vol. 5) by John Holloway and 'Banquo and Edgar; Character or Function' (Vol. 7) by L. Kirschbaum; the Editors of *Modern Language Quarterly* for 'The Architecture of George Eliot's Novels' (Vol. 9) by Walter Naumann; the University of California Press and the Editors of *Nineteenth Century Fiction* for 'A Preface to *Middlemarch*' (Vol. 9) by F. G. Steiner and 'Structure and Imagery in Adam Bede' (Vol. 10) by M. Hussey; the Editors of *The Kenyon Review* for 'Fiction and the Analogical Matrix' (Vol. 11) by M. Schorer; the Editors of *The Sewanee Review* for 'Spatial Form in the Modern Novel' (Vol. 53) by J. Frank; Messrs Charles Scribner's Sons for *The Writing of Fiction* (1925) by Edith Wharton; and Messrs Rinehart & Co. for *The English Novel: Form and Function*, copyright 1953, by Dorothy Van Ghent; the Yale University Press and Professor Gordon S. Haight for quotations from Professor Haight's edition of *The Letters of George Eliot*.

Introduction

In his book on D. H. Lawrence, Dr Leavis writes that 'learning to recognize the success and the greatness of *Women In Love*—I speak for myself—was not merely a matter of applying one's mind in repeated re-readings and so mastering the methods of the art and the nature of the organization; it was a matter, too, of growing—growing into understanding'. It is doubtful whether very much criticism exists which can vitally help one's growth into understanding, private and prolonged as such a process must be. Certainly the present book has no such ambition; it aims more moderately at the study of 'the methods of the art and the nature of the organization'. Its title, therefore, is deliberate, though cast in a conventional form. Despite the enthusiasm of some of her late-Victorian admirers, George Eliot has little in common with Shakespeare; but she has this much, at least—that like Shakespeare she has for too long been regarded as a 'natural' genius, deficient in art, her distinctive talent hampered by outworn conventions. This book seeks to redress the balance by stressing the formal characteristics of her work.

For this reason I have not followed the fashionable practice of devoting a chapter to each of her novels but have attempted instead a general study. This has its disadvantages —looking back, I see that I have sadly neglected *Silas Marner*—but it does allow the essential points to be made in a fairly logical order and it does avoid a good deal of repetition. It has also allowed me an easier transition from the study of a particular work to some relevant point of general critical theory, from which we may return—I hope with greater understanding—to the work again.

Indeed, some readers may think that I have taken too great an advantage of this and that the book tends to fall between two stools. My defence must shape itself on two different levels. On the lowest level I have been careful to cite and discuss the findings of other critics since I must substantiate my general thesis that much modern criticism has essentially misconceived the nature of George Eliot's achievement. We all know the dangers of the type of book in which the author is more concerned with other critics than he is with any actual work of art—and yet if criticism is to advance at all, it must surely be by way of discussion and disagreement.

On another level my excursions into critical theory proved to be necessary because I found that George Eliot was not alone in being misunderstood; what I have to say in my opening chapter is also largely true of most Victorian novelists. We stand, I believe, on the brink of a great leap forward in our understanding and appreciation of Victorian fiction; we must, therefore, be all the more sure of our present foothold. One way forward is by way of historical understanding; we should be able to see more clearly the aims, methods, concerns and conventions of the Victorian novelists in their historical context and to see how they differ from those distinctive strategies of modern fiction which have so preoccupied modern critics. The way in which literary history may serve the interests of criticism is well exemplified by a book like Mrs Tillotson's *Novels of the Eighteen Forties*. But historical understanding, while it may anatomize more clearly the various *kinds* of fiction, cannot estimate their quality. That is the critic's concern, and the refined tools of modern criticism offer at once both great opportunities and great dangers. Our concern with symbolism, for instance, has discovered for us a new dimension in Dickens; but we must be careful not to replace the merely comic, sentimental, melodramatic or social reformist Dickens by the merely symbolic Dickens. So with George Eliot; we need to discover first the kind of fiction she wrote and then adapt our critical methods—sharpened on quite other kinds of fiction—to her distinctive achievement. This book is intended primarily to assist such a process; to point out where we have gone wrong in the past may well be to take the first step in the right direction.

Since this book is both a study of George Eliot and a survey of recent tendencies in the criticism of fiction, my debts must be many and varied. I hope I have acknowledged the more definite of them in my notes and bibliography. But I must thank in particular F. R. Leavis and John Holloway for the stimulus of disagreement, and also Barbara Hardy for the academic 'shop' we have exhanged. Mrs Hardy's book was published too late for me to take advantage of it, but I did profit from her articles on George Eliot. I have referred to these in my notes, but listed her book only in the bibliography. We discussed our work together in order to prevent any overlapping in our books; we have reached much the same conclusion but, I think, by different routes. All students of George Eliot are deeply indebted to Professor Gordon S. Haight.

Parts of this book were published in a different form in *Anglia* and in *Nineteenth Century Fiction*. I must thank my colleagues at Keele for help which they can hardly be aware of having given. Since this book derives directly from my teaching I must thank the scores of undergraduates with whom I have read and discussed George Eliot; Mr Dion Webb in particular will recognize how much I have benefited from one of his suggestions. Finally I must thank my wife, who has endured the irritabilities of academic labour, who scrutinized the manuscript with a philosophic eye and who, more than once, has rescued it from the all too practical criticism of my children.

University College of North Staffordshire.   W. J. H.

CHAPTER I

George Eliot and the Criticism of Fiction

IDO not wish to attempt even a brief history of the critical reputation of George Eliot's novels; that has been done, ably and exhaustively, in its proper place elsewhere.[1] I intend rather to discuss in this chapter those factors in the modern criticism of fiction which may distort a proper reading of her work. Criticism of fiction is of so recent origin, is still so innocent of generally accepted terms and has to deal on so many levels with such a multitudinous and confusing subject-matter that it is not surprising to find an absence of method or even of clear thought about general principles. By and large, such criticism has been based on analogies with other arts—with painting, sculpture and architecture (Henry James), or with music (E. M. Forster); such analogies may often be enlightening but are always dangerous. More recently E. M. W. Tillyard has argued in his study of *The Epic Strain In The English Novel* for an assimilation of the novel to other traditional kinds of literature. I agree that a doctrine of kinds is a desirable and necessary part of our critical equipment, but I think such a notion should operate *within* the novel rather than by imposing on fiction criteria relevant to altogether different modes of literature. Dr Tillyard's book seems to me evidence of the dangers of this latter procedure; he is always at his best when ranging furthest from his conceptual categories, and the poverty which results when he tries to apply the idea of epic to the novel—how little good fiction actually filters through the term—is significant. It would be disastrous if we followed Dr Tillyard's method to its logical extremes;

---

[1] In two unpublished Ph.D. theses on 'The Literary Reputation Of George Eliot'; one by J. D. Barry (Evanston, Illinois, 1955) and one by R. J. Owens (Liverpool, 1958).

what, one wonders, would result from the application to fiction by some academic Polonius of a 'tragical-comical-historical-pastoral' mode?

A less radical but more fruitful attempt at such assimilation has been made between the novel and poetic drama. (If Bradley tended sometimes to see Shakespearian tragedy as a novel manqué we have reversed the position; Dr Leavis's essays, for example, were originally published in *Scrutiny* under the symptomatic title of *The Novel as Dramatic Poem*.) Indeed, the tremendous advances made in Shakespearian criticism during the last thirty years seem to me one of the major factors determining the course and scope of fictional criticism. Some of these—for example, the interest in image-patterns or the change in the concept of character—are discussed later in relevant chapters; what I wish to stress here is that this advance on the Shakespearian sector is part of a general critical transformation which may hold out tempting but dangerous promises to the critic of fiction, promises of analytical precision and finality. We can see something of these dangers if we examine the fate of Henry James.

I shall discuss James in detail later in this chapter; it is sufficient to say here that it is from his precepts and practice that modern criticism of the novel has received its main bias. It is clear that the practice of James represents a considerable technical advance—or at least, complication—over that of his predecessors and that his precepts are mainly rationalizations of his particular creative interests, techniques and strategies. His collected prefaces may fairly be called the *Poetics* of the novel, and he shares with Aristotle the fate that his observation of particulars and subsequent rationalization have been transmuted by his commentators and disciples into general and normative principles. His insistence on dramatic representation, point of view, elimination of the author—all this and much more has undergone a subtle critical change into something like dogma, while his characteristic techniques have been frequently considered as in some way inherently better than the conventions and strategies of earlier novelists.

Clearly there are many interacting reasons for this critical shift; the one I wish to isolate here for particular emphasis lies within the critical process itself. Let us for the moment view the novel—as James so often does—as a little world, a fictional microcosm created by the novelist which we may compare with the factual macrocosm, the world we conveniently label 'real life' and too easily assume as a given and fixed datum in our criticism of fiction. The fictional microcosm has its own nature, its own natural laws and we can criticize it as obeying or disobeying these, as achieving or failing to achieve internal coherence and consistency. These natural laws are created within each novel, are peculiar to it alone and need not be referred to 'real life'. A work which is not in any usual sense, realistic—*Alice in Wonderland, The Waves, As I Lay Dying*—will still have and still obey its own laws. The demonstration of these natural laws of fiction— the relationship of this part to that, the functions of this image-pattern, the importance of that parallel or contrast, and so on—is in fact the main substance of critical analysis. It is a main object of the present study. Baffled generally by its inability to scrutinize the language of fiction with the same intensity that it devotes to poetry, criticism is distinctively occupied with the tracing out of patterns, themes, imaginative structures. Done very well, this is, of course, valuable and necessary and it is something difficult to do very well. But it is *not* difficult to do reasonably well. It is certainly much easier than that strenuous confrontation of microcosm and macrocosm which we may call moral criticism and which is exemplified in the work, say, of Dr Leavis. This is surely a fact of academic life that any university teacher will endorse. An intelligent student will confidently outline, let us say, the nature and structural importance of imagery drawn from music in the novels of E. M. Forster where he will lack the maturity to estimate the quality of experience residing in those novels. The dead-end and rat's alley of this approach is that stereotyped, mechanical and jargon-ridden type of analysis which has sometimes brought the name of criticism into disrepute.

Ideally these two critical procedures—the analytic and the moral—should not be divorced. But we must face the sad fact that they generally are, unpropitious though such a separation is to the health of criticism as a whole. On the one hand, unless the moral critic is aware of all that analysis can achieve, his criteria will tend to be drawn in the case of the novel from crude or naïve ideas about 'real characters' or 'truth to life'. But it is the opposite danger which is more important at present, the danger that the analyst will think that his procedures provide in themselves sufficient criteria for judgment. Certainly, and this is another aspect of the same problem, the analyst tends to stress the autonomy of the fictional world and to resent any manifest connection between it and the real world. (The omniscient author is the most obvious and—to such a critic—most obnoxious of such connections.) The fact that the post-Jamesian novel has involved unprecedented technical experiment gives added strength to such a critic, since technical complication gives him a better chance to exercise his analytical skills. The satisfaction he derives from such exercise may easily lead him into errors of judgment.

Even without this technical revolution, criticism of the novel would undoubtedly have been transformed in the twentieth century which, as I say, has seen great advances all along the critical front. But if poets like Pound and Eliot gave direction to the criticism of poetry, then equally the criticism of fiction has been largely determined by modern creative experiment. It is significant that apart from academics nearly all the important modern critics of fiction have been, on a greater or lesser scale, creative writers; apart from James, one thinks of Edith Wharton, D. H. Lawrence, E. M. Forster, Virginia Woolf—even Percy Lubbock, whose popularization of James had such a tremendous influence, had a tenuous and minor but genuine creative talent.

Naturally the academic critic could not but be influenced by such examples; indeed, one feels that today the wheel has come full circle and that the novels of, say, Mark Schorer are written directly out of a critical position which he elaborated in his academic role. Critical theory, then, is peculiarly adapted to contemporary practice and critical principles tend to work better with modern rather than with traditional examples. Yet seen in the long perspective of the history of fiction, the surge of twentieth-century technical experiment must appear as a special case, as something of a freak. The critical weapons we have subsequently evolved are ill adapted to deal with more than a few of the great traditional novelists.

This revolution in practice and theory must be seen as beginning with Henry James. Scholarship may blur the distinctions, may point out precedents for nearly every one of his innovations, but when all is said and done he marked the watershed. And the essential nature of this revolution is fumblingly foreshadowed by James in his early article on *The Novels of George Eliot*. He has been criticizing, acutely, the end of *Adam Bede*, in particular the marriage of Adam and Dinah which he thinks too arbitrary and explicit. Instead, at the most, he would have liked the reader left with the suggestion that such a marriage was possible:

> The assurance of this possibility is what I should have desired the author to place the sympathetic reader at a standpoint to deduce for himself. In every novel the work is divided between the writer and the reader, but the writer makes the reader very much as he makes the characters. When he makes him ill, that is, makes him indifferent, he does no work; the writer does all. When he makes him well, that is, makes him interested, then the reader does quite half the labour. In making such a deduction as I have just indicated, the reader would be doing but his share of the task; the grand point is to get him to make it. I hold that there is a way. It is perhaps a secret; but until it is found out, I think that the art

B

of storytelling cannot be said to have approached per-
fection.

Of the changing relation of reader to novel I shall say
more in a later chapter; it is here enough to point out that
from it derived all those aspects of James's theory and practice which had been so heavily stressed by later critics—the
passion for dramatic representation, point of view, the elimination of the omniscient author, all the various strategies of
indirection and obliquity. It is worth noting that these find
their freest play in the later novels of James, those written in
the 1890's and after. It is hard not to feel that this stress has
been misplaced or at least exaggerated. Even here James is
more traditional than is generally recognized, even here the
technique of omniscience is more important than is usually
thought. And one cannot but feel that in these later novels
there is a growing disproportion between what is said and
the elaborate means of saying it, that technique proliferates
in a thinning human atmosphere and that James's conventions, pushed to their extremes, result in precisely the same
awkwardness that in a different form has been felt so strongly
in the traditional novelists. As Mrs Wharton remarks of
The Golden Bowl:

> The same attempt to wrest dramatic forms to the uses
> of the novel that caused *The Awkward Age* to be written
> in dialogue seems to have suggested the creation of
> Colonel and Mrs Assingham as a sort of Greek chorus to
> the tragedy of *The Golden Bowl*. This insufferable and
> incredible couple spend their days in espionage and dela-
> tion, and the evenings in exchanging the reports of their
> eaves'-dropping with a minuteness and precision worthy
> of Scotland Yard. The utter improbability of such conduct
> on the part of a dull-witted and frivolous couple in the
> rush of London society shows that the author created
> them for the sole purpose of revealing details which he
> could not otherwise communicate without lapsing into
> the character of the mid-Victorian novelist chatting with
> his reader of 'my heroine' in the manner of Thackeray and

Dickens. Convention for convention (and both are bad), James's is perhaps even more unsettling to the reader's confidence than the old-fashioned intrusion of the author among his puppets.[2]

Certainly in what is for me James's great creative decade, 1880-90, which sees the publication of *The Portrait Of A Lady, The Bostonians, The Princess Casamassima* and *The Tragic Muse*, he is much more like George Eliot than like any modern novelist. It is surprising how firmly the intervening hand of the omniscient author guides and directs the progress of *The Portrait Of A Lady* in the manner just described by Mrs Wharton.

' "Tell me what they do in America," pursued Madame Merle, who, it must be observed parenthetically, did not deliver herself all at once of these reflexions, which are presented in a cluster for the convenience of the reader. . . . I am bound to confess, though it may cast some discredit on the sketch I have given of the youthful loyalty practised by our heroine toward this accomplished woman, that Isabel had said nothing whatever to her about Lord Warburton. . . . While this sufficiently intimate colloquy (prolonged for some time after we cease to follow it) went forward. . . .' These are just a few examples of the dominant narrative convention of the novel; of course, where James differs crucially from George Eliot is the fact that he does not use omniscience for moral comment or generalization. My main point, however, is that a critical temper which can find greater interest in *The Ambassadors, The Wings of The Dove* and *The Golden Bowl* rather than in the novels of the 1880's is more likely to do serious injustice to a pre-Jamesian novelist like George Eliot.

Some facts are necessary at this point to place James firmly in historical relation to George Eliot. He wrote in all ten essays or reviews about her; of these, five are important for our present purpose. They are a review of *Felix Holt (The*

[2] Edith Wharton, *The Writing of Fiction*, pp. 90-91. London: Charles Scribner's Sons, 1925.

Nation, 1866), an article on *The Novels of George Eliot*
(*Atlantic Monthly*, 1866); a review of *Middlemarch* (*The
Galaxy*, 1873); *Daniel Deronda*; *A Conversation* (*The Nation*,
1876) and a review of Cross's *Life* (*Atlantic Monthly*, 1885).[3]
Thus they span a great deal of his creative and critical life
and we can trace his opinions changing and developing from
the undergraduate smartness and cocksureness of the early
Felix Holt review to the mature and grave survey of the *Life*
review. James was 23 when he first wrote about George
Eliot and he had only recently started reviewing and pub-
lishing sketches and short stories in magazines; his first
novel, *Roderick Hudson*, was not published until 1875; only
the last item in the list postdates the publication of his
seminal essay, *The Art of Fiction*, in *Longman's Magazine* for
September 1884. Although these essays and reviews are only
groping towards the critical position elaborated in the
Prefaces, they do nevertheless at every stage reveal his own
developing creative interests.

They reveal them most clearly in a rather peculiar way.
James once wrote, 'To criticize is to appreciate, to appropriate, to take intellectual possession, to establish in fine a
relation with the criticized thing and make it one's own.'
For James, to whom as the *Notebooks* reveal, even the slightest
hint of a story was enough to start his imagination working,
we can interpret this remark in a limited and special way;
there is indeed a particular sense in which he makes the
criticized thing his own. At several points in his reviews we
can see the frustrated artist behind the critic, longing to
correct flaws and to rewrite the story according to his own
conceptions.* There is a hint of this in the criticism of the
ending of *Adam Bede* which I have already quoted; we can
glimpse it again in his conversation piece about *Daniel
Deronda*. For James, Gwendolen Harleth is clearly the centre
of the novel and clearly he would have wished all else to be
subordinated to her; had he written *Daniel Deronda* she

---

[3] For full details see the note on Henry James in the bibliography.
* See p. 246.

would have been to the novel what Isabel Archer is to *The Portrait Of A Lady*. Indeed, Constantius conjectures at one point in the dialogue:

> The irony of the situation, for poor Gwendolen, is almost grotesque, and it makes one wonder whether the whole heavy structure of the Jewish question in the story was not built up by the author for the express purpose of giving its proper force to this particular stroke.

We may agree that Gwendolen is the most living thing in *Daniel Deronda*, but to view the novel in these terms is to distort the whole of its structure. The clearest example of the artist-critic at work, however, is to be found in James's criticism of the ending of *The Mill On The Floss* (*The Novels of George Eliot*):

> As it stands, the dénouement shocks the reader most painfully. Nothing has prepared him for it; the story does not move towards it; it casts no shadow before it. Did such a dénouement lie within the author's intentions from the first, or was it a tardy expedient for the solution of Maggie's difficulties? This question the reader asks himself, but of course he asks it in vain. For my part, although, as long as humanity is subject to floods and earthquakes, I have no objection to see them made use of in novels, I would in this particular case have infinitely preferred that Maggie should be left to her own devices. I understand the author's scruples, and to a certain degree, I respect them. A lonely spinsterhood seemed a dismal consummation of her generous life; and yet, as the author conceives, it was unlikely that she would return to Stephen Guest. I respect Maggie profoundly, but nevertheless I ask, Was this after all so unlikely? I will not try to answer the question. But one thing is certain; a dénouement by which Maggie should have called Stephen back would have had far more in its favour than can be put to confusion by a mere exclamation of horror.

James was in many ways baffled by the kind of achievement represented in George Eliot's novels. For this reason the dialogue of *Daniel Deronda*; *A Conversation*, distributed between the enthusiastic Theodora, the hostile Pulcheria and the judicial (and rather infuriatingly superior) Constantius, is a precise formal index of James's own mixed feelings. He is often acute—for instance in his diagnosis of the aesthetic weakness of Dorothea—sometimes astonishingly wrong, as in his opinion that Bulstrode is a superfluous failure. Some of his major judgments are difficult to follow even on the basis of his own critical remarks. We can take as a fair example his opinion of *Romola*. In his essay on *The Novels of George Eliot* he calls *Romola*:

> the most important of George Eliot's works . . . not the most entertaining nor the most readable, but the one in which the largest things are attempted and grasped . . . the book strikes one less as a work of art than as a work of morals.

After this backhanded compliment he goes on in his review of *Middlemarch* to maintain that:

> *Romola* sins by excess of analysis; there is too much description and too little drama; too much reflection (all certainly of a highly imaginative sort) and too little creation. Movement lingers in the sory, and with it attention stands still in the reader.

Finally, in his review of Cross's *Life* he writes:

> It was in *Romola*, precisely, that the equilibrium I spoke of just now was lost, and that reflection began to weigh down the scale. *Romola* is pre-eminently a study of the human conscience in an historical setting which is studied almost as much . . . . More than any of her novels it was evolved, as I have said, from her moral consciousness—a moral consciousness enriched by a prodigious amount of literary research. Her literary ideal was at all times of the highest, but in the preparation of *Romola* it placed her under a control absolutely religious. She read innumerable books, some of them bearing only remotely on her subject, and consulted without stint contemporary records

and documents. She neglected nothing that would enable her to live, intellectually, in the period she had undertaken to describe. We know, for the most part, I think, the result. *Romola* is on the whole the finest thing she wrote but its defects are almost on the scale of its beauties. The great defect is that except in the person of Tito Melema, it does not seem positively to live. It is overladen with learning, it smells of the lamp, it tastes just perceptibly of pedantry. In spite of its want of blood, however, it assuredly will survive in men's remembrances, for the finest pages in it belong to the finest part of our literature. It is on the whole a failure, but such a failure as only a great talent can produce; and one may say of it that there are many great 'hits' far less interesting than such a mistake. A twentieth part of the erudition would have sufficed, would have given us the feeling and colour of the time, if there had been more of the breath of the Florentine streets, more of the faculty of optical evocation, a greater saturation of the senses with the elements of the adorable little city. The difficulty with the book, for the most part, is that it is not Italian; it has always seemed to me the most Germanic of the author's productions.

One must agree with the general drift of James's observations; this is what makes his general judgment that '*Romola* is on the whole the finest thing she wrote' all the more surprising and isolated. Contrast that judgment with the other, made only a few lines later, that *Romola* 'is on the whole a failure' and the discrepancy between his initial critical perceptions and his final verdict becomes still more obvious. There may be some nuance of meaning, some subtle discrimination which has not been fully worked out, but I doubt it; these passages reflect a mind in doubt, a tension unresolved between recognition of substantial merits and awareness of great defects, an inability to make a final critical placing of the subject under discussion. James has intermittently appreciated but he has not, in any sustained manner, appropriated George Eliot.

This local indecision is a minor result of a problem that

always confronted James, a problem we may for convenience crudely call the issue of 'form' versus 'life'. What James means by form is most succinctly summed up when he writes of Flaubert. We do not read *Madame Bovary*, he says, because of its subject matter; it does not deal

> with things exalted or refined; it only confers on its sufficiently vulgar elements of exhibition a final unsurpassable form. The form is in *itself* as interesting, as active, as much of the essence of the subject as the idea, and yet so close is its fit and so inseparable its life that we catch it at no moment on any errand of its own. That verily is to *be* interesting—all round; that is to be genuine and whole. The work is a classic because the thing, such as it is, is ideally *done*, and because it shows that in such doing eternal beauty may dwell.[4]

Opposed to this kind of achievement are those 'loose, baggy monsters' he treated with a mixture of fascination, admiration, annoyance, bewilderment and repulsion. The supreme example of this category is *War and Peace*, and comparing Tolstoy with his beloved Turgenev, he writes:

> Turgenieff is in a peculiar degree what I may call the novelist's novelist—an artistic influence extraordinarily valuable and ineradicably established. The perusal of Tolstoy—a wonderful mass of life—is an immense event, a kind of splendid accident, for each of us; his name represents nevertheless no such eternal spell of method, no such quiet irresistibility of presentation, as shines close to us and lighting our possible steps, in that of his precursor. Tolstoy is a reflector as vast as a natural lake; a monster harnessed to his great subject—all human life! —as an elephant might be harnessed, for purposes of traction, not to a carriage, but to a coach-house. His own case is prodigious, but his example for others dire;

---

[4] James, *The Art of Fiction and other essays*, ed. M. Roberts, p. 134. N.Y.: O.U.P., 1948. This is perhaps a more accessible source than *Notes on Novelists* (1914) in which the essay on Flaubert is also to be found.

disciples not elephantine he can only mislead and betray. . . .[5]

For James the issue was complicated; on the one hand he
was by no means disrespectful of the claims of 'life' while on
the other hand his admiration for Flaubert was severely
qualified; thus he declares that Frederic Moreau and
Madame Bovary are defective in that they are 'such limited
reflectors and registers, we are forced to believe it to have
been by a defect of his mind. And that sign of weakness
remains even if it be objected that the images in question
were addressed to his purpose better than others would have
been; the purpose itself then shows as inferior'.[6]

Once we remember the nature of his own creative genius,
his mixed and reserved attitude to Tolstoy (and, to a lesser
extent, George Eliot) is clearly explained; they are to him
what Milton was to T. S. Eliot—'his own case is prodigious,
but his example for others dire; disciples not elephantine he
can only mislead and betray'. In general, then, Henry James
deals with this problem in a delicate and scrupulous manner,
but he does not always quite save himself from absurdity.
Thus he says that we in England ignore considerations of
style and form 'because the novel is preponderantly culti-
vated among us by women, in other words by a sex ever
gracefully, comfortably, enviably unconscious (it would be
too much to call them even suspicious) of the requirements
of form'. This note, exaggerated to the point of aberration,
is to be found also in the early review of *Felix Holt* (the
reference to Charles Reade is extremely revealing):

> In our opinion, then, neither *Felix Holt*, nor *Adam
> Bede*, nor *Romola* is a masterpiece. They have none of the
> inspiration, the heat, nor the essential simplicity of such a
> work. They belong to a kind of writing in which the
> English tongue has the good fortune to abound—that
> clever, voluble, bright-coloured novel of manners which

---

[5] Roberts, *op. cit.*, p. 119. This essay, on *Ivan Turgenieff*, was originally printed
in the *Library of World's Best Literature*, ed. C. D. Warner, 1897.
[6] Roberts, *op. cit.*, pp. 135-6.

began with the present century under the auspices of Miss Edgeworth and Miss Austen. George Eliot is stronger in degree than either of these writers, but she is not different in kind. She brings to her task a richer mind, but she uses it in very much the same way. With a certain masculine comprehensiveness which they lack, she is eventually a feminine—a delightfully feminine—writer. She has the microscopic observation, not a myriad of whose keen rotations are worth a single one of those great sympathetic gestures with which a real master attracts the truth, and which, by their occasional occurrence in the stories of Mr Charles Reade (the much abused *Griffith Gaunt* included), make him, to our mind, the most readable of living English novelists, and prove him a distant kinsman of Shakespeare. George Eliot has the exquisitely good taste of a small scale, the absence of taste on a large (the vulgar plot of *Felix Holt* exemplifies this deficiency), the unbroken current of feeling and, we may add, of expression, which distinguishes the feminine mind.

For James the formal defects of George Eliot's novels lie in an over-expansive and discursive manner resulting in a lack of concentration and onward dramatic drive. Thus of *Janet's Repentance* he writes, acutely, that:

> I cannot help thinking that the stern and tragical character of the subject has been enfeebled by the over-diffuseness of the narrative and the excess of local touches. The abundance of the author's recollections and observations of village life clogs the dramatic movement, over which she has as yet a comparatively slight control.

and of *Adam Bede*:

> It is as a picture, or rather as a series of pictures, that I find *Adam Bede* most valuable. The author succeeds better in drawing attitudes of feeling than in drawing movement of feeling.

while in general he remarks on:

> the excellence of what I have called her pictures, and the comparative feebleness of her dramatic movement. . . .

Of the four English stories, *The Mill On the Floss* seems to me to have the most dramatic continuity, in distinction from that descriptive, discursive method of narration which I have attempted to indicate.

James evidently prefers *The Mill On The Floss* because the rest of the novel is relatively subordinated to the strong central figure of the heroine. In contrast:

> In all those of our author's books which have borne the name of the hero or heroine . . . the person so put forward has really played a subordinate part. The author may have set out with the intention of maintaining him supreme; but her material has become rebellious in her hands, and the technical hero has been eclipsed by the real one.

This emphasis is significant (we remember his remarks about the status of Gwendolen Harleth in *Daniel Deronda*). In these quotations, all from the early essay on *The Novels of George Eliot*, James is groping towards the conception of a *disponible* or a fine central intelligence which was to play such a major role in the shaping of his own novels. To think of George Eliot's novels as a pattern of subordinate parts governed by a dominating central character is essentially to misconceive their structural principle. They are built rather around a balance or conflict of a number of centres of interest all of which solicit our attention. It is the relationship of these parts, the various tensions existing between them, which make up the pattern of the novels and we shall read them more truly if we think of a network of relations rather than of a single governing character. I would, then, deny one of James's critical assumptions; the antithesis between 'form' and 'life' (or in his later terms, between 'selection' and 'saturation') seems to me to break down if closely examined and tested. But if we grant him this premise his next criticism of George Eliot is a logical development. In his review of *Felix Holt*, he concludes that the novel displays a 'disproportion between the meagre effect of the whole and the vigorous character of the different parts'. This is developed in his review of *Middlemarch*:

> We can well remember how keenly we wondered, while its earlier chapters unfolded themselves, what turn in the way of form the story would take—that of an organized, moulded, balanced composition, gratifying the reader with a sense of design and construction, or a mere chain of episodes, broken into accidental lengths and unconscious of the influence of a plan. We expected the actual result, but for the sake of English imaginative literature which, in this line is rarely in need of examples, we hoped for the other. . . . *Middlemarch* is a treasure-house of detail, but it is an indifferent whole.

Such judgments have been frequently repeated, but perhaps even more influential has been James's diagnosis of the causes underlying this alleged failure of form. These he locates in an inherent split in George Eliot's creative powers. The classic statement of his occurs in his review of the *Life*:

> The truth is, perception and reflection, at the outset, divided George Eliot's great talent between them; but as time went on circumstances led the latter to develop itself at the expense of the former. . . . Her early novels are full of natural as distinguished from systematic observation, though even in them it is less the dominant note, I think, than the love of the 'moral', the reaction of thought in the face of the human comedy.

This develops from a more generalized statement of the case, earlier in the same review:

> We feel in her, always, that she proceeds from the abstract to the concrete; that her figures and situations are evolved, as the phrase is, from the moral consciousness, and are only indirectly the products of observation.

In such a manner James lays down the main line of subsequent critical attack. But there is another critical approach demanding our consideration which also descends, though more indirectly, from him. At the outset of his review of the

Life James expatiates on one of his favourite themes, which perhaps receives its most eloquent treatment in his Preface to *The Tempest*—the mystery of artistic creation and the essential impersonality of the artist. He writes:

> It is certain that George Eliot had this characteristic of the mind *possessed*; that the creations which brought her renown were of the incalculable kind, shaped themselves in mystery, in some intellectual back-shop or secret crucible, and were as little as possible implied in the aspect of her life.

But then James goes on to contradict himself in a curious manner. He outlines George Eliot's life and it is at the point when he is discussing her union with Lewes that one can discern the novelist behind the critic. James was always fascinated by the relation of the artist's life to his art—it forms the basis of several of his stories—and one can feel his interest quickening at this point as he comes upon what must have been to him a particularly interesting case. He writes:

> It would be too much to say that George Eliot had not the courage of the situation she had embraced, but she had, at least, not the levity, the indifference; she was unable, in the circumstances, to be sufficiently superficial. Her deep, strenuous, much-considering mind, of which the leading mark is the capacity for a sort of luminous brooding, fed upon the idea of her irregularity with an intensity which doubtless only her magnificent intellectual activity and Lewes's brilliancy and ingenuity kept from being morbid. The fault of most of her work is the absence of spontaneity, the excess of reflection; and by her action in 1854 (which seemed superficially to be of the sort usually termed reckless), she committed herself to being nothing if not reflective, to cultivating a kind of compensating earnestness.

In other words, James does feel able to relate the art of the novels, the 'excess of reflection', the 'compensating earnestness' to the circumstances of George Eliot's life. He states this relation modestly and tentatively, and clearly such an approach is more dangerous than a direct scrutiny of the novels' form since it relies much more on speculation. Just how easily this line of enquiry can be debased is illustrated by Anthony West's review of Professor Haight's edition of the *Letters*, reprinted in his collection of essays, *Principles and Persuasions*. The crudity of this needs no comment. What does need careful consideration, however, is the far more delicate and critically relevant comment of Dr Leavis, who writes of *The Mill On The Floss*:

> We feel an urgency, a resonance, a personal vibration, adverting us of the poignantly immediate presence of the author . . . the emotional quality represents something, a need or hunger in George Eliot, that shows itself to be insidious company for her intelligence—apt to supplant it and take command.[7]

There is, undoubtedly, this element of emotional intrusion in the novels and in a later chapter we shall have to consider its results in some detail.

It may seem, from this chapter, that I have made James the villain of the piece. Of course, I have no wish to imply anything so absurd; indeed, I have quoted him at such length in order to present his case as fairly as possible. But it must be said that there is something in James's criticism which if exaggerated or treated crudely—and that it has been so treated I hope to show in later chapters—would result in a fundamental distortion of our view of George Eliot's fiction, or indeed, of fiction in general. In particular, the idea of form is vulnerable to debasement, is liable to a reduction from something 'as much of the essence of the subject as the idea' to a collection of structural properties and stylistic devices. James's noble 'house of fiction' will be seen as a series of blueprints. Perhaps some such reduction is inevitable by the very nature of the critical process; certainly I am well aware that the present study has not

[7] F. R. Leavis, *The Great Tradition*, p. 39. London: Chatto and Windus, 1948

escaped it. James himself summed up the danger in a sentence which every critic should learn by heart and repeat daily:

> The critic who over the close texture of a finished work shall pretend to trace a geography of items will mark some frontiers as artificial, I fear, as any that have been known to history.[8]

We have seen how James qualifies his view of Flaubert's achievement and yet—how potent are such qualifications in the face of his central concern with what is 'ideally done'? To have given the moral seriousness of great fiction a concomitant aesthetic seriousness is one of James's major achievements. But it is a precariously poised achievement and has often been thrown off balance by the enthusiastic excesses of subsequent critics. How easy it would be, with a crude notion of form, to say that *The Rape of The Lock* is more 'ideally done' and therefore better than *The Dunciad*? And if we oppose *War and Peace, Middlemarch, The Rainbow* to *Madame Bovary, The Ambassadors, Mrs Dalloway*, does it not appear that the 'loose, baggy monsters', the representatives of 'life' in James's terms, triumph over the champions of form? Put thus, of course, the absurdity of the antithesis and the limitations of James's view become obvious. There must be some ordering and controlling principle in the novels of 'life', and any concept of form which does not include them will be applicable only to a small segment of our great fiction.

To sum up the various points I have tried to make in this chapter: we can see three main trends or influences which may possibly distort our reading of George Eliot. These are the general advance in critical analysis and especially in the criticism of Shakespearian drama, the unprecedented amount of technical experiment in the post-Jamesian novel with its subsequent critical rationalization, and lastly the precept and practice of James himself. From the interaction of these three

[8] Roberts, *op. cit.*, p. 13.

influences two main criticisms of George Eliot emerge. The first is that her novels betray a dissociation between the artist and the moralist, between the imaginative and the intellectual modes. This reveals itself both by major structural defects and by an excess of reflection, description and omniscient comment. The second is that George Eliot, because of the circumstances of her life, intrudes personally in her novels, that the artist is forced to meet the emotional needs of the woman. Both these criticisms are sometimes justified; it is one of the purposes of this book to discover how far they may limit or qualify our view of George Eliot's total creative achievement. Clearly, much light may be thrown on this achievement—both in its strength and its weakness—by an examination of George Eliot's own views on the nature and function of her art. This I shall attempt in the next chapter.

CHAPTER II

Moral and Aesthetic Bases

W E know a great deal, too much perhaps, about George Eliot's views on the aims and methods of art in general, and of her own novels in particular. There are three main sources of evidence; her essays and reviews, her letters, and the novels themselves. So much has been written about the aesthetic implications of George Eliot's criticism that although this will be my starting point, I shall place greater emphasis on the letters and the novels, First, however, I must consider briefly those external forces which one might expect to exert a constricting pressure on her precepts and practice. The two chief forces of this kind are the nature of publication in George Eliot's day and the nature of her audience.

How she published her novels is a story soon told. The three stories which make up *Scenes of Clerical Life* were first published in parts in *Blackwood's Magazine*, but she did not write them with serialization in mind. Her only novel to be written under these conditions was *Romola*, which first appeared in *The Cornhill Magazine*. This was allowed to appear in much larger instalments than was usual and one would have to examine the novel very closely indeed before one could discover what influence serialization might have had upon its composition. *Middlemarch* and *Daniel Deronda* were not serialized, but were first published in bi-monthly and monthly parts. This was Lewes's idea and his letters reveal that he constantly interfered with the arrangement of the parts; thus he wrote to Blackwood about *Middlemarch*:

> We have added on to the end of part I that portion of part II which closes with the scene at the miserly uncle's —a capital bit to end with; and this new arrangement not only pitches the interest forward into part II and prepares

c

the way for the people and for Dodo's absence from part II, but also equalizes quantities better, though making part I rather longer than II which however is desirable. (*Haight*, V, p. 184)

Lewes's kind officiousness, inspired largely by a keen business sense, was accepted by George Eliot, though there is some evidence that at times she resented it. 'I wanted,' she wrote to Blackwood, 'for the sake of quantity, to add a chapter to the Third Book, instead of opening the Fourth with it. But Mr Lewes objects on the grounds of effectiveness' (*Haight*, V, p. 237). Later, about *Daniel Deronda* she complained, 'I cannot drill myself into writing according to set lengths' (*Haight*, VI, p. 182). The result was, that except for minor adjustments, the instalments were not written to set lengths; the pattern of the novel dictated the pattern of publication and not vice-versa as was so often the case with serialization. It is difficult to see that this kind of publication had any intimate or significant effect upon the structure of the novels. Occasionally a jarring note is struck; thus the passage of omniscient comment which ends Chapter 11 of *Daniel Deronda* would have been far more appropriate and unobtrusive if Chapter 11 had, as was originally intended, closed Book I, instead of opening Book II. But this is a matter of local detail and does not vitally affect our judgment of the total work. The rest of her books were written without even these limitations and if we feel that the endings of some of her stories—notably *The Mill On The Floss*—are muddled and over-compressed, this was not due to any arbitrary pattern imposed by the conventional three-decker novel but rather to her tendency to dawdle over the early part of her narrative. George Eliot had, in fact, unusual freedom in the construction and writing of her novels; the exigencies of time, space and money did not press unduly upon her, and she was extremely lucky in having the accommodating and enlightened Blackwood as publisher for all her work save *Romola*. (The intrigue over the publication of *Romola* was a shady business and throws a dubious moral light on George Eliot, although one feels that Lewes was again the cause of the affair. Blackwood, by comparison, comes out of it with great decency and dignity.)

The pressure of the reading public on George Eliot is naturally less easily defined than the conditions of publication. It probably had injurious effects in that it reinforced her tendency to evade certain areas of human experience, notably those involving sexual relationships. We should however retain some sense of historical perspective and remember that even Blackwood protested at the realism of Dempster's attack of D.T.s in *Janet's Repentance* while one reviewer attacked *Adam Bede* for its 'obstetric accuracy'![1] *The Mill on the Floss* aroused the moral indignation of a good many contemporary critics, including Swinburne, whose shrill rhetoric now seems absurdly hysterical (strong feeling has betrayed him into bad grammar):

> If we are really to take it on trust, to confront it as a contingent or conceivable possibility, resting our reluctant faith on the authority of so great a female writer, that a woman of Maggie Tulliver's kind can be moved to any sense but that of bitter disgust and sickening disdain by a thing—I will not write, a man—of Stephen Guest's; if we are to accept as truth and fact, however astonishing and revolting, so shameful an avowal, so vile a revelation as this; in that ugly and lamentable case, our only remark, as our only comfort, must be that now at least the last word of realism has surely been spoken, the last abyss of cynicism has surely been sounded and laid bare.[2]

George Eliot was not less outspoken than most of her contemporaries. Moreover, the limitations imposed by the reading public were not all harmful. They probably helped George Eliot to express her religious views with an indirection and obliquity that could only do good by checking any

---

[1] A fair cross-section of contemporary opinion is conveniently summarized by M. Parlett in 'The Influence of Contemporary Opinion on George Eliot', *Studies in Philology*, XXX, 1930.

[2] A. C. Swinburne, *A Note on Charlotte Brönte*, pp. 32-3. London: Chatto and Windus, 1877.

impulse to dogmatize. George Eliot would not have achieved general and immediate popularity had she stated her philosophic position directly in her novels. Not, I think, that there was ever much danger of this, as we shall see when we examine both the quality of George Eliot's humanism and her conception of the way that viewpoint related to her art. But the reading public probably helped.

Before she wrote a word of fiction—if we discount tales of an early unfinished story—George Eliot had fully worked out her basic aesthetic principles. She had also been forced, by her rejection of orthodox Christianity, to work out her own philosophy of life. She had already achieved a reconciliation between the mainsprings of her creative talent and the main intellectual currents of her day. She was already at the centre of contemporary intellectual life. In many ways she was lucky to have Lewes as her partner; he acted as a buffer between her and the world, shielding her from criticism, organizing her life to give full scope for her talent, charming away her diffidence about her own powers, providing her with an emotional stability she had hitherto lacked. He was intelligent enough for her without being too intelligent; he could stimulate and extend her views without challenging or destroying her painfully won convictions. Aesthetically, perhaps, he was less helpful. I do not agree with those critics who maintain that Lewes shaped or influenced in any significant way her basic aesthetic concepts. It is doubtful whether the author of *Ranthorpe* could teach the author of *Adam Bede* a great deal about her art. In so far as he directly influenced her work during composition the results were not generally happy—witness his suggestions about the ending of *Adam Bede*. Nevertheless he was, on balance, an excellent partner for George Eliot; without him the novels might well never have been written.

Of George Eliot's philosophical formulations I shall say more later. But that her moral outlook, her fundamental humanism, cannot be separated from her aesthetic views is easily seen from a reading of her essays and reviews, particularly *Worldliness and Other-Worldliness: The Poet Young*. This is one of the great critical essays of the nineteenth century and it contains in embryo nearly all we need to know about the moral and aesthetic bases of George Eliot's novels. It is a distinctly modern essay both in its method—the close scrutiny of particular passages—and its treatment of problems that have been central to much of the New Criticism —the concrete universal, poetry and belief, literature and morality and many others. Her attack on Young is based on two general points—that he is too abstract and that consequently he fails to transmute dogma into imaginative literature by engaging us in a sufficient body of felt life, dramatically realized. Young, she says, lacks

> those living touches by virtue of which the individual and particular in Art becomes the universal and immortal. Young could never describe a real, complex human being . . . when he ceases to sing his sorrows, and begins to insist on his opinions,—when that distaste for life, which we pity as a transient feeling, is thrust upon us as a theory, we become perfectly cool and critical, and are not in the least inclined to be indulgent to false views and selfish sentiments . . . his insincerity is the more likely to betray him into absurdity, because he habitually treats of abstractions, and not of concrete objects or specific emotions . . . emotion links itself with particulars, and only in a faint and secondary manner with abstractions.

This is interesting since the criticism she here levels at Young has often been levelled at her own novels. As we have seen, critics have frequently found in her work a dichotomy between George Eliot the creative artist and George Eliot the didactic intellectual. She herself realized that no such dissociation could be allowed; time and time again she insists that she is not dogmatic or didactic, that her work is art and not mere opinion. Thus in a famous letter to Frederic Harrison she writes:

> I think aesthetic teaching is the highest of all teaching because it deals with life in its highest complexity. But if

it ceases to be purely aesthetic—if it lapses anywhere from the picture to the diagram—it becomes the most offensive of all teaching. (*Haight*, IV, p. 300)

Again, she writes to Blackwood, commenting on Alexander Main's selection of *Wise, Witty and Tender Sayings:*

Unless my readers are more moved towards the ends I seek by my works as wholes than by an assemblage of extracts, my writings are a mistake. I have always exercised a severe watch against anything that could be called preaching, and if I have ever allowed myself in dissertation or in dialogue [anything] which is not part of the *structure* of my books, I have there sinned against my own laws.

I am particularly susceptible on this point, because it touches deeply my conviction of what art should be, and because a great deal of foolish stuff has been written in this relation.

Unless I am condemned by my own principles, my books are not properly separable into 'direct' and 'indirect' teaching. (*Haight*, V, pp. 458-9)

We must now ask in what ways the moral seriousness which so clearly pervades George Eliot's work is to be distinguished from didacticism—what, in short, does she mean by '*aesthetic* teaching'? Part of the answer to this question is to be found in a letter to Mrs Taylor:

My function is that of the *aesthetic*, not the doctrinal teacher—the rousing of the nobler emotions, which make mankind desire the social right, not the prescribing of special measures, concerning which the artistic mind, however strongly moved by social sympathy, is often not the best judge. (*Haight*, VII, p. 44)

This clearly excludes only one kind of didacticism; in an early essay, however, George Eliot, commenting upon the social-reformist type of novel, states in a more positive and inclusive way the kind of morality that inheres in a work of art:

Our social novels profess to represent the people as they are, and the unreality of their representations is a grave

evil. The greatest benefit we owe to the artist, whether
painter, poet, or novelist, is the extension of our sympathies. Appeals founded on generalizations and statistics
require a sympathy ready-made, a moral sentiment already
in activity, but a picture of human life such as a great
artist can give, surprises even the trivial and the selfish
into that attention to what is apart from themselves, which
may be called the raw material of moral sentiment. . . .
Art is the nearest thing to life; it is a mode of amplifying
experience and extending our contact with our fellow-men
beyond the bounds of our personal lot. All the more
sacred is the task of the artist when he undertakes to paint
the life of the people. Falsification here is far more per-
nicious than in the more artificial aspects of life. It is not
so very serious that we should have false ideas about
evanescent fashions, about the manners and conversation
of beaux and duchesses; but it *is* serious that our sympathy with the perennial joys and struggles, the toil, the
tragedy, and the humour in the life of our more heavily-
laden fellow-men, should be perverted, and tuned towards
a false object instead of the true one. (*The Natural History
of German Life*)

I am not sure that George Eliot has not here fallen into the
kind of fallacy associated with some of the cruder varieties
of Socialist Realism—the idea that some areas of life—areas
usually defined in terms of social classes—are inherently
more worthwhile subjects for the artist because they are
intrinsically more real. *Real*, of course, is a notoriously tricky
word; the reality of a work of art does not depend in any
simple way upon the alleged reality of characters, classes or
societies existing outside the world of art. In one important
aesthetic sense of the word, Pope's belles and beaux are more
'real' than a good many of Wordsworth's peasants; while
with the example of Proust before us we are not likely to
suppose, with George Eliot, that social classes can be judged
as more or less real by criteria which depend on a crude antithesis between ephemeral manners and enduring passions
common to all men. Perhaps the peasant seemed intrinsically

more real to George Eliot than a duchess because he was aesthetically so; that is to say, George Eliot knew she could realize the peasant as a fictional character whereas the duchess was less easily accessible to her powers of observation and imaginative sympathy. We shall notice later an oscillation in her attitude to this topic depending on the shifting emphasis she places on the importance of the subject-matter's intrinsic qualities as opposed to the artist's treatment of his subject-matter.

In any case this variety of naïve realism is not of central importance to George Eliot's aesthetic. What *is* centrally important is the process of awakening and extending moral insight and sympathy through the agency of the imagination working upon particulars. It is an emphasis which reverberates in the novels themselves; characters frequently have to struggle, often painfully, towards this enlargement of sympathetic vision—thus Adam Bede, the hard man, the man of fixed principles and rigid categories, comes at last to this recognition:

> It seems to me it's the same with love and happiness as with sorrow—the more we know of it the better we can feel what other people's lives are or might be, and so we shall only be more tender to 'em, and wishful to help 'em. The more knowledge a man has, the better he'll do's work; and feeling's a sort o' knowledge. (52)

As with the character, so with the reader; if he closes the book with his vision enlarged and his sympathy extended through an imaginative participation in, or contemplation of, the particular destinies portrayed, then the novel has been morally successful. This view is not, of course, original; the important thing to notice about the process of moral enlargement is that it has clear aesthetic concomitants; it determines, as we shall see later, not only George Eliot's use of the omniscient author convention, but also the way in which she presents her characters and builds up the structure of her novels. The moral purpose and the aesthetic means cannot be divorced. If her novels are to succeed in creating 'a mode of amplifying and extending our contact with our fellow men beyond the bounds of our personal lot', they must be so contrived as to demand of the reader that kind of sympathy which is based on his own deepest and most mature understanding. This George Eliot achieves by controlling our vision of her fictional world so that we see it through a series of interconnected but ever-enlarging perspectives which demand of us greater and greater knowledge, sympathy and insight. By this means each of her characters is seen in a number of interacting relationships—man in relation to himself, his family, trade, local community and to the whole of his historical society. In *Adam Bede*, for example, the Napoleonic wars impinge in various ways even on the sheltered and isolated community of Hayslope. The wars keep up the price of the Poysers' corn, Arthur goes off to them, Adam hasn't yet married because he had to use his savings to buy Seth out of the army—and so on. The largest of these relationships, the most inclusive of contexts, is of course the reader's deepest comprehension of the whole novel. He is granted an omniscience akin to that of the author. A character will know so much of himself and of his fellow-men, but the reader, by virtue of the wider perspective allowed him, will know more and understand more than any character. Standing outside the novel, he will be able to connect and compare in a way that the inhabitants of the fictional world, of their very nature, cannot. The very effort on the part of the reader to connect and compare—in short, to understand—is part of the moral process that the novel aims to stimulate. From his vantage point the reader will perceive, let us say, a relationship between Bessy Cranage and Hetty Sorrel of which both these characters must necessarily be unaware; namely, that Bessy is a kind of comic parody of Hetty. The reader's perception of this relationship—I have deliberately chosen a minor instance which I will later elaborate—will slightly increase his understanding of the whole fictional world of which these characters are a part.

This increase of understanding, multiplied many times, is what George Eliot aims to achieve; it is thus that the book will succeed in extending our sympathies.

The two main obstacles, in George Eliot's view, to this process of moral enlargement are dogmatism and egoism. They are, of course, closely related; in particular, George Eliot regards many doctrinal perversions of Christianity as having an egoistical basis. Of that moral system based upon a scheme of eternal rewards and punishments—a doctrine which was the fundamental cause of her own rejection of Christianity—she writes, making explicit what is frequently implicit in the action of her novels:

> Fear of distant consequences is a very insufficient barrier against the rush of immediate desire. Fear of consequences is only one form of egoism, which will hardly stand against half-a-dozen other forms of egoism bearing down upon it. And in opposition to your theory that a belief in immortality is the only source of virtue, I maintain that, so far as moral action is dependent on that belief, so far the emotion which prompts it is not truly moral,—is still in the stage of egoism, and has not yet attained the higher development of sympathy.

Later in the same essay, on Young, she argues that he 'has no conception of religion as anything else than egoism turned heavenward'. She rarely attacks such doctrinal perversion in her novels; perhaps Bulstrode and the Reverend Tyke in *Middlemarch* come closest to it. One limiting factor was obviously her audience. But in any case debate, the mere countering of opinion by opinion, would have led her into the kind of didacticism she deplored. Her method is more in keeping with the account of her given by Lewes to Black-wood, when submitting the first of the *Scenes of Clerical Life*:

> It will consist of tales and sketches illustrative of the actual life of our country clergy about a quarter of a century ago; but solely in its *human* and *not at all* in its *theological* aspect; the object being to do what has never yet been done in our Literature, for we have had abundant

religious stories polemical and doctrinal, but since the 'Vicar' and Miss Austen, no stories representing the clergy like any other class with the humours, sorrows, and troubles of other men. He begged me particularly to add that—as the specimen sent will sufficiently prove—the tone throughout will be sympathetic and not at all antagonistic. (*Haight*, II, p. 269)

And George Eliot herself, writing to Blackwood about *Janet's Repentance*, declares that:

My irony, so far as I understand myself, is not directed against opinions—against any class of religious views—but against the vices and weaknesses that belong to human nature in every sort of clothing. (*Haight*, II, p. 348)

But if she rarely attempts direct satire it is noticeable that her sympathetic clergymen—Irvine, Dr Kenn, Farebrother and the rest—are never in the least doctrinal; their pastoral care is always conceived in essentially human terms. The point is summed up by Mrs Poyser when she is talking to her Methodist niece, Dinah:

I'm quite willing you should go and see th'old woman, for you're one as is allays welcome in trouble, Methodist or no Methodist; but, for the matter o'that, it's the flesh and blood folks are made on as makes the difference. Some cheeses are made o' skimmed milk and some o' new milk, and it's no matter what you call 'em, you may tell which is which by the look and the smell. (8)

The same point is made more generally and explicitly when George Eliot describes Irwine:

He really had no very lofty aims, no theological enthusiasm: if I were closely questioned, I should be obliged to confess that he felt no serious alarms about the souls of his parishioners, and would have thought it a mere loss of time to talk in a doctrinal and awakening manner to old 'Feyther Taft' or even to Chad Cranage the blacksmith. If he had been in the habit of speaking theoretically he would perhaps have said that the only healthy form religion could take in such minds was that of certain dim but strong emotions, suffusing themselves as a hallowing influence over the family affections and neighbourly duties. He thought the custom of baptism more important than its doctrine, and that the religious benefits the peasant drew from the church where his fathers worshipped and the sacred piece of turf where they lay buried, were but slightly dependent on a clear understanding of the Liturgy or the sermon. (5)

The dogmatic man is the egoist capable of intellectual formulation. There are, however, many kinds of egoists in her novels, from the fixed and irredeemable coldness of Grandcourt, through Tito, the man who steadily degenerates, through Casaubon and Bulstrode to the egoist who can, like Rosamund Vincy, for a moment transcend herself and the egoist who painfully and gradually achieves some kind of moral growth, like Gwendolen Harleth. At the very end of the scale is somebody like Hetty Sorrel, whose moral life is so stunted and inarticulate that she can hardly be said to reach the status of egoist at all. The key-word that George Eliot uses in describing Hetty's inner life, or rather, her lack of an inner life, is 'narrowness'. The antithesis of narrow and broad, of closed and open, recur throughout her work. Narrowness has its literal counterpart in the novels; Hetty knows no other community than Hayslope until she starts out to find Arthur at Windsor; Rosamund has only once been to London. George Eliot speaks in *Middlemarch* of 'the pinched narrowness of provincial life at that time'; Dorothea 'was disposed rather to accuse the intolerable narrowness and the purblind conscience of the society around her', while Lydgate's failure can in part be attributed to the cramping pressures of Middlemarch society. Again, George Eliot writes in more general terms of Dorothea:

> The intensity of her religious disposition, the coercion it exercised over her life, was but one aspect of a nature altogether ardent, theoretic and intellectually consequent, and with such a nature struggling in the bonds of a

narrow teaching, hemmed in by a social life which seemed
nothing but a labyrinth of petty courses, a walled-in maze
of small paths that led no whither, the outcome was sure
to strike others as at once exaggeration and inconsistency. (3)

This passage glances not only at the narrowness of provincial life but also at the dogmatic element we have already
noticed. It is one of the novel's ironies that Dorothea seeks
to escape 'a labyrinth of petty courses' by marrying Casaubon
who is consistently characterized by images of labyrinths,
tombs, gloomy rooms and other claustrophobic metaphors.
Dorothea attempts this false escape because of defects in her
character; her too theoretical nature is the counterpart both
of genuine innocence of the ways of the world and of a kind
of moral myopia which mistakes prison for liberty. Dorothea
is metaphorically as well as literally shortsighted. But there
is more to her than this. George Eliot in fact attempts with
her—as also with Maggie Tulliver—an analysis of a subtler
variety of egoism, a point we must bear in mind when we
consider later the charges of idealization often levelled at
George Eliot in her treatment of these two characters. If
'narrow' is the key-word in Hetty's case, the equivalent
terms for Dorothea are 'ardent' and 'theoretic'. Ardour is
seen as having a positive weight; it is a good and necessary
element of sympathetic vision, but it can lead to dangerous
excesses, especially when it is allied with the theoretic. Just
how the two are linked is indicated by this passage, describing the impact of Rome on Dorothea, 'a girl whose ardent
nature turned all her small allowance of knowledge into
principles, fusing her actions into that mould, and whose
quick emotions gave the most abstract things the quality of
a pleasure or a pain' (20). *Principles, mould, abstract*—these
are all danger signals since by being based on 'a small allowance of knowledge', Dorothea's principles cannot prove
adequate to the complexities of life. Dorothea's 'mind was
theoretic and yearned by its nature after some lofty conception
of the world' (1); she expresses 'her usual eagerness for a

binding theory which could bring her own life and doctrine into strict connection with that amazing past, and give the remotest sources of knowledge some bearing on her actions' (10). This is dogmatism all over again and the novel insists that there is no easy formula, no such binding theory by which life can be governed. Dorothea's yearnings have their fitting and ironic reward; she finds no binding theory but only Casaubon's dusty and sterile key to the Mythologies. (We remember that Maggie, too, sought a key to all life's problems and was also disillusioned.) Dorothea's moral growth is slow and painful but is skilfully charted in the novel; it begins with the change in her attitude to her husband, with the 'first stirring of a pitying tenderness fed by the realities of his lot and not by her own dreams'.

This theoretic bias differentiates Dorothea from her parallel protagonist. Like her, Lydgate is defeated partly by circumstance and environment, partly by personal defects—in his case certain 'spots of commonness'—but although he has his own brand of idealism he bases it much more on the facts of life than on theories; thus he is dominated by 'the conviction that the medical profession as it might be was the finest in the world; presenting the most perfect interchange between . . . intellectual conquest and the social good. Lydgate's nature demanded this combination; he was an emotional creature with a flesh-and-blood sense of fellowship which withstood all the abstractions of special study. He cared not only for "cases" but for John and Elizabeth, especially Elizabeth.' (15)

Dorothea's limited point of view is criticized and qualified not only by George Eliot's description and analysis but also by the comments and reactions of other characters in the novel. There is Mr Brooke, wise even in his bumbling foolishness—'Young ladies are a little ardent you know—a little one-sided, my dear'; there is Celia who continually harps on the foolishness of her sister's notions (another keyword and danger signal); and there is Will Ladislaw. Will is himself an 'ardent fellow . . . without any neutral region of indifference in his nature, ready to turn everything that befell him into the collisions of a passionate drama' (82). (One notices in this last clause a qualifying attitude which George Eliot adopts towards him elsewhere in the novel.) But Will can point out Dorothea's defects to her; he accuses her of having 'the fanaticism of sympathy' (22). (What is morally good in Dorothea is exaggerated until it turns into its opposite, so the phrase suggests.) He takes up this attack later in a letter to Dorothea; 'it was a lively continuation of his remonstrance with her fanatical sympathy and her want of sturdy neutral delight in things as they are' (20). This suggests precisely the correction that must be made to Dorothea's moral outlook, but we should notice that neutrality in itself is bad, a sign of the complete egoist; the word *neutral* opposes the quality implied by *ardour* in the same way that *narrow* is established in opposition to *broad*. In *Middlemarch* it is applied particularly to Rosamund who speaks in her 'silvery neutral way' (58), and who goes to meet Dorothea 'inwardly wrapping her soul in cold reserve . . . she prepared herself to meet every word with polite impassibility' (81). It is a term which later attaches itself to Grandcourt.

Neutrality, indifference, narrowness, the refusal to enlarge one's views or to extend one's sympathies by modifying one's dogmatic principles to fit the facts of life—all these are aspects of George Eliot's analysis of egoism and as such constitute a large though negative part of the moral burden of her novels. As we should expect, these are failures which operate entirely on the level of human relationships since the moral vision of her work is essentially humanistic. The novels lack any supernatural or metaphysical framework; George Eliot is concerned solely with man's moral struggle in this world. The quality of that humanism and its aesthetic consequences is conveyed time and again in her letters; two examples will suffice:

My books . . . are deliberately, carefully constructed on a basis which even in my doubting mind is never shaken

by a doubt. . . . The basis I mean is my conviction as to
the relative goodness and nobleness of human dispositions
and motives. And the inspiring principle which alone
gives me courage to write is, that of so presenting our
human life as to help my readers in getting a clearer
conception and a more active admiration of those vital
elements which bind men together and give a higher wor-
thiness to their existence; and also to help them in gradually dissociating these elements from the more transient
forms on which an outworn teaching tends to make them
dependent. (*Haight*, IV, p. 472)

Later she writes to another correspondent that there can
be found in her books 'a conclusion without which I could
not have cared to write any representation of human life—
namely, that the fellowship between man and man which has
been the principle of development, social and moral, is not
dependent on conceptions of what is not man: and that the
idea of God, so far as it has been a high spiritual influence, is
the ideal of a goodness entirely human (i.e. an exaltation of
the human)' (*Haight*, VI, p. 98).

Whatever we may think of this as a philosophical position
we are not likely to consider that George Eliot arrived at it in
a shallowly rationalistic way nor that it leads to a facile
optimism. It springs not merely from the intellectual topsoil
of her mind but from the whole maturing personality. It is a
position to be respected because of the weight of experience,
of long consideration and painful struggle that we feel to lie
behind it. Moreover, it is a position peculiarly adapted to the
demands and opportunities of the novel—I say nothing of
George Eliot's poetry. And it is necessary to insist that she
proceeds from philosophy to art in a generally tactful and
delicate way; the philosophy, though it pervades and informs
the novels, is never obtruded or advanced as doctrine for its
own sake as we may feel it sometimes is in the work of
Hardy.

There might seem to be one exception to this rule;
namely, George Eliot's variety of determinism, her idea of

Nemesis. 'Our deeds determine us as much as we determine our deeds' or 'Anyone watching keenly the stealthy convergence of human lots, sees a slow preparation of effects from one life on another, which tells like a calculated irony on the indifference or the frozen stare with which we look at our unintroduced neighbour. Destiny stands by sarcastic with our *dramatis personae* folded in her hand' (*Middlemarch*, II).

It is easy to take comments of this kind from their context and use them as evidence for the view of George Eliot as a crude type of the novelist-philosopher. George Eliot is in fact a philosophic novelist, a very different thing. We do *not* feel Destiny as an abstract force working in *Middlemarch*; what we do feel is 'the stealthy convergence of human lots' as something dramatically worked out in the structure of the narrative. Whether she is dealing with the moral consequences of one individual act or with the interaction of character and society, George Eliot submerges her philosophy in the very texture of her novels.

Moreover, her variety of determinism is not crude or mechanical; it is subtle and flexible, allowing the kind of play of free-will that we feel does actually operate in life as we know it. As it happens, one of George Eliot's friends was very troubled by this question, so we have the full testimony of her letters on this point. She writes:

As to the necessary combinations through which life is manifested, and which seem to present themselves to you as a hideous fatalism, which ought logically to petrify your volition—have they, *in fact*, any such influence on your ordinary course of action in the primary affairs of your existence as a human, social, domestic creature? And if they don't hinder you from taking measures for a bath ... why should they hinder you from a line of resolve in a higher strain of duty to your ideal, both for yourself and others? But the consideration of molecular physics is not the direct ground of human love and moral action, any more than it is the direct means of composing a noble picture or of enjoying great music. (*Haight*, VI, pp. 98-9)

D

Later she writes:

> I shall not be satisfied with your philosophy till you
> have conciliated necessitarianism—I hate the ugly word
> —with the practice of willing strongly, willing to will
> strongly, and so on. (*Haight*, VI, p. 166)

In other words, although we may be *ultimately* governed
by a non-human necessity, by the movement of atoms or by
genetic patterns, human beings are rarely concerned with
such ultimates. There is plenty of room for manœuvre in the
foreground. Much more obviously, we are directed and
conditioned by social pressures of various kinds, yet this
denies neither us nor George Eliot's characters the opportunity of making moral choices, of taking decisions. The
artist is limited by the size of his canvas; within that frame
he can paint what he likes. So we are limited by our various
social canvases, yet within these limits we are free.

George Eliot's views on this point demand our respect and
square well enough with life as we experience it; certainly
the impression we derive from the novels is not that of a
malignant Fate or of an impersonal historical force; it is
rather a full portrayal of the 'necessary combinations through
which life is manifested'. Moreover, when discussing George
Eliot's determinism we must remember always to distinguish
between her philosophy and the successful effect of her
creative powers. By vividly realizing a character she may
stimulate in us the reaction, 'Yes, of course, he would act
like that in the circumstances.' This, of course, is not in any
philosophical sense deterministic; in other words, we must
distinguish between the kind of inevitability which derives
from the philosophy and the impression of inevitability
which is the effect of a successful aesthetic whole. Many
critics of George Eliot have, I feel, assigned the right effect
to the wrong cause.

George Eliot's humanism and her conception of the
relation of art to morality almost inevitably led her to endorse
some kind of realist aesthetic. I do not want to get bogged

down in definitions of the word *realism* nor do I want to describe in detail the various naturalistic techniques exploited by George Eliot. In general it seems to me that her kind of realism is governed by three imperatives—it must be true, it must be normal, it must be connected—and I want briefly to analyse each of these principles in turn.

Truth in this context I wish to approach by way of negative definition, by suggesting what, in George Eliot's opinion, a work of art must *not* be. It must not be idealized. She was concerned particularly with two kinds of idealization which we may call the romantic and the moral. Romantic idealization is much the less important; George Eliot simply observed it as a characteristic of much contemporary fiction and reacted against it. The sort of thing I have in mind is conveyed by a typical passage like this from the end of Chapter 3 of *Adam Bede*:

> Considering these things, we can hardly think Dinah and Seth beneath our sympathy, accustomed as we may be to weep over the loftier sorrows of heroines in satin boots and crinoline, and of heroes riding fiery horses, themselves ridden by still more fiery passions.

Moral idealization is a more serious matter; it generally derives from the kind of didacticism George Eliot disliked so much; thus in one of her essays she writes:

> This perversion is not the less fatal because the misrepresentation which gives rise to it has what the artist considers a moral end. The thing for mankind to know is, not what are the motives and influences which the moralist thinks *ought* to act on the labourer or the artisan, but what are the motives and influences which *do* act on him. We want to be taught to feel, not for the heroic artisan or the sentimental peasant, but for the peasant in all his coarse apathy, and the artisan in all his suspicious selfishness. (*The Natural History of German Life*)

If the writer can distort, so can the reader; as she says in a letter:

> In writing any careful presentation of human feelings,

you must count on that infinite stupidity of readers who are always substituting their crammed notions of what ought to have been felt for any attempt to recall truly what they themselves have felt under like circumstances. (*Haight*, V, p. 471)

The writer, then, must present things as they are, not as they ought to be. Clearly the process of moral idealization taken to the extreme would result in a simple division of humanity into black and white, the sheep and the goats. This danger George Eliot is aware of from the beginning; thus she writes to Blackwood about *Mr Gilfil's Love Story*:

> I am unable to alter anything in relation to the delineation or development of character, as my stories always grow out of my psychological conception of the dramatis personae. For example the behaviour of Caterina in the gallery is essential to my conception of her nature and to the development of that nature in the plot. My artistic bent is directed not at all to the presentation of eminently irreproachable characters, but to the presentation of mixed human beings in such a way as to call forth tolerant judgment, pity, and sympathy. And I cannot stir a step aside from what I *feel* to be *true* in character. (*Haight*, II, p. 299)

A little later she answers one of Bulwer-Lytton's criticisms of *The Mill On The Floss*:

> The other chief point of criticism—Maggie's position towards Stephen—is too vital a part of my whole conception and purpose for me to be converted to the condemnation of it. If I am wrong there—if I did not really know what my heroine would feel and do under the circumstaces in which I deliberately placed her, I ought not to have written this book at all, but a quite different book, if any. If the ethics of art do not admit the truthful presentation of a character essentially noble but liable to great error—error that is anguish to its own nobleness—*then*, it seems to me, the ethics of art are too narrow, and must be widened to correspond with a widening psychology. (*Haight*, III, pp. 317-18)

Apart from an emphasis on the naturalistic surface of things and a keen sense of the mixture and complexity existing within individual characters, George Eliot's other aesthetic imperatives act as safeguards against the two kinds of idealization I have described. Since I shall discuss this question in some detail in my chapters on George Eliot's techniques of characterization, we may pass directly to her second demand—it must be normal. 'My design', she writes of *Middlemarch*, 'is to show the gradual action of ordinary causes rather than exceptional.' No other novelist has succeeded so well in expressing the humdrum, the normal, the commonplace, the bread-and-butter texture of our everyday world. From the very first George Eliot places the routine and the mediocre at the centre of her canvas; her achievement is to reveal the significance of the apparently insignificant. She is explicit on this; thus at the opening of Chapter 5 of *Amos Barton* she writes:

> The Rev. Amos Barton, whose sad fortunes I have undertaken to relate, was, you perceive, in no respect an ideal or exceptional character; and perhaps I am doing a very bold thing to bespeak your sympathy on behalf of a man who was so very far from remarkable,—a man whose virtues were not heroic, and who had no undetected crime within his breast; who had not the slightest mystery hanging about him, but was palpably and unmistakably commonplace . . . it is so very large a majority of your fellow-countrymen that are of this insignificant stamp. . . . Yet these commonplace people—many of them—bear a conscience, and have felt the sublime prompting to do the painful right; they have their unspoken sorrows, and their sacred joys; their hearts have perhaps gone out towards their first-born, and they have mourned over the irreclaimable dead. Nay, is there not a pathos in their very insignificance—in our comparison of their dim and narrow existence with the glorious possibilities of that human nature which they share?
> Depend upon it, you would gain unspeakably if you would learn with me to see some of the poetry and the

pathos, the tragedy and the comedy, lying in the experience of a human soul that looks out through dull gray eyes, and that speaks in a voice of quite ordinary tones.

This naïve and awkward address to the reader is implicitly supported by the rest of the tale; what strength there is in *Amos Barton* lies not so much in the story itself, nor in the pathos of the death-bed scene, nor even in the comedy provided by the chorus of rustic characters, but rather in the sober and unemphatic description of Mrs Barton wearily going about the daily round and the common tasks taken for granted by most novelists.

We may feel sometimes that she insists too much on the importance of the usual and the insignificant, that there is no need, for example, to lay such stress upon details like this description of one of Maggie's favourite walks which 'was to a spot that lay beyond what was called the "Hill"—an insignificant rise of ground crowned by trees, lying along side of the road which ran by the gates of Darlcote Mill. Insignificant I call it, because in height it was hardly more than a bank; but there may come moments when Nature makes a mere bank a means towards a fearful result, and that is why I ask you to imagine this high bank crowned with trees . . .' (V. 1). By laying such stress on the apparent insignificance of details which are *really* insignificant, George Eliot defeats her own ends; the result is merely portentous. This kind of thing may result from the wrong kind of stress on subject matter which I noticed earlier. (Some things are intrinsically more real than others; the average is more real than the extreme; the commonplace is more real than the extraordinary—these may be true for the social services but they do not necessarily hold for the work of art.) But this is a minor flaw; what is remarkable is the amount of stress George Eliot can lay on the commonplace and the mediocre without ever sacrificing a keen sense of the individual, without ever descending to the merely typical. This is because of her perception that the commonplace is often anything but simple. Her fine sense of the complexity of things

is largely derived from the third of her aesthetic imperatives
—it must be connected.

The moral enlargement of many of George Eliot's characters is essentially a recognition of the complex relations of
things, that life is rarely a matter of simple categories;
similarly the moral effect of the novels is accomplished for
the reader if his vision is enlarged in the same way. To this
end all aspects of George Eliot's technique are subordinated;
hence, for example, her usual method of interweaving concurrent stories within one narrative framework, hence all the
devices of gradually enlarging perspectives that I have
already mentioned. It is only necessary here to notice the
intricacy of pattern in the usual George Eliot novel, the
careful marshalling of all the many kinds of relationships
which go to make up her picture of life. There are the interaction of private and public within one character, of past and
present, of the small society and the great world outside, of
one character and another, of all the various interactions
between character and society. All of these build up that
'solidity of specification' so much desired by Henry James
and it is a solidity we never feel to be theoretic. It is remarkable, for example, how much social analysis George Eliot
can pack into a novel without ever swamping the individuality of her characters and without ever allowing the novel to
degenerate into a sociological treatise. As she wrote in her
essay on *The Natural History of German Life*:

> The tendency created by the splendid conquests of
> modern generalization, to believe that all questions are
> merged in economical science, and that the relations of
> men to their neighbours may be settled by algebraic
> equations . . . none of these diverging mistakes can co-
> exist with a real knowledge of the people, with a thorough
> study of their habits, their ideas, their motives.

It is a lesson she never forgot in her novels. Perhaps the
best way of discovering how vital to a right appreciation of
her work is a full understanding of the various and complex
modes of connection, both social and aesthetic, is to examine

in some detail one incident from one novel. This should help to show the local density and richness, the packed-without-being-clotted quality of her prose and also how firmly and subtly local detail is related both to its immediate context and to the book as a whole. For these purposes I have chosen a passage from the end of Chapter 31 of *Middlemarch,* the scene describing Lydgate's engagement to Rosamund; although it is a fairly lengthy passage I print it here for convenience.

Miss Vincy was alone, and blushed so deeply when Lydgate came in that he felt a corresponding embarrassment, and instead of any playfulness, he began to speak at once of his reason for calling, and to beg her, almost formally, to deliver the message to her father. Rosamund, who at the first moment felt as if her happiness were returning, was keenly hurt by Lydgate's manner; her blush had departed, and she assented coldly, without adding an unnecessary word, some trivial chainwork which she had in her hands enabling her to avoid looking at Lydgate higher than his chin. In all failures, the beginning is certainly the half of the whole. After sitting two long moments while he moved his whip and could say nothing, Lydgate rose to go, and Rosamund, made nervous by her struggle between mortification and the wish not to betray it, dropped her chain as if startled, and rose too, mechanically. Lydgate instantaneously stooped to pick up the chain. When he rose he was very near to a lovely little face set on a fair long neck which he had been used to see turning about under the most perfect management of self-contented grace. But as he raised his eyes now he saw a certain helpless quivering which touched him quite newly, and made him look at Rosamund with a questioning flash. At this moment she was as natural as she had ever been when she was five years old; she felt that her tears had risen, and it was no use to try to do anything else than let them stay like water on a blue flower or let them fall over her cheeks, even as they would.

That moment of naturalness was the crystallizing feather-touch; it shook flirtation into love. Remember

that the ambitious man who was looking at those Forget-
me-nots under the water was very warm-hearted and rash.
He did not know where the chain went; an idea had thrilled
through the recesses within him which had a miraculous
effect in raising the power of passionate love lying buried
there in no sealed sepulchre, but under the lightest, easily
pierced mould. His words were quite abrupt and awkward, but the tone made them seem like an ardent,
appealing avowal.

'What is the matter? you are distressed. Tell me, pray.'

Rosamund had never been spoken to in such tones
before. I am not sure that she knew what the words were:
but she looked at Lydgate and the tears fell over her
cheeks. There could have been no more complete answer
than that silence, and Lydgate, forgetting everything else,
completely mastered by the outrush of tenderness at the
sudden belief that this sweet young creature depended on
him for her joy, actually put his arms round her, folding
her gently and protectingly—he was used to being gentle
with the weak and the suffering—and kissed each of the
two large tears. This was a strange way of arriving at an
understanding, but it was a short way. Rosamund was not
angry, but she moved backward a little in timid happiness,
and Lydgate could now sit near her and speak less in-
completely. Rosamund had to make her little confession,
and he poured out words of gratitude and tenderness with
impulsive lavishment. In half an hour he left the house an
engaged man, whose soul was not his own, but the
woman's to whom he had bound himself.

I will start by briefly sketching in the context of this
passage. It is Lydgate's profession that first brings him into
contact with the Vincy family. In Chapter 26 Fred falls ill
and Lydgate is called in to replace Dr Wrench: 'the event
was a subject of general conversation in Middlemarch'. The
function of gossip as a connecting and relating agent in the
novel is extremely important; it is a kind of crude social oil
which soon clings to Lydgate and Rosamund. Not without
cause, for Rosamund admirably acts the part of a sister

concerned for her brother's health (we may contrast this with Dorothea's anxiety for Casaubon) and Lydgate's professional duties soon entangle him in a personal relationship. 'Her presence of mind and adroitness in carrying out his hints were admirable and it is not wonderful that the idea of Rosamund began to mingle itself with his interest in the case.' A flirtation soon springs up which of course does not escape the attention of the Middlemarchers since 'it was not more possible to find social isolation in that town than elsewhere'. Mrs Bulstrode gossips about it with Mrs Plymdale (a masterly piece of cattish dialogue), catechizes Rosamund and hints to Lydgate through her husband that his attentions are not desired. The irony of this is a very common one in George Eliot, the irony of a character acting to produce one result and actually producing the reverse of his intentions. Gossip and social pressure as represented here by Mrs Bulstrode combine to force the flirtation to such a degree of explicitness that some irreversible decision has to be taken. (In a minor way Farebrother unwittingly abets Mrs Bulstrode in this.) Lydgate decides to end the flirtation and does not visit her for ten days—hence Rosamund's distress and hence Lydgate's downfall. On the eleventh day he does go to the Vincy's house, ostensibly for professional reasons, though 'It must be confessed, also, that momentary speculations as to all the possible grounds for Mrs Bulstrode's hints had managed to get woven like slight clinging hairs into the more substantial web of his thoughts.' (A very characteristic and revealing image.) Thus the scene we are about to examine takes place in a wide social context; George Eliot sharpens her focus to concentrate on the two individuals, but once the scene is over and the engagement made, she broadens her vision again; the chapter ends with a social occasion, with Lydgate visiting Mr Vincy to gain his approval and being welcomed into the family circle.

George Eliot does not in this scene attempt to portray directly the developing emotional relationship between Lydgate and Rosamund; the reason for this we shall discuss later.

The scene is conveyed to us mainly by description and comment, yet at the same time it does achieve a peculiar kind of concreteness and immediacy. On analysis we find, I think, that this is due to the sharply visualized nature of the passage, the way in which emotions are expressed by physical postures or gestures. Rosamund refusing to look at Lydgate, her dropping the chainwork, his stooping, looking up at her, his embrace; these are all the physical correlatives of their developing relationship. This is a common and recurring technique in George Eliot's novels; the peaks of *Middlemarch* are nearly always conveyed at least in part by sharply defined stances—we remember Casaubon in the posture of death, Bulstrode in the posture of despair, Dorothea and Will in the stance of love. In this passage the sense of physical presence is the unobtrusive but necessary condition for the other effects George Eliot wishes to achieve. It defines, for instance, the quality of Rosamund at this moment. Rosamund, the pathetic product of Mrs Lemon's academy for young ladies, is analysed throughout the novel in terms of artifice; her egoism expresses itself largely through dramatic stance and imagery. (Drama, as we shall see later with *Daniel Deronda*, is nearly always in George Eliot's novels a metaphor for the self-deluding, dream-spinning, narcissistic type of egoism of which Rosamund is an example.) Earlier in this chapter Rosamund has withstood Mrs Bulstrode's questions 'with a great sense of being a romantic heroine, and playing the part prettily'; later, when she thinks Lydgate has broken off the flirtation she 'felt as forlorn as Ariadne—a charming stage Ariadne left behind with all her boxes full of costumes and no hope of a coach'. But at this moment—and only for the moment—the self-control wavers, the artifice drops away and it is, ironically, the unusual naturalness of the girl that captivates Lydgate, which traps him into marriage and so ruins both their lives. The moment of naturalness which here does the damage is balanced by the one other moment in the novel when Rosamund transcends her egoism and breaks through the mask of artifice to do good; if here she ruins herself and Lydgate, later she saves Will and Dorothea. I am thinking, of course, of Chapter 81, the great scene—again marked by a keen sense of physical presence, in which Rosamund tells Dorothea the truth about her relationship with Will. In the one case, things go wrong, in the other things are put right.

Of course, the ironic effectiveness of Rosamund's moment of naturalness in this scene depends vitally upon the character of Lydgate. Lydgate, we know, has his 'spots of commonness', and one of them is to regard women as a relaxation and an adornment to life—hardly an attitude likely to lead to a successful marriage. (It is an attitude not far removed from Casaubon's to Dorothea.) But Lydgate is also, as George Eliot tells us, 'warm-hearted and rash' (we have the previous evidence of his affair with the French actress), and these qualities betray him. Moreover, even here he is a doctor as well as a man; one notices the revealing force of the parenthesis, 'he was used to being gentle with the weak and the suffering'; indeed, in many ways the whole interview has the incongruous flavour of a doctor's visit—'In half an hour he left the house. . . .' Love dwindles down to an emotional therapy.

I have said that George Eliot evades any direct expression of a complicated human relationship and indeed, at first glance, this whole passage might be taken as evidence of her failure to deal adequately with that area of life which involves mature sexual relationships. Such a criticism has its point elsewhere, but it does not apply here. For the whole passage is precisely concerned to show the failure of such a relationship, without which marriage will almost certainly come to disaster. In fact, it is not love in any full sense of the word which binds Lydgate to Rosamund; it is affection, tenderness, compassion, the consciousness of having hurt her, the sense that she depends on him for her joy—admirable qualities but insufficient as a basis for marriage. (This is clearly paralleled by the relationship of Dorothea and Casaubon; that Dorothea can regard Casaubon as a father as much as a husband bodes no good for their union.) This genuine, but fatally limited, relationship is expressed most clearly when Lydgate embraces Rosamund, 'folding her gently and protectingly—he was used to being gentle with the weak and the suffering'.

As Lydgate begins, so he must go on; he will be dis-illusioned—at best his marriage will never amount to much more than what is implied in this passage; the beginning foreshadows the end. Excluding the Epilogue, the Lydgate-Rosamund story in *Middlemarch* finishes thus:

> Poor Rosamund's vagrant fancy had come back terribly scourged—meek enough to nestle under the old despised shelter. And the shelter was still there; Lydgate had accepted his narrowed lot with sad resignation. He had chosen this fragile creature, and had taken the burthen of her life upon his arms. He must walk as he could, carrying that burthen pitifully.

The tone of the two passages, with its basic image of nestling, folding, sheltering, is strikingly similar. The wheel has come full circle; the working out of the whole of this part of the novel has given substance to George Eliot's touch of omniscient generalization in this passage—'In all failures, the beginning is certainly the half of the whole.'

There is one other important way in which this passage relates to its context. Lydgate's aroused emotion is described in a striking, rather odd image:

> An idea had thrilled through the recesses within him which had a miraculous effect in raising the power of passionate love lying buried there in no sealed sepulchre, but under the lightest, easily pierced mould.

This image, which risks blasphemy, gains in power and relevance if we see it in relation to the pattern of tombs, closets, sealed rooms which cluster around Casaubon. Casaubon is 'a sealed sepulchre'; that is one reason why his marriage comes to grief. Lydgate's will come to grief for exactly the opposite reasons. Thus language itself is an important mode of connection in the novel. One might possibly notice another instance of the same sort of thing in this passage though I hesitate to press the point since I am not sure that it is genuinely there to be pressed. At any rate, it will serve as a good index of the difficulties and delicacies involved in discussing language as creatively used. Rosamund, at the beginning of the scene, is doing some 'trivial chainwork', later 'she dropped the chain . . . Lydgate instantaneously stooped to pick up the chain . . . he did not know where the chain went. . . . In half an hour he left the house an engaged man, whose soul was not his own, but the woman's to whom he had bound himself'.

We may not be justified in seeing any symbolic significance in the insistently repeated chain motif; but we should give full weight to the note of Lydgate binding himself. Imagery of entanglement, of bonds, yokes, fetters, bridles is, as we shall see later, a dominant though unobtrusive pattern in the book.

To sum up; the modes of connection revealed by this passage are many and complex. Within the subject matter, the actual life portrayed, they include the relation of private life to public society, with particular reference to gossip as a social force, and also the relation of private to public within the individual—Lydgate the man cannot be separated from Lydgate the doctor. His profession involves and in part betrays him. Aesthetically, they include structural contrasts and parallels, anticipations and recollections, and various patterns of language. The result is a characteristic density and solidity which is an important element both in George Eliot's realism and in her moral intention.

I have attempted this lengthy and possibly exhausting—though by no means exhaustive—analysis of one particular passage in an attempt to check the inevitably abstract and theoretic nature of this chapter. We have been speaking in general of George Eliot's intentions; how far these are fulfilled in her novels is another question, one which the rest of this book will attempt to answer. But if I may anticipate my conclusions, I should say that she ranks with Cowper—ranks in kind but surpasses in degree—whom she contrasts with Young at the end of her essay on that poet:

> The sum of our comparison is this: In Young we have the type of that deficient human sympathy, that impiety towards the present, and the visible, which flies for its motives, its sanctities, and its religion, to the remote, the vague and the unknown; in Cowper we have the type of that genuine love which cherishes things in proportion to their nearness, and feels its reverence grow in proportion to the intimacy of its knowledge.

CHAPTER III

The Omniscient Author Convention

IN my first chapter I maintained that many of James's dicta, based either on his own creative experience or on his experience of particular works, have gradually and unconsciously been transmuted into general principles. This can, I think, be seen both in the modern critical treatment of pre-Jamesian novelists and in the pejorative connotations frequently attached to pre-Jamesian literary conventions. Too often, even now, critics fault earlier novelists for not being like James or else—perhaps more damaging because more insidious—they attempt to convert earlier modes of fiction into pseudo-Jamesian achievements. Equally it is noticeable that a phrase like the 'omniscient author convention' often carries with it overtones of dispraise. The purpose of this chapter is three-fold; I shall attempt a clearer definition of the distinctive *kind* of fiction written by George Eliot; I shall suggest that though her narrative techniques are non-Jamesian they are more rewarding than is generally thought, and finally I shall try to throw some light on modern critical procedures where they seem to me to distort both the failures and the successes of George Eliot and, indeed, of a great deal of Victorian fiction. To focus the issues more sharply I shall concentrate on *Adam Bede*, *The Mill On The Floss* and *Middlemarch*. *Scenes of Clerical Life*, which exploits the omniscient mode in so blatant and distressing a manner, can fairly be dismissed as the work of a novice who has received her literary training largely through the writing of essays while the other mature novels do not modify in any significant way the conclusions arrived at from a study of the three novels I have chosen.

The three critics I shall cite all illustrate the critical bias I have outlined in my first chapter, and it is perhaps significant that the more sympathetic the critic, the more unconscious he is of this bias. Of my three witnesses, Mr F. G. Steiner is the most explicit about the theoretic bases from which he works, perhaps because he is the most concerned with evaluation.[1] His judgment of *Middlemarch*, in so far as it concerns the omniscient author convention, follows familiar lines. Comparing George Eliot and Flaubert—and surely the fair comparison here is between Emma and Rosamund and not, as he suggests, between Emma and Dorothea—he writes of

> the total lack of technique on George Eliot's part. . . . By interfering constantly in the narration George Eliot attempts to persuade us of what should be artistically evident. . . . At other times George Eliot adds to her omniscience deliberate comments and summaries of events. It should be noted that omniscience is an author's most lazy approach and that personal interference in the action must be compared to what occurs in a Chinese theatre where the manager comes on during the play to change props.

I am not here concerned to defend *Middlemarch* against Mr Steiner; my interest in his article is in its revelation, in an unusually pure form, of the critical bias I have outlined. Mr Steiner is aware of this bias and accepts it; indeed he constructs from it a distinction between novelist and story-teller, a distinction primarily of technique:

> A novelist is one whose material need not differ from the story-teller's; it can, in fact, be more modest and commonplace. But he will rely on a very different order of response, on a reader aware of technique, of indirect narration, of point of view; on a reader alert for the tactics used in a single paragraph and for the over-all strategy whereby the artist demonstrated that he has seen from the inside. The story-teller depends essentially on the nature of his material and on the associations it will evoke in the

---

[1] All my references to Mr Steiner are from his article, 'A Preface To *Middlemarch*', in *Nineteenth Century Fiction*, 9, 1954, pp. 262-279.

reader's imagination. Incident is the springboard of this effect, and his characters are marked for easy recognition.

Mr Steiner admits that most Victorian writers are, by his definition, story-tellers rather than novelists and while he allows that both story and novel have their characteristic excellences, he strongly implies that the novel is inherently a better kind of literature than the story. One's first impulse is to deny Mr Steiner's premise—one could deny some of his conclusions too, but on the whole they follow as logically as any aesthetic argument can. If James is the Aristotle of the novel, then one might say that Mr Steiner is the Thomas Rymer; surely his assumptions are no more appropriate here than were Rymer's neo-classical tenets to Shakespearian drama.

One is soon confronted, however, with the fact that his assumptions are present in a milder, more diluted form in much modern criticism of Victorian fiction—even, as I have said, in the most sympathetic of such criticism. In Dorothy Van Ghent's case, for instance, this bias does not appear so much in her valuable essay on *Adam Bede* as in the extensive notes which form an appendix to the main work.[2] There, she instances the openings of Chapters 5 and 6 of *Adam Bede*, and asks:

> What specific damage does the chosen convention of narration do to the fictional illusion? . . . Do you feel that the convention of the 'omniscient author' is actually not the right one for this book, or do you feel that it is the only adequate one for the materials, but that George Eliot has allowed it too much licence? Glance over the first four or five pages of Chapter 15, where Hetty is indulging her fantasy before the mirror; point out specific places where the 'omniscient' point of view allows the author to load the dice against Hetty in such a way that we become uncomfortably conscious that we are not being given the opportunity to make up our own minds but are having a *parti pris* forced upon us.

[2] Dorothy Van Ghent, *The English Novel, Form and Function*, pp. 401-2. N.Y.: Rinehart, 1953.

This passage contains three interesting points; firstly, Mrs Van Ghent realizes that the omniscient author convention includes many different elements and operates in diverse ways; secondly, she raises the question of the author intruding to 'load the dice' and lastly, she stresses the damage this convention does to the 'fictional illusion'. The question of fictional illusion is also raised by my final witness, Joan Bennett, who writes of the weakness of presentation in *Adam Bede* that:

> The principal defect of this kind is that the didactic essays, explaining the characters or the moral import of their stories, are too long and of too frequent occurrence.[3]

She later instances Chapter 17 as an example of this, but immediately following the passage I have quoted, she goes on to distinguish between George Eliot and Thackeray. The omniscient author convention, she says, was necessary to Thackeray's satiric purpose, but it is a pity that George Eliot:

> should accept a method of presentation that was current and that was used by the author she most admired. Her manner of using the asides to the reader is also partly the result of distrust in her own creative power. She is not convinced that the fruits of her imagination will convey to the reader all that her own intelligence discerns. So, from time to time, she breaks the illusion that she has so successfully built up, the illusion that we are actually in Hayslope.

I have chosen these three critics because they seem to me fair representatives of the modern critical approach to George Eliot, and indeed to Victorian fiction in general. They all have valuable and shrewd things to say and it would be futile and absurd to attempt a complete defence of George Eliot, to maintain that she shows a complete and consistent mastery of technique. Indeed, a good deal of this chapter will be devoted to her failings. Nevertheless, I think it can

---

[3] Joan Bennett, *George Eliot*, p. 106. C.U.P., 1948.

be argued that these three critical approaches lose a good deal of their point partly because they are based on insufficiently broad theoretical assumptions, partly because they misconceive or over-simplify the nature of the omniscient author convention, and partly because they misunderstand—or understanding, fail to allow—the kind of fiction attempted by George Eliot.

Before we discuss the novels in detail, it would be as well to make one preliminary general point. The 'omniscient author convention' is only a convenient shorthand term describing one kind of relationship existing between the writer and his work. But clearly, this relationship is complex and contains many elements that will manifest themselves in the novel through a variety of techniques. Thus the use of the convention will differ as between author and author and will further depend upon the *quality* of the work involved. Leavis has made the point succinctly in another connection when, writing of E. E. Stoll's Shakespearian criticism, he says, 'When Shakespeare uses the "same" convention as Beaumont and Fletcher, Dryden and Voltaire, his use is apt to be such that only by a feat of abstraction can the convention be said to be the same.'[4] This is obvious enough, yet of the three critics I have cited, only Mrs Van Ghent reveals even limited recognition of the fact. Mrs Bennett, it is true, distinguishes between George Eliot and Thackeray, but only on the grounds that Thackeray needed the convention and George Eliot didn't. She does not recognize any difference in the kind or quality of the convention being used, but assumes that it is something external to particular novels, a ready-made technique that the novelist may simply adopt or reject. Yet if we compared the use of the convention in, say, Fielding, Scott, Thackeray and George Eliot, we should find that the one critical term covers four different techniques adapted to very different ends. Strictly speaking, I suppose we ought to say that the omniscient author convention does not exist apart from any particular manifestation of it and that only

[4] F. R. Leavis, *The Common Pursuit*, p. 156. London: Chatto and Windus, 1952.

these manifestations are the proper objects of critical study. This, however, would be extreme; few critics would wish to be so stranded high and dry upon the particular since they would lose a useful, if potentially dangerous, critical abstraction. But abstractions may be checked by particulars; George Eliot's use of the convention in *Adam Bede* is clumsy compared with her use of it in *Middlemarch*, and I shall hope to make later some of the relevant and necessary discriminations.

We may well begin with Chapter 17 of *Adam Bede* which Mrs Bennett singles out for special comment. It is a vital chapter for its revelation of George Eliot's conception of her art. At first sight that kind of interest might seem extraneous to the novel and might be dismissed simply as a clumsy intrusion by the author. I do not wish by any means to offer a complete defence of the chapter—Mrs Bennett's criticisms are largely just—but I do think that it can be shown to have a function in the novel and not to be a mere piece of tacked-on comment. I take it as axiomatic—though Mr Steiner would probably disagree with me—that the omniscient technique only becomes objectionable when the author intrudes directly into her fiction either by way of stage-directions or of moral commentary. Granted this, Chapter 17 of *Adam Bede* is probably the extreme instance in George Eliot's work of such intrusion and is therefore worth detailed analysis, quite apart from its ideological content. As we shall see, the content cannot in fact be separated from the mechanics of the convention; the very purpose and manner of the intrusion are part of the ideology.

George Eliot begins the chapter with an arch brightness that betrays her nervousness and uncertainty; she assumes a reaction by the reader about the Reverend Irwine which is supposed to follow—and the connection is pretty tenuous—from the preceding chapter:

'This Rector of Broxton is little better than a pagan!' I hear one of my readers exclaim.

The infuriating thing about this, of course, is that she hears nothing of the sort; the reader is repelled by having his reactions determined for him; he feels himself, and not the character, to be a puppet manipulated by the author. Earlier I defined the omniscient author convention in terms of the relation of author to novel, but this is clearly insufficient and we have to extend the term to cover also the relationships existing, or assumed to exist, between writer and reader. Seen thus, a successful use of the convention depends upon the author's tact, upon delicacy of tone, and George Eliot is here being tactless; we feel insulted at being identified with such a crass reaction as George Eliot assumes us to have. (I discount the fact that many of George Eliot's contemporary readers may well have had precisely this reaction; I do not think we can allow historical relativism to rescue us in quite this way. The problem of portraying decency without doctrine in a clergyman may have been a real one for George Eliot but it did not compel her to use the methods she does.)

Granted this shaky opening to the chapter, George Eliot continues with a disquisition on the nature of her art in which she champions a realist as opposed to an idealist position. She deals, in fact, with the problem of idealization, which I glanced at in the previous chapter. It is significant that her realism—with its usual approving side-glance at Dutch painting—is not opposed here, as it often is, to romance in its various forms, but to its more complete antithesis, that type of art which improves on life by simplifying the stubborn facts of existence. This simplification, in order that life as it is may be identified with life as ideally it ought to be, may be moral in nature—'Let all people who hold unexceptionable opinions act unexceptionally. Let your most faulty characters always be on the wrong side and your virtuous over on the right.' Or it may be aesthetic, a simple retreat from 'common coarse people' to the depiction of ideal states, the painting of 'an angel . . . with a violet floating robe and a face, paled by the celestial light . . . a Madonna, turning her mild face upward and opening her arms to welcome the divine glory'.

After this excursion into aesthetic theory she returns, still in her own person, to the 'real life' of the novel, to the Reverend Irwine. Here she puts into the mouth of Adam Bede, in his comments on Irwine, a realist as opposed to an idealist view which parallels the antithesis she has already drawn in the field of aesthetics. As applied to religion, this takes the form of the familiar contrast between right feeling and dogma, between morality and metaphysics. But we must notice that although the ideological positions are parallel, we have slipped from the omniscient author expounding her own views to one of the characters expounding his. We have crossed, probably without realizing it, the vague boundary between the fictional microcosm of the characters and the macrocosm of George Eliot and the real world. The omniscient author is the bridge or link between the two worlds; beginning the chapter in her own right, George Eliot slides imperceptibly into a persona *within* the novel by the simple device of making herself an audience for the now aged and reminiscent Adam. The implications of this process are important for our view of the kind of fiction George Eliot is writing. What starts up by seeming a clumsy intrusion of the author may now be seen to have a necessary function in establishing the kind of 'reality' of the story being told, the kind of assent we are asked to accord the novel. And surely the 'illusion of reality' aimed at in this kind of fiction is not that of a self-contained world, a fictional microcosm intact and autonomous as in the Jamesian mode, but a world coterminous with the 'real' world, with the factual macrocosm. The author bridges the two worlds; we accept her opinions about the real world (i.e. her aesthetic argument) *on the same level and in the same way* as we accept the opinions of Adam Bede from within the novel. In this same chapter George Eliot speaks of life as a 'mixed entangled affair' and that phrase aptly expresses not only the nature of life within the fictional microcosm but also the relationship of that

microcosm to the real world that you and I and George Eliot
inhabit. She is not aiming at the insulation, the self-suffici-
ency of the Jamesian novel; no sharp boundaries between
real and fictional are to be drawn here; the edges are blurred
and the author allows us an easy transition from one world
to the other.

A hostile critic, even if he grants that this is the kind of
fiction written by George Eliot, will still declare her vulnerable where James is immune, and his attack will probably
follow roughly similar lines to Mrs Van Ghent's criticism of
Hardy. She quotes two passages from *Tess of the D'Urbervilles* in which Hardy intrudes a personal opinion, and then
comments:

> What philosophical vision honestly inheres in a novel
> inheres as the signifying form of a certain concrete body
> of experience; it is what the experience 'means' because it
> is what, structurally, the experience *is*. When it can be
> loosened away from the novel to compete in the general
> field of abstract truth—as frequently in Hardy—it has
> the weakness of any abstraction that statistics and history
> and science may be allowed to criticize; whether true or
> false for one generation or another, or for one reader or
> another, or even for one personal mood or another, its
> status as truth is relative to conditions of evidence and
> belief existing outside the novel and existing there quite
> irrelevant to whatever body of particularized life the novel
> itself might contain.[5]

How successfully George Eliot may be defended against
a similar attack depends on several factors. These include
the quality and successful realization of the 'body of particularized life' within the novel, the relevance of this life to
the opinion expressed, the intrinsic quality of this opinion
(its inclusiveness, balance, maturity), the frequency and
extent of intrusion, the relation of the intruded opinion to
the author and, finally, its relation to the reader. Perhaps I
should stress once again that I am not dealing with the

[5] Van Ghent, *op. cit.*, p. 197.

omniscient author convention as a whole but only that most vulnerable part of it which relates to the intrusive author. Even within this limited frame of reference it will be seen from the list of factors I have just made that the convention is more complex than most critics have assumed and that this complexity demands in all fairness a good deal of particular scrutiny before any general judgment can be made. The laborious and exacting task of building up to a general judgment from such particular scrutiny should not be short-circuited by a too easy use of general critical terms such as the one we are examining. And if comparative excellence is the critic's self-appointed task—as it is with Mr Steiner—then no amount of dogmatic self-assurance will serve if the difficult step-by-step ascent from the particular to the general is evaded. If I say, for instance, that George Eliot is a much greater novelist than Hardy, one tiny part of what I mean is that she is not so vulnerable as Hardy to Mrs Van Ghent's attack. This in turn depends upon an examination of her intruded opinions from the various points of view listed above.

This may be labouring the obvious, and yet one glance at the criticism of George Eliot shows the obvious to be the overlooked. The rest of this chapter will be devoted to the kind of particular scrutiny I have just mentioned and if it raises doubts about a too common and too unexamined use of general terms in the criticism of fiction—and 'omniscient author' is only one of many such terms—then it will have achieved one of its main aims.

I will begin by commenting further on the body 'of particularized life' if I may appropriate Mrs Van Ghent's useful phrase. Clearly the nature and quality of the omniscient author's intrusions will depend very largely upon the nature of the imaginative world that is intruded upon. If George Eliot does not succeed in creating a sufficiently large, complex and imaginatively realized body of life—as, it may be argued, she fails to do in *Romola*—it will be pointless to discuss her omniscience or her intrusive comments. The fictional world must be a world, not merely a map of a world.

The question in dispute is not this; rather it is whether we should agree so readily to the Jamesian (or pseudo-Jamesian) critic's demand that the body of particularized life should be autonomous and that the author's comments should be implicit in the organization and representation of that body of life. Criticism shows that these two questions have been muddled together and it would be as well to begin by making some simple discriminations.

An essential part of this imaginative realization—and one which is obviously far removed from the intrusive author—is the dramatic self-revelation of a character through speech and action. From this point of view, *Middlemarch* is by general consent George Eliot's most successful novel. I would point here to the brilliant way in which characters are not only revealed but also differentiated and placed by the quality of their speech. When Mr Steiner remarks that 'the break between descriptive prose and passages in quotation is often obscured by their similarity . . . she hardly attempts to differentiate styles of expression', I can hardly believe that we are reading the same novel. But it would only be fair to take the weakest novel from this point of view—*Adam Bede*—and similarly the weakest character, Hetty Sorrel. I will return to this example shortly; first I must discuss another of Mr Steiner's dicta, again representative of much modern criticism of George Eliot: 'The author speaks through her characters and not in them.'

I must isolate three cases which might seem to support Mr Steiner's remark. There is, firstly, the case of the persistently moralizing character. These abound in the novels, but so long as the moral comments are consistent with the nature of the character expressing them, we cannot really object. A good example is Adam Bede; Mrs Bennett rightly stresses that his 'gratuitous didacticism' is inherent in him, is an essential trait of his character.* So far is Adam from being simply George Eliot's mouthpiece that his growth in the book is portrayed in terms of this didacticism breaking

* See p. 246.

down before the hard facts of life; his moral categories prove inadequate to experience. A second, related case is discussion by two characters of a moral problem which is related, directly or obliquely, to one of the novel's major themes—for example, the discussion between Arthur and Irwine in Chapter 16 of *Adam Bede*. Again, we cannot assume that either of them is simply speaking for their creator and again we must consider how appropriate to their characters are the moral positions they adopt and how appropriate, also, is the discussion as a whole to the situation in the novel at this point. My final case might seem to concede Mr Steiner's point. There are in George Eliot's novels—as probably in most works of equal scope—characters who represent some norm, who are touchstones or points of moral reference by which all other characters may be measured or judged. Frequently these characters expound, preach, comment, offer advice and so on. Examples would include Dinah, Irwine and Bartle Massey in *Adam Bede*, Farebrother in *Middlemarch* and—perhaps the purest example of all—Dr Kenn in *The Mill On The Floss*. But even here, I believe, we should beware of seeing these characters as simply mouth-pieces for George Eliot. Certainly the views they express are often meant to be endorsed by us, but nevertheless they, too, are fallible human beings and their views are seen as limited and partial in the larger perspective which the author bestows on us. Irwine fails with Arthur, Farebrother is really in the wrong vocation, even Dr Kenn has to give way to the pressure of public opinion. If George Eliot compels us—as I believe she does in nearly every instance—to return a qualified response to these characters, we cannot make a simple identification of their views and hers.

Turning from these three cases and coming a stage nearer the intrusive omniscient author, we encounter George Eliot's analysis of her characters. We should notice here how much more easy is the transition from analysis to intrusive comment as compared with dialogue or even non-analytical description. This is perhaps the reason why critics have sometimes confused the two. Moreover, George Eliot's analysis is often not of an individual but of a society. (A good example is Book IV, Chapter 1 of *The Mill On The Floss*.) The individual is related to a wider social context in a way that is parallel to the mixture of individual analysis and intrusive comment, since this comment is usually of an expansive and generalizing nature. Nevertheless, although analysis and comment are frequently and intimately connected, it must be stressed that they are not one and the same thing. Analysis, in George Eliot's hands, is an important element in the creation of a body of particular life. I would maintain that superbly handled, as it generally is by her, analysis is a literary mode in no way inferior to full dramatic representation. The Jamesian critic would probably deny this, and deny it in terms of the spatial metaphor I have already mentioned; Mr Steiner, for example, denies that George Eliot speaks *in* her characters and would maintain that her treatment of them remains external. There is in this metaphorical antithesis an implication of imaginative frigidity that can only be met by an appeal to experience. Surely in the case of Bulstrode or Casaubon or Rosamund Vincy, analysis produces a sense of intimacy, of human reality as profoundly felt and as subtly conveyed as any 'inside' representation? Surely Leavis is right when he says that in George Eliot's hands analysis becomes creative? Bulstrode, Casaubon, Rosamund—these, however, represent George Eliot at her most mature; let us return to the relatively inexperienced and imperfect novelist and consider her treatment of Hetty Sorrel.

George Eliot's problem here was how to express in the rich fulness of her art an impoverished reality without either appearing paradoxical or allowing her art to suffer an impoverishment corresponding to the reality. One can easily see how this problem would have appealed to the author of *What Maisie Knew* and what a fascinating novel would have resulted. (Indeed, we know that for James, Hetty Sorrel was the central and finest achievement of *Adam Bede*.) But *Adam*

Bede is, after all, a different story and Hetty Sorrel is not an interestingly crippled central intelligence whose very blindness illuminates, but only one strand in the total pattern. She cannot be allowed to become too important. The problem, then, is two-fold; there are the exigencies of economy, balance and proportion and there is the problem of presenting a narrow, stunted imagination, a pathetically limited sensibility which, of its very nature, must be inarticulate. George Eliot attacks these problems boldly by giving us at the outset, in Chapters 9 and 15, a full analysis of Hetty. It is perhaps the *placing* of this analysis that arouses so many objections. Later in the story Hetty is fully and dramatically presented in a way that not even the most rigid Jamesian could fault. But even here, in the journey to and from Windsor, she is presented through action; only once, in the prison scene, does she achieve anything like adequate articulation of her experience, and this, contrasting so sharply with her previous moral inexpressiveness, strikes us perhaps more forcibly than it should, since it throws too clear a light on Dinah's exhortation. (Dinah is the *too* articulate character; we accept her in her actions and through other characters' estimates of her, but once she opens her mouth she fails. Perhaps this has something to do with the Methodist idiom George Eliot has to give her.) This realization of Hetty comes late in the book; consequently we have to take the early analysis on trust and George Eliot cannot completely overcome this structural difficulty. (With Maggie Tulliver, she has learnt her lesson and the position is reversed; the first extended analysis of Maggie occurs only after her childhood life is firmly established for us.) There are other objections to George Eliot's treatment of Hetty, but my concern here is simply to show that there are at least good reasons why analysis in this case should be necessary and why it must precede, rather than accompany or follow, dramatic presentation.

The most offensive case of the intrusive author—one where we may fully agree with Mrs Bennett that George

Eliot displays a distrust of her creative power—is not, however, related to analysis or to moral comment. I refer to George Eliot's use of the historic present. She generally juggles with her tenses in this way either to introduce us to a new aspect of her subject or to give greater dramatic force to a moment of crisis or climax. Mrs Van Ghent's instances, the openings of Chapters 5 and 6 of *Adam Bede*, exemplify the first function; the most striking example of the second is Chapter 47, the brief scene in which Arthur gallops up in the nick of time, waving Hetty's pardon.† I cannot conceive a reasonable defence of this practice; one might seek an explanation of it in contemporary taste, but this would be irrelevant to judgment. The only thing one can say by way of extenuation is that it is not so widespread as is generally thought; while it irritates considerably in *Adam Bede*, there are only two or three brief instances in *The Mill On The Floss* and I cannot recall one single instance in *Middlemarch*. Even in *Adam Bede* it is not so much the frequency as the placing of the device which annoys. Let us agree that it is a blemish. It still remains of interest to examine more closely the precise charges the modern critic brings against the practice. Mrs Van Ghent is explicit. 'What specific damage does the chosen convention of narration do to the fictional illusion?' she asks. I think Mrs Van Ghent is here framing the wrong question. The dominant convention of narration in *Adam Bede* as a whole is that of the omniscient author writing in the past tense; the switch into the historic present is an aberration from this dominant mode, all the more infuriating because it is unnecessary. If this violation of the dominant mode of narration is all that Mrs Van Ghent means by 'damage to the fictional illusion', then one cannot but agree with her. But I suspect that by 'fictional illusion' she means a good deal more and it is this critical term that here interests me. Mrs Bennett, as we have seen, also refers to the damage George Eliot does to 'the illusion that she has so successfully built up, the illusion that we are actually in Hayslope'.

† See p. 246.

Nearly all critics use the term 'fictional illusion' or its various equivalents.‡ It is a useful and fashionable phrase—more, it is a necessary part of the Jamesian critic's equipment. And when we apply it to the Jamesian mode we know, in a rough and ready way perhaps, what we mean by it. But are we sure that we still know what we mean by it when we use it of George Eliot? May it not, in fact, hinder our perception of what kind of fiction her novels represent? One thing we surely *cannot* mean is that we believe 'we are actually in Hayslope'. The fictional microcosm that George Eliot creates is, as Leavis would say, *there* in all its rich truth and complexity, but it is a world surely designed for our contemplation, not for our imaginative participation. We do not leave the 'real' world behind when we are confronted with the world of the novels; in fact, George Eliot compels us to keep both worlds and their interrelationships firmly in our minds. Thus whatever damage the switch into the historic tense does, it is not exactly damage to a fictional illusion; it does not suddenly expel us from the fictional microcosm since, as I have tried to show, the kind of fiction attempted by George Eliot depends on our awareness of the links between microcosm and macrocosm, links of which the omniscient author is the most important. It would be tempting to pursue the whole question of the fictional illusion further, but it is too complex and theoretical an issue to receive here the treatment it deserves. I would only point out that the term disguises a good many assumptions that may be appropriate to the Jamesian mode but which are dangerous if applied to George Eliot or, indeed, to most Victorian fiction. My own disguised assumption, I should hasten to add, is that the reader-novel relationship I have termed contemplation is in no way inferior to that labelled imaginative participation; it is simply different.

We may now move directly to that aspect of the omniscient author convention—the instrusive moral comment—which is the main concern of this chapter. I wish to deal first

‡ See p. 247.

with the frequency, extent and intrinsic quality of these intrusions. The number and length of such comments is not as great as some critics assume. Mrs Bennett certainly over-states her case when she writes of *Adam Bede* that 'the didactic essays, explaining the characters or the moral import of their stories, are too long and of too frequent occurrence'. In fact, the great majority of intrusive comments last for only two or three sentences and with rare exceptions are surely passed over by the impetus of any non-analytical reading. Moreover, if we take the novels in their chronological order there is a steady decline in the frequency of intrusion, until in *Middlemarch* intrusion is comparatively rare.§ This might lead one to assume that George Eliot was transcending the omniscient author convention and looking towards a James-ian mode of fiction. This would be a false assumption. *Middlemarch* is firmly within the omniscient author conven-tion; the difference is one of quality, not of kind. George Eliot has become more expert in handling her chosen con-vention and one element of expertise is economy.

Generally speaking, we may say that the great majority of these moral comments share roughly the same characteristics and function. They are generalizing, expansive and con-cerned to involve the reader in a particular way. As such, they are essential to George Eliot's purpose, both moral and aesthetic, and to that mode of contemplation which I have suggested is the right relationship of reader to novel. This contemplation is emphatically not akin to intellectual frigid-ity, to a merely cerebral scrutiny of human nature or to any crude didactic purpose. George Eliot did not create her characters simply to exemplify the moral comments she interpolates nor are these comments mere captions to the picture she draws. There is, of course, inherent in the con-templative attitude a certain detachment. But this detach-ment is that of the ironic and yet sympathetic observer who is seeking to understand what he observes by placing it in a larger context, standing back to view it in a wider perspect-

§ See p. 247.

ive. This search for understanding—unflinching and patient, sometimes clinical but never inhuman—is, as I tried to show in the previous chapter, basic to George Eliot's purpose. Of course—again as I pointed out in Chapter II—her characters create their own perspectives, they are partial or limited in their view of each other, and the reader perceives relationships of which they are necessarily ignorant. Mr Brooke is unaware of his failings and unaware, as we shall see later, that these failings illuminate the character of Casaubon; it is the reader who contemplates and connects and understands. But apart from this dramatic creation of perspective, George Eliot creates the widest, most inclusive of contexts by her intrusive comments. Unwilling that the reader should stand outside the fictional world which she has so carefully left open and uninsulated, George Eliot challenges the reader to bring this fictional world into the most inclusive context he is capable of framing; that is, his own deepest sense of the real world in which he lives.

If this is so, then clearly the intrinsic quality of these comments is of the greatest importance. If they repel the reader or provoke his dissent they will fail in their purpose and the reader will be diverted from his proper taste of contemplation and understanding into debating the pros and cons of the opinion expressed. This would be fatal to George Eliot's purpose, for these comments are a means to an end; they are one of the bridges between our world and the world of the novel. They are not ends in themselves, not the proper objects of our contemplation. And we are meant to pass easily and quickly over these comments, these bridges; if we halt to discuss the rights and wrongs of a particular comment we shall find that it has turned into a cul-de-sac, leading us nowhere, or worse, into a path leading us *away* from the novel into an area of intellectual discourse remote from the body of particular life in the novel. A good example of this kind of failure is George Eliot's defence of Irwine at the end of Chapter 5 of *Adam Bede*. At first sight this might seem to be a simple case of special pleading and on those grounds

F

alone to be irritating. But there is more to it than this. The interesting point is that the passage involves opinions and attitudes common in the novels and which we do not find offensive elsewhere. Then why here? Because, I think, George Eliot is not so much making a special plea for one of her characters as using that character to score a debating point. At first her generalizing technique is familiar; Irwine is a representative figure, there are many like him—so far, so good—but then she concludes:

> Such men, happily, have lived in times when great abuses flourished, and have sometimes even been the living representatives of the abuses. That is a thought which might comfort us a little under the opposite fact— that it is better sometimes *not* to follow great reformers of abuses beyond the threshold of their homes.
>
> But whatever you may think of Mr Irwine now, if you had met him that June afternoon . . . etc. etc.

But we are *not* concerned here—or, for that matter, anywhere in the novel—with the private morality of 'great reformers of abuses'; we have been led away from Irwine towards a point which we cannot really relate to the novel we have left behind. The abrupt jerk with which George Eliot pulls us back to Irwine and the novel merely emphasizes the wrong turning she has taken.

This, however, is to anticipate. My immediate concern is to note that if we analyse these intrusive comments we shall find that most of them are commonplaces, truisms, platitudes about life and human behaviour. Indeed they are necessarily so since it is a part of their function that we should accept them quickly and without question; if they were idiosyncratic or tendentious they would draw the reader's attention away from the proper object of his contemplation. This is one way in which George Eliot's handling of the convention is superior to that of most nineteenth-century novelists; her intrusive comments are generally neither dramatic gestures, rhetorical embellishments demanding an overwrought emotional response from the reader, nor are they the dogmatic assertions of a particular philosophy; rather they are, in the main, the sober, unemphatic and mature statement of those great commonplaces of human nature, those basic facts of life that underlie all human situations, real or imaginary. I say facts of life, and especially facts of the moral life; one reason why George Eliot is here greater than, say, Hardy, is that his comments derive from a debatable metaphysic whereas she is careful to subdue her own brand of determinism so that the various psychological and economic forces moulding her characters are submerged in the very texture of the novel and rarely appear in the aggressive directness of an author's comment. Her whole bias, as I have said, is anti-dogmatic and anti-doctrinal and it is precisely when Hardy's comments issue in something akin to doctrine that we feel uncomfortable about his novels. Moreover, George Eliot has a far better mind than Hardy or, for that matter, most novelists. I have said that most of her comments are commonplaces, but I must immediately qualify this in two ways. Many of her comments, though expressing commonplaces, are not in themselves commonplace. I would instance the end of Book VII, Chapter 2 of *The Mill On the Floss*, though many more such passages might be cited. For my second qualification I would once again invoke Dr Leavis, commenting on another author; writing on Dr Johnson's poetry, he remarks on 'the conditions that enable Johnson to give his moral declamation the weight of lived experience and transform his eighteenth century generalities into that extraordinary kind of concreteness'.[6] We may fairly apply this remark to George Eliot; behind her moral generalities, too, we feel the 'weight of lived experience' in a way that guarantees their validity. The main part of that weight is, of course, expressed in the body of particular life in the novels, both in the characters as realized and in the structure of the work. We shall examine the architecture of George Eliot's novels later; what I want to do in the rest of this

* Leavis, *op. cit.*, p. 119.

chapter is to examine structures of another kind; namely, those that derive from the various relationships existing between author and reader, dramatic representation and moral comment. These relationships are at least as important as the content of the novels to the final effect that they produce.

I will begin with *Adam Bede*. And since most of what I have to say concerns George Eliot's failures, I will quote first an example of her success, a minor and unobtrusive success, but all the more representative for that. Towards the end of Chapter 26 Adam walks home, tormented by doubts about Hetty; he finally consoles himself and George Eliot writes:

> And so Adam went to bed comforted, having woven for himself an ingenious web of probabilities—the surest screen a wise man can place between himself and the truth.

That is all; we may, in a casual reading, hardly notice the presence of a generalized comment. Yet it is potently and successfully placed; it arises naturally from the immediately preceding description and analysis of Adam's turmoil; through the image of the web it relates to one of the main strands of imagery and one of the main themes of the novel, and it makes, quietly and unemphatically, its own ironical point. This is not a spectacular success; it is one of many such touches in the book which are cumulatively far more important than George Eliot's more noticeable failures.

I have already pointed out one kind of structural flaw in George Eliot's defence of Irwine—the case of the author taking, so to speak, the wrong turning. But this is a subsidiary defect; most of the failures in this book derive from an instability in George Eliot's attitude towards her characters. The stylistic symptoms of this instability are easy to detect; I will merely point to three of them. The first, and rarest, is a certain stridency in George Eliot's address to the reader, marked by aggressive questions and emphatic assertion. This is a good example from Chapter 29; it concerns Arthur's evasive rationalizations about Hetty:

> Are you inclined to ask whether this can be the same Arthur who, two months ago, had that freshness of feeling, that delicate honour which shrinks from wounding even a sentiment, and does not contemplate any more positive offence as possible for it?—who thought that his own self-respect was a higher tribunal than any external opinion? The same, I assure you, only under different conditions.

The second symptom is a certain archness or whimsicality; in this instance, from the end of Chapter 3, it emerges mainly as a mock-modesty and an over-heavy irony:

> Still—if I have read religious history aright—faith, hope and charity have not always been found in a direct ratio with a sensibility to the three concords; and it is possible, thank Heaven! to have very erroneous theories and very sublime feelings.

Finally there is a rhetorical floridity which betrays George Eliot's uneasiness at being required to deal with passionate feeling; this, for instance, from Chapter 12, describing Hetty and Arthur:

> Love is such a simple thing when we have only one-and-twenty summers and a sweet girl of seventeen trembles under our glance, as if she were a bud first opening her heart with wondering rapture to the morning. Such young unfurrowed souls roll to meet each other like two velvet peaches that touch softly and are at rest; they mingle as easily as two brooklets that ask for nothing but to entwine themselves and ripple with ever-interlacing curves in the leafiest hiding-places.

Underlying these symptoms are two main kinds of instability in the author-novel relationship, the first of which is very rare in George Eliot. This is a form of snobbery, the author inviting the reader to share with her an attitude of lofty condescension towards one of her characters. ('Poor deluded man,' she says in effect, 'but *we* know better, don't we?') The problem here is again one of the author's failure of delicacy in manipulating the reader's response; what happens is that by intruding in such a way she sets up a pattern of emotional reaction (i.e. rejection of the author's overtures) which interferes with a right response to the story itself. This fault occurs only once, I think, in a severe form in *Adam Bede*, in Chapter 33, where George Eliot is discussing Adam's love for Hetty. This is significant in that it is Hetty who is the cause and object of the main kind of instability in the novel. This derives, not from a wrong author-reader relationship like the snobbery I have just mentioned, but from a wrong author-character relationship. Critics have frequently and rightly noted some failure of objectivity here and the consequent presence of something like personal animus in George Eliot's attitude to Hetty. The reasons for this are irrelevant here; what we should notice is that the result is that heavy, ponderous irony I have already noted, which repels because it is in excess of the facts which cause it. It appears in an acute form at least five time in the novel,[7] and represents perhaps the major lapse in George Eliot's handling of the omniscient author convention. Mrs Van Ghent stresses it when she asks the reader to notice how George Eliot 'loads the dice' against Hetty; I wish to examine this phrase briefly since it is a possible source of confusion. We do not mean by it that George Eliot is not playing fair in the actual presentation of Hetty's character, that she is suppressing evidence or allowing a wrong kind of inconsistency. Nor do we mean—as we might with Hardy—that she makes events conspire unfairly against Hetty; the inevitability, almost the naturalness of Hetty's downfall is indeed one of the minor triumphs of the book. What we mean is that the reactions we have, given the character and the situation, are not those George Eliot supposes us to have or wishes to arouse in us by her comments. It is not merely that there exists a gap between the particular body of life

[7] Chapters 9, 15, 22, 29, 30.

and the attached comment; it is that the one negates the other. Moreover, granted the nature of Hetty, ironical comment is *too* easy; she is too vulnerable a target for such an attack and this sense of intrinsic unfairness adds to our sense of unjustified hostility on the part of the author. George Eliot's treatment of Hetty in the first two-thirds of the book is a flaw we can only regret; but it does not occur again.

I have spent a disproportionate amount of time on *Adam Bede* because it exhibits in the purest form those kinds of successes and failures most important in George Eliot's handling of the convention. Thereafter, as her technical assurance increases, her failures become fewer and less obvious. There is, for example, no equivalent to Hetty Sorrel in *The Mill On The Floss*. Any instability in George Eliot's treatment of her characters here—and the obvious case, though still debatable, is her idealization of Maggie—does not derive from the omniscient author convention. The major defects of the novel are structural and only one such defect is in any way related to the convention. An analysis of the frequency of intrusions shows that a relatively high proportion of them occur in Book II, that section of the novel devoted to Tom's education. I have always felt a want of economy in this section. We may grant that the theme of education is related in various ways to the main themes of the book. Tom's book learning is contrasted with the hard facts of life he has to learn. Mr Tulliver's conception of education reveals the materialistic nature of his society and so on. But the education theme is not in itself central or very important—if we say that the centre of the book is Maggie's education we are using the word in an entirely different way—and the suspicion that in Book II George Eliot is indulging herself in one of her pet topics is increased by the number and length of her intrusions. But if this is a failure it can, I think, be balanced by a successful use of the convention which is unique to this novel. I mean the extended intrusion of the author in the opening chapters, the conflation of her past and present selves which creates a more intimate and personal

tone than anything else in her work. Some critics have
thought this intrusion a flaw (largely, I suspect, just because
it *is* an intrusion), but it seems to me to fulfil its purposes
delicately and economically. Locally, the control of the contrasting past and present is deft and successful, while in
relation to the whole novel, it gives the author a status within
her fictional microcosm in a way more audacious, complete
and secure than the equivalent device in Chapter 17 of
Adam Bede, which I have already analysed.

In *Middlemarch* George Eliot achieves the steadiness and
clarity of ironic contemplation which belongs to full maturity. Where she wavers or where her vision is blurred for a
moment—as sometimes in her treatment of Dorothea and
Will—the reason is hardly ever to be found in her handling
of the omniscient author convention. (The exception that
proves the rule—the opening of Chapter 55—is not very
important.) The steady, clear ironical gaze derives from the
stability of the author-novel relationship and it results in
local touches that the early George Eliot would have found
unthinkable; we cannot imagine the author of *Adam Bede*,
commenting in her description of an auction sale that:

> This was not one of the sales indicating the depression
> of trade; on the contrary it was due to Mr Larcher's great
> success in the carrying business, which warranted his
> purchase of a mansion near Riverston already furnished
> in high-style by an illustrious spa physician—furnished
> indeed with such large framefuls of expensive flesh paint-
> ing in the dining-room, that Mrs Larcher was nervous
> until reassured by finding these subjects to be scriptural.‖

This steadiness of ironic contemplation is given the stamp
of full maturity by a device new to George Eliot's art
(although it is embryonically there in *Felix Holt*), a device
whereby the irony becomes self-inclusive and is directed not
simply at the fictional microcosm but also at the omniscient
author herself in her relation to that microcosm. (It is, in a

‖ See p. 247.

minor way, much the same device that Chaucer uses when he gives himself the tales of Sir Topas and Melibeus in *The Canterbury Tales*.) In several cases George Eliot opens a chapter with a paragraph or two of omniscient comment, all of which shows a confidence and poise quite new to her art. In Chapter 15, by referring to the intrusive devices of Fielding, she makes fun of the whole convention. The phrases she uses to make the transition from comment to story reveal the same attitude. 'These things are a parable' (Chapter 27); 'Having made this rather lofty comparison' (Chapter 41); 'This fine comparison has reference to . . .' (Chapter 59)—phrases like these, viewed in their context, reveal a new awareness in George Eliot of what she can do within the convention, an awareness which is paralleled in general by the much greater degree of stylistic self-conscious-ness and control displayed throughout the novel. The ironic treatment of the convention itself is a point peculiar to *Middlemarch*, but George Eliot's general handling of the convention shows an equally great technical advance; I would cite as a typical instance the opening of Chapter 10, one of the times in the novel when Will Ladislaw is not in any way idealized. I wish to end these comments by stressing as I did at the outset, this usual level of success. The failures are so much more obvious that we may be inclined to judge the whole convention by them and to infer some causal rela-tion between convention and failure. In fact, the successes are cumulatively far more significant.

CHAPTER IV

Structure I

Some Theoretical Preliminaries

A N interesting example of the way in which a pseudo-
Jamesian view of George Eliot's novels can mislead
even a sympathetic critic is to be found in 'The
Architecture Of George Eliot's Novels' by Walter Naumann.[1] After quoting various dicta of James, Mr Naumann
continues:

> George Eliot's works give us but little of that par-
> ticular intellectual pleasure which we experience in watch-
> ing the conception and the development of a story, or, in
> other words, its formal beauty aside from the subject-
> matter. *Middlemarch* is not 'ideally done'; it is set down
> just as it arose in the mind of the author, without arrange-
> ment and without any previous consideration of the form,
> everything being left in the confusion of life. There is a
> similarity of construction throughout her novels, just as
> there is a repetition of characters. The architecture of her
> books does not serve to enhance the subject-matter, but
> is intimately connected with it; form is not an artistic
> procedure or adornment, but part of the novelist's convic-
> tions.

This is, I think, intended as a summary of James's view;
how just a summary I leave the reader to decide in the light
of my first chapter. Certainly, as it stands, it seems to me a
very muddled view, with a number of apparent contradic-
tions which can only be resolved if we bring to light the
dichotomy between form as 'artistic procedure or adornment' (surely not a Jamesian view) and form as 'part of the

---

[1] Walter Naumann, 'The Architecture of George Eliot's Novels', *Modern
Language Quarterly*, IX, 1945, pp. 37-50.

novelist's convictions'. Does such a dichotomy exist in the work of any great novelist—in James himself, for example? Surely not. We have examined some of George Eliot's convictions in Chapter II and have seen how inevitably her moral aim of sympathetic enlargement of vision leads on to her various aesthetic imperatives.

This summary, however, is certainly endorsed by Mr Naumann, who a little later in his essay makes explicit this dichotomy which is at first submerged. He writes:

> George Eliot had an incredibly easy effortless manner, the manner of the spinner of tales who passes from one chapter to the next, from one object to another even when remote, without the slightest difficulty. Unable to control or to direct her creative power, she is carried away by it. The element which predominates in her world, the quality which makes her novels great, lies deeper. It springs from an inner source—sympathetic feeling.

Such a view obviously has much in common with Mr Steiner's distinction, which we noticed in the last chapter, between the novelist and the story-teller. It will be the purpose of the next few chapters to maintain that George Eliot *is* a novelist and not a mere story-teller; that there exists no such dichotomy as Mr Naumann suggests between 'the novelist's convictions ... an inner source ... sympathetic feeling' and the form of her novels; that the form of her novels cannot be considered in terms of 'adornment' but is rather the necessary correlative of her vision of life—in brief, that her novels are, as James said, 'triumphs of applied and achieved art'. *Form* is a large and vague word and could cover many aspects of her art; I am here concerned only with the larger structural properties of her work and I would rather allow the term *structure* to achieve its own definition in the next two chapters than attempt some abstract or generalized statement of it at the outset.

Nobody, of course, would maintain that George Eliot is a perfect or even a consistently good artist so far as the structure of her novels is concerned. But we should notice that she was acutely conscious of her defects. Just as she does not conform to Mr Naumann's conception of the effortless spinner of tales—all the evidence we have points to the pain and effort of her creative labour—so she does not fall into the category of the naïve, spontaneous, uncalculating artist. She writes, for instance, to Blackwood about the end of *The Mill On The Floss*:

> Your letter yesterday morning helped to inspire me for the last 11 pages—if they have any inspiration in them. They were written in a furor, but I dare say there is not a word different from what it would have been if I had written them at the slowest pace. (*Haight*, III, p. 278)

Thus far the 'inspirational' artist—but immediately she goes on in the same letter to suggest certain corrections and emendations to the text! Again, Mr Jerome Beatty has shown how a detailed study of the manuscript of *Middlemarch* disproves the notion, engendered by Cross's biography, that she wrote parts of that novel in an inspired state.[2]

With two such intimate critics as Lewes and Blackwood, George Eliot could hardly have been unselfconscious about her art. As I have said, the efforts to show that Lewes had any great theoretical effect on George Eliot's conception of her art seem to me unproven, but there is plenty of evidence of day-to-day intervention by Lewes, on the whole with bad results. Blackwood, on the other hand, was not only an ideal publisher but also a shrewd critic and his comments were nearly always valid, penetrating and helpful. George Eliot was not, I think, as sheltered from contemporary criticism as is generally thought, but even if she had been completely insulated from all other comment, the interventions of Lewes and the acute insights of Blackwood could not but have stimulated her to a self-conscious concern for her craft, a

---

[2] Jerome Beatty, 'Visions and Revisions: Chapter 81 of *Middlemarch*', *P.M.L.A.*, 72, 1952, pp. 662-79.

concern which already had well-nurtured roots in her experience as a reviewer. We have already examined the broader aspects of this concern in Chapter II; but when we are concerned with the structural nature of her work we cannot, surely, ignore comments and assertions like these:

(*a*) On *Romola*

Perhaps even a judge so discerning as yourself could not infer from the imperfect result how strict a self-control and selection were exercised in the presentation of details. I believe there is scarcely a phrase, an incident, an allusion, that did not gather its value to me from its supposed subservience to my main artistic objects. But it is likely enough that my mental constitution would always render the issue of my labour something excessive—wanting due proportion. (*Haight*, IV, p. 97)

(*b*) On *Felix Holt*

I feel sure that there are deficiencies if not absurdities in what the Germans call the *Motivirung* seen from a legal point of view. Unhappily there is a great deal of slow matter in the volume which is only indirectly necessary to the completeness of your revision. I wish I could with confidence write 'Skip' to everything that does not touch on law. But the threads are so woven together that I do not know how to separate them without leaving you in a state of mystification as to my intentions. (*Haight*, IV pp. 237-8)

(*c*) On *Middlemarch*

I don't see how I can leave anything out, because I hope there is nothing that will be seen to be irrelevant to my design, which is to show the gradual action of ordinary causes rather than exceptional, and to show this in some directions which have not been from time immemorial the beaten path—the Cremorne walks and shows of fiction. But the best intentions are good for nothing until execution has justified them. (*Haight*, V, pp. 168-9)

(d) On *Daniel Deronda*

It seemed inadmissible to add anything after the scene with Gwendolen, and to stick anything in, not necessary to development, between the foregoing chapters, is a form of 'matter in the wrong place' particularly repulsive to my authorship's sensibility. (*Haight*, VI, p. 240)

I meant everything in the book to be related to everything else there. (*Haight*, VI, p. 290)

At least three things emerge clearly from quotations like these. George Eliot is critically concerned with her own work; she has brought her fine intelligence to bear upon her own craft, confirming one's *a priori* expectations that so intellectually eminent a novelist would not tend to be a simple teller of tales. Moreover, her comments reveal the kind of structure she intended although, since her comments are tied to particular novels and particular problems, she never achieves the grandeur of generality exemplified by James in *The Art of Fiction*:

I cannot imagine composition existing in a series of blocks, nor conceive in any novel worth discussing at all of a passage of description that is not in its intention narrative, a passage of dialogue that is not in its intention descriptive, a touch of truth of any sort that does not partake of the nature of incident, or an incident that derives its interest from any other source than the general and only source of the success of a work of art—that of being illustrative. A novel is a living thing, all one and continuous, like any other organism, and in proportion as it lives will it be found, I think, that in each of the parts there is something of each of the other parts.[3]

Yet granted the different nature of their critical utterances it does not seem to me that the notion of structure implicit in George Eliot's remarks is far removed from that of James. Of course we must distinguish between intention and achievement. Once we have read George Eliot's letters we hardly need this warning; the passages I have quoted display

[3] James, *The Art of Fiction*, ed. Roberts, p. 13; cf. p. 24, n. 4.

her acute awareness of her own failings and limitations. This again makes her quite remote from the simple and effortless story-teller, supposedly innocent of those fine problems of technique that engaged James.

The external evidence, then, so far as it can take us, suggests a novelist concerned with her craft and particularly with an idea of structure as something transcending mere plot, as some integrating power bringing all the disparate elements of the novel together into significant relationship. This is, however, the view of the mature novelist; as one might expect, the early works display much greater defects of craft from a structural point of view. Before considering these there is one important theoretical problem that must be faced. This is the problem of reconciling, if possible, what are commonly called in the jargon of critics the temporal and spatial modes of fiction. I have not tried to trace the ancestry of the term 'spatial mode', but I should be surprised if its history extends much further than that seminal study of Shakespeare, Professor Wilson Knight's *The Wheel Of Fire*. In his first chapter he writes:

> One must be prepared to see the whole play in space as well as in time. It is natural in analysis to pursue the steps of the tale in sequence, noticing the logic that connects them, regarding those essentials that Aristotle noted, the beginning, middle and end. But by giving supreme attention to this temporal nature of drama we omit what, in Shakespeare, is at least of equivalent importance. A Shakespearian play is set spatially as well as temporally in the mind. By this I mean that there are throughout the plays a set of correspondences which relate to each other independently of the time-sequence which is the story.[4]

Before we examine the critical revolution stemming from this passage there is much to be cleared out of the way. Knight links this spatial pattern with something he calls 'atmosphere', and both are further connected with the special and sometimes highly idiosyncratic metaphysical themes he

[4] G. Wilson Knight, *The Wheel of Fire*, p. 3. London: Methuen, 4th ed., 1949.

discovers in the plays. Neither of these extensions of the idea of spatial pattern has been found very fruitful by later critics and we may safely ignore them. On the other hand, Knight's concern with spatial pattern has led him to deal largely with clusters of associated images, a central mode of Shakespearian criticism in the last thirty years. Indeed his 'spatial pattern' has often been reduced to 'patterns of imagery', a reduction he did not intend and which has often impeded the true task of criticism. The study of a work's imagery has become so common and so important a method that I shall deal with it later in a separate chapter. What I shall be concerned with here is the notion of spatial pattern as reflected in the larger structural properties of George Eliot's novels.

We should notice first of all how easily the concept of spatial pattern fits in with the other interests and activities of post-Jamesian critics of fiction. For evidence of this we need only turn to James's *Prefaces*; I quote, almost at random, three passages covering well-nigh the whole of his creative life:

(*a*) Really, universally, relations stop nowhere, and the exquisite problem of the artist is eternally but to draw, by a geometry of his own, the circle within which they shall happily *appear* to do so. (*Roderick Hudson*)

(*b*) I remember that in sketching my project for the conductors of the periodical I have named I drew on a sheet of paper—and possibly with an effect of the cabalistic, it now comes over me, that even anxious amplification may have but vainly attenuated—the neat figure of a circle consisting of a number of small rounds disposed at equal distance about a central object. The central object was my situation, my subject in itself, to which the thing would owe its title, and the small rounds represented so many distinct lamps, as I liked to call them, the function of each of which would be to light with all due intensity one of its aspects. (*The Awkward Age*)

(*c*) There was the 'fun' to begin with, of establishing one's successive centres—of fixing them so exactly that the portions of the subject commanded by them as by happy points of view, and accordingly treated from them, would constitute, so to speak, sufficiently solid *blocks* of wrought material, squared to the sharp edge, as to have weight and mass and carrying power, to make for construction, that is, to conduce to effect and to provide for beauty. (*The Wings Of The Dove*)

Clearly James often conceived the structure of his novels in spatial terms. His frequent analogies with geometry, with paintings, sculpture and with architecture have been inherited by subsequent critics of fiction. A good example of this mode of approach is to be found in Joseph Frank's essay, *Spatial Form In The Modern Novel,* which originally appeared in three parts in *The Sewanee Review* (1945) and which has since been widely anthologized. At least two varieties of spatial form may be discovered ambiguously entwined in Frank's essay; we may call these local and extensive. The local variety of spatial form is illustrated by his discussion of one particular scene in *Madame Bovary,* on which he comments:

> For the duration of the scene, at least, the time-flow of the narrative is halted; attention is fixed on the interplay of relationships within the limited time area. These relationships are juxtaposed independently of the progress of the narrative; and the full significance of the scene is given only by the reflexive relations among the units of meaning.[5]

But this interplay of relationships which is independent of the narrative may extend throughout the whole novel, may indeed become its structural basis. Frank's example is *Ulysses*; he maintains that Joyce presents:

> the elements of his narrative—the relations between Stephen and his family, between Bloom and his wife, between Stephen and Bloom and the Daedalus family— in fragments, as they are thrown out unexplained in the

[5] These quotations are taken from the version of Mr Frank's essay published in *Critiques and Essays In Modern Fiction,* ed. J. W. Aldridge, pp. 43-66. N.Y.: The Ronald Press, 1952.

G

course of casual conversation, or as they lie embodied in the various strata of symbolic reference; and the same is true of all the allusions to Dublin life and history, and the external events of the twenty-four hours during which the novel takes place. *In other words, all the factual background —so conveniently summarized for the reader in an ordinary novel—must be reconstructed from fragments, sometimes hundreds of pages apart, scattered through the book. As a result, the reader is forced to read Ulysses in exactly the same manner as he reads modern poetry—continually fitting fragments together and keeping allusions in mind until, by reflexive reference, he can link them to their complements.*

I have italicized this last passage because it underlines the relationship between the relative importance of the spatial mode in any novel and the amount of creative activity that novel imposes upon the reader. As we have already seen, it has become a commonplace of modern criticism to stress as one of the salient features of post-Jamesian fiction the disappearance of the author from his novel. This withdrawal, as Leon Edel remarks, has 'made necessary a significant shift in narrative; it created the need to use the memory of the characters to place the reader in a relationship with their past. There was no "story", no "plot". And above all the novel seemed to turn the reader into an author; it was he, ultimately, who put the story together, and he had to keep his wits about him to accumulate his data.'[6]

This is undeniably true of much modern fiction, but we can take Edel's point a little further by noticing the probable consequences of this greater creative activity demanded of the reader. For this kind of creative co-operation is very close to the kind of activity we normally call critical. There is little chance of an ordinary, relaxed reading of *Ulysses* or *The Waves* or *The Sound And The Fury*; the common reader when confronted with such novels is compelled to use faculties of perception and interpretation, of analysis and synthesis, that we generally assign to the literary critic. And because the

[6] L. Edel, *The Psychological Novel*, p. 15. London: Hart-Davis, 1955.

reader is compelled by the nature of this fiction to 'put the story together' or to accumulate fragmentary pieces of evidence until 'by reflexive reference, he can link them to their complements', he will naturally tend to find spatial patterns in these novels. One simple form of spatial pattern is the jigsaw puzzle, and if we are honest we must admit that p. of the pleasure of much modern fiction is of the jigsaw puzzle variety.

As I have mentioned already, the techniques and strategies of the modern novelist have dictated the techniques of the critic. These techniques are, on one level, comparatively easy to acquire; a concern with spatial forms, patterns of imagery, symbolic structures, thematic configurations and the rest has come to be the stock-in-trade of modern criticism of fiction. As such, it has frequently been debased or exploited for its own sake, has developed its own jargon and rhetoric and its own over-rigid conventions. It has offered satisfying opportunities for intellectual ingenuity and has appeared to guarantee analytical precision and finality. It has undeniably thrown much light on many novels and has made impossible the retreat to certain older fashioned inanities, but it has also tended to petrify into a mechanical routine which substitutes a skill in handling formal properties for a full and responsible reaction to the total work.

As such, it has naturally provoked a reaction. This has taken the form of an appeal to common sense, a faith in the common reader rather than in the routines of the new critic. (Though can there ever be a common reader of *Ulysses?*) Take, for example, this passage from an essay by John Holloway in which he discusses the Chicago critics, a group who have reacted in various ways against the kind of critical reading I have just tried to describe:

> I have still, however, to suggest the distinctive mode of reading which underlies the critical work of the Chicago school. It is that at any rate *one* legitimate and significant way to read a work is to begin at the beginning and advance page by page to the end. Further, these critics

argue that with a good book the ensuing experience is of a wholly individual, a unique sequence of interests, sympathies, concerns, excitements and the rest, which (whatever their objects) have it as their characteristic to be sequential; to be aroused and then subsequently to be resolved. . . . This is not a wholly innocent account, of course, simply because it is not an account of one way to read a book at all. It is just how people do read. It is, one is inclined to say, *the* way. It is a vastly more central and significant conception than that of reading and turning to and fro the pages of a book (one we have already read the Chicago way several times) in order to complete a 'spatial analysis' or to find out what words 'take up' or 'anticipate' others.[7]

My excuse for disinterring my original comment on this passage from the obscure columns of an academic journal must lie in the fact that Mr Holloway's essay raises many large issues, some of which have played a major part in the shaping of this book. His essay, then, originally provoked me to remark that:

Mr Holloway's purpose is, of course, largely and laudably strategic; to correct an emphasis, to readjust a misbalance. But, as he says, his account is not wholly innocent, and if for a moment we regard the work of art in its aspect of a sequence of interests in the reader's mind, and combine with this the idea of an enforced creative activity in the case of the psychological novel, we shall see that the situation is more complicated than he allows. For the various stream of consciousness techniques . . . chiefly demand the 'spatial' approach that he brands as marginal; the creative activity of the reader is in a large measure this perception of a pattern which is independent of the temporal sequence of the novel. Mr Holloway can reply that modern psychological fiction is a special case, and this is indeed so. . . . But even with the traditional novel, the idea of narrative structure as a simple sequence of interests

7 J. Holloway, 'The New and The Newer Critics', *Essays In Criticism*, 5, 1955, pp. 365-81.

aroused and resolved is more complicated than Mr Holloway allows—complicated, for instance, by the fact that most of our readings are actually re-readings. How do memory and foreknowledge affect the temporal mode of reading? It is a question that Mr Holloway reduces to a parenthesis, but it must be faced without protective brackets. For how can a critical attention to the temporal mode of narration be founded on anything but knowledge of the whole work, the same kind of knowledge that in fact underlies 'spatial analysis'? Mr Holloway also distinguishes between ordinary and critical reading but he exaggerates it, for his strategic purpose, to the point of unacceptibility. There is surely a kind of reading that must be called critical, but which does not issue in the special academic activity that provides so easy a target for Mr Holloway. This critical reading results from a compound of many 'ordinary' readings, a compound which goes far beyond a temporal mode of attention and interest and which, once achieved, cannot but inform any subsequent 'ordinary' reading.[8]

This account as it stands is clearly vulnerable to attack at various points and Mr Holloway's subsequent courteous challenge to clarify certain confusions in the argument and to elaborate other issues does in fact involve some radical thinking about the nature of fiction and particularly about the apparent contradiction between temporal and spatial modes. I am sure this contradiction is more apparent than real; one feels uncomfortable about either approach only when it is pushed to extremes. A determinedly naïve temporal reading leaves too much out of account, a determinedly ingenious spatial reading puts too much in. But between these extremes there is ample room for the kind of manœuvre and adjustment that most of us in fact unconsciously make whenever we are reading a novel. While I cannot pretend to offer anything in the way of a solution to the theoretical problems involved—and some of these problems, such as the ontological status of the work of art, I shall evade

[8] *Essays in Criticism*, 7, 1957, pp. 190-3.

entirely—I shall hope at least to clarify some of the questions which are raised. I shall maintain, as I originally did, that much modern fiction is a special case to which Mr Holloway's remarks do not apply. But since our main concern is with George Eliot, we need not worry too much about the problems posed by Proust or Joyce or Faulkner.

I should like to repeat one sentence of my initial quotation from *The Wheel Of Fire*—'A Shakespeare play is set spatially as well as temporally in the mind.' What we must primarily concern ourselves with are acts of mind, modes of perception and apprehension. We are not for the moment concerned with what objective properties of a novel's structure might provoke us to this or that kind of reading, but rather with the different possibilities latent in the art of reading. We may begin by trying to construct a rough scale of the ways in which it is possible to read a novel. Such a scale would have extremes of naïveté and sophistication, or perhaps—since some spatial analyses are very naïve—extremes of minimum and maximum critical activity. Certain constants would have to be assumed if such a scale were to be possible; constants of intelligence, sensibility and experience. Because these constants are in fact variables—and variables not simply between reader and reader but also within the same reader— no such scale could ever approach scientific stability. But very roughly, at one end of the scale there would be the ordinary, relaxed, non-analytical reading that most of us indulge in when we are reading a novel for the first time. This is perhaps the only occasion when our reading conforms fully with the 'central' mode of reading suggested by Mr Holloway. And if we limit ourselves to the kind of novel which aspires to be a serious work of art, this kind of reading is probably more infrequent than one might at first imagine. At the other end of the scale there is the kind of reading undertaken—one hopes—by an undergraduate attempting an essay or a critic attempting a book, a reading which involves full critical awareness and the constant effort to translate one's experience as reader into an intellectual mode which will order and clarify one's insight without doing too much injustice to the raw, entangled and often chaotic experience resulting from the book's direct impact upon us. This intellectual activity tries to take into account all the evidence, and the prime piece of evidence is the book *as a whole*. Critical discussion of a novel would not get very far if it ignored the question of the book's unity or left untouched the relation of part to part and of part to whole. Discussion of this kind must involve a view of the novel that may fairly be called spatial although it need not involve the kind of page-turning spotting of patterns deplored by Mr Holloway. This kind of reading is surely not invalid or even peripheral; it only becomes so when one feels that the intellectual mode of critical discussion has imposed a pattern on the raw experience of reading instead of eliciting a pattern from it. Such activity then becomes the sterile academic routine attacked by Mr Holloway, a routine in which intellectual ingenuity or even the desire for simple tidiness usurps the place of sensitive and sensible perception and comprehension.

These, then, are the two extremes of the scale. But in between them there are a variety of readings, hard to differentiate but which, for me, make up the 'central' way in which we read a book. This central range depends on a great variety of circumstances, all of which complicate and modify Mr Holloway's thesis. I will mention only three of these. In so far as a novel is difficult or complex, or even in so far as it is a serious, mature piece of work, it challenges the relaxed, casual quality of our reading, provokes us into an activity that must be called critical since it involves a progressive evaluation of the work as we go through it page by page. But this evaluation is progressive in more than a merely temporal or linear manner; it involves summary and recapitulation and the modifying of judgments made at an earlier stage in our reading. If, moreover, we are reading a novel for the second time, or even if we are reading a novel— say a historical novel—for the first time, in which the narrative is in any way circumscribed by facts we already know, then that foreknowledge must affect our page-by-page progress through the book so that what had previously passed unremarked now takes on a new anticipatory or retrospective significance. We are, then, already on our way to a spatial reading of the book. We are making a journey through country we already know, at least as a map. Finally, our experience as readers is cumulative. If we have read, say, ten novels by Henry James, then we are to that extent better equipped for the eleventh, we tend to know in advance that we can ignore *this* scene while *that* is a warning sign or a symptom of something important ahead. Theoretically this need not be so, but in fact it generally works this way. If we stay long enough in the country of any novelist we learn a kind of weather-wisdom; we guess that there are storms or calms to come, we can forecast the pressures and temperatures of chapters still in the future. In these ways, then, our naïve temporal progression through the novel is disturbed and generally this disturbance leads to something like a spatial view of the novel. In fact, spatial and temporal are not, of course, the simple antithesis the words suggest; they are indeed interdependent and mutually enriching. It is really only in the very special and somewhat artificial area of critical theory that they need to be reconciled; if we examine our own experience as readers we shall find that they co-exist and complement each other to such an extent that we are often unaware of any duality. To separate them may be to violate our full reading; nevertheless, such a separation is often in the interests of critical clarity and order. Granted this, I want first of all to view George Eliot's novels in a distinctively temporal mode; once we have done that, we may be able to see more clearly that the structure of her novels is in some sense spatial, independent of the normal processes of time.

The word 'temporal' is in itself ambiguous. It may refer to two kinds of sequence which for convenience I shall call the narrative chronology and the reader's chronology. Narrative chronology is easy enough to define; it is simply the sequence of the action as we have it, a sequence which may be straightforward or complicated. The story may, for instance, start in 1799 and advance simply into 1800 as in *Adam Bede*, or the author may disturb the chronology of his story by the use of flashbacks and multiple time-levels as, for example, in *Wuthering Heights*. The reader's chronology, on the other hand, is the process by which he gains his experience of the novel as he reads it through from beginning to end, the way in which the significance of the story accumulates in his mind. Basically this kind of chronology is determined by the sequence and speed with which the reader gains his knowledge of what, in the widest sense, is going on, the amount of illumination granted him at any given moment in his reading. This reader's chronology is obviously related to the narrative chronology, but it is not necessarily *directly* related. One can easily construct a case where the narrative chronology of two books is exactly the same and yet the reader's chronology is quite different. Take, for example, the genre in which the novelist's control of the reader's chronology is of supreme importance—the detective story. We may imagine such a story beginning 'The shadowy figure shot the butler and leapt out of the window before anyone else arrived on the scene.' The story would then follow a straightforward narrative chronology leading up to the revelation of the murderer's identity by the detective in the last chapter. Suppose, however, we make one small but vital change in our opening sentence, so that it runs 'Harry James shot the butler and leapt out of the window, etc.' The narrative chronology of this version could then be identical with that of the first version, but the effect of the book would be totally different. In the first version the interest would probably lie in our trying to discover with the detective, or ahead of him, the identity of the shadowy figure; in the second version our interest would probably centre on the murderer as we watched him in the subsequent action, narrowly escaping detection and finally being caught. The different effect would be due to the simple but radical change in the reader's chronology; we know something in the second version of which we are ignorant in the first, and this piece of information alters the entire way in which we read the book.

I have chosen a crude instance to clarify the distinction between the two kinds of chronology which are ambiguously contained in the single word 'temporal'. But subtler examples could be found. William Golding's *Pincher Martin*, for instance, is an extended example of self-deception; his lonely protagonist contrives a series of self-dramatizations to ward off his recognition of the fact that he is dead. Gradually his defences crumble, gradually he is forced to recognize the truth. Mr Golding chooses to relate this gradual recognition to the reader's dawning consciousness of what in fact is going on; in other words, with great skill he matches the narrative chronology to the reader's chronology. But he need not have done so; he could easily have told us at the outset that Martin is in fact dead. The effect of the book would then have been completely altered; our involvement in the protagonist's predicament would have been replaced by an attitude of ironic, omniscient contemplation. With one slight alteration in the reader's chronology and with no alteration at all in the narrative chronology, Mr Golding would have written not a better but an entirely different book.

Even less alteration would be needed in a novel like James's *The Princess Casamassima*. In this book James always makes the reader's awareness of the true situation slightly precede that of the hero, Hyacinth Robinson. The result is that we have a double view of the Princess; we see her objectively and through Hyacinth's eyes. This double vision is necessary since by it we judge not only the Princess but the hero himself. The reader gradually becomes aware that the Princess is in part a fraud, and this awareness colours our attitude to Hyacinth with irony and pity. When Hyacinth realizes the truth about the Princess it hardly matters to him, but to the reader it matters a great deal. The reader's attitude to the Princess is at first largely qualified by the use of nuance, overtone and the unconsciously revealing inflections of speech. With stylistic changes so slight that they would not in any way affect the narrative chronology the reader's view of the Princess could have been made to coincide with Hyacinth's and the whole quality of the novel would have been altered. Here, then, is a case where the two kinds of chronology in a novel are remarkably independent of each other.

Clearly it is often very difficult to distinguish these two kinds of chronology. And it should be stressed that the relative simplicity or complexity of either of these temporal processes offers no basis for evaluation. One can think of novels in which the narrative chronology is simple and straightforward, but where the author's control of the reader's chronology, his growing sense of what, in the fullest sense, is happening, is extremely subtle and complex—for example, *A Passage To India* or *Portrait Of A Lady*. On the other hand, there are cases where the narrative chronology is extremely complicated and yet where the author's control over his reader's developing experience remains crude—for example, *Eyeless In Gaza*. Or there is the third case where both chronologies match each other in such a complexity that the actual value of the novel seems disappointingly inadequate to the elaboration of technique—for instance, *The Sound And The Fury*.

I may seem to have laboured to make a distinction which is theoretically possible but which has little practical consequence for our actual reading of novels. But I think the distinction helps to clear up possible critical ambiguities especially when we are considering the various relations of the temporal to the spatial mode. I have talked in this chapter of the spatial mode as part of the process of reading, as an act of mind. Strictly speaking, this is the only way in which we can talk of a spatial mode of fiction. No novel as an artifact can have actual spatial properties; one page *must* follow another; the novel can only have to a greater or lesser extent temporal qualities which may provide a spatial reading. So much is obvious, and yet it is easy to confuse the two, the artifact and the act of mind. When we discuss the relationships existing between these two, we shall often find, I think, that what we are in fact discussing is the relationship of narrative chronology to reader's chronology. Any disparity between the two chronologies will tend to provoke the reader to a spatial reading. And the omniscient author convention as I have described it remains the most economical way of producing such a disparity; by a prophetic comment or by a passage of simple exposition the omniscient author may bestow foreknowledge on the reader so that his insight into the future can reflect upon the necessary ignorance of the characters acting in the dramatic present. This is the nineteenth century's ample equivalent for the greater creative activity forced on the reader by the experimental novel of the twentieth century. Opposite means may equally produce the same end, the same process of reading spatially. Omniscience, then, makes easy the control of the reader's chronology; it is, of course, not the only structural property of the novel which may provoke a spatial reading. Before I examine such structural properties I wish to discuss in greater detail George Eliot's treatment of time, her control of the two kinds of chronology I have tried to distinguish.

CHAPTER V

Structure II
George Eliot's Treatment of Time

IN this chapter I shall deal first with the way in which George Eliot controls her narrative chronology. At first glance her method seems simple and straightforward if we dismiss as a special case *The Lifted Veil* which, dealing as it does with a hero cursed with pre-visionary powers, obviously involves an abnormal and unique tampering with time. But apart from this, the stories seem to plod straightforwardly on, relieved only by a simple flashback whenever—as is frequent—George Eliot has to show by other than expository means the various pressures of the past on the present.

We should notice, however, two rather more complicated instances of flashback. The first of these occurs in *Mr Gilfil's Love Story*. We are led into this tale in a devious anecdotal manner, but the very first sentence contains a precise temporal placing—'When old Mr Gilfil died, thirty years ago.' Immediately a gap is opened up between the past, Mr Gilfil in old age, and the present which we, through the narrator, inhabit. Translated into literal contemporary terms it is a gap between 1859 and about 1830. Towards the end of this first chapter the room which contains the touching relics of Gilfil's youth is described:

> a faded satin pincushion, with the pins rusted in it, a scent bottle, and a large green fan, lay on the table; and on a dressing-box by the side of the glass was a work-basket, and an unfinished baby-cap, yellow with age, lying in it. . . . Such were the things that Martha had dusted and let the air upon, four times a year, ever since she was a blooming lass of twenty; and she was now, in

this last decade of Mr Gilfil's life, unquestionably on the wrong side of fifty. Such was the locked-up chamber in Mr Gilfil's house; a sort of visible symbol of the secret chamber in his heart, where he had long turned the key on early hopes and early sorrows, shutting up forever all the passion and the poetry of his life.

By such trivial details as Martha's age we are prepared for another jump in the time scheme, a preparation continued by the gossip of Mr Hackit in which Gilfil's story suffers the vagueness and distortion of an old legend, while at the very end of the chapter the author directly invites us to leap this gap—'if you care to know more about the Vicar's courtship and marriage, you need only carry your imagination back to the latter end of the last century, and your attention forward into the next chapter'. This second chapter—which impels us over this second time-gap by opening in the historic present—is even more precise in its temporal placing than the first; it is now, we are told, 'the evening of the 21st of June, 1788'. We thus view the main action at two removes; Chapter One serves the purpose of taking us, in two clearly distinguished leaps from 1859 to 1830 to 1788. A similar double distancing also occurs in *Adam Bede*. In the case of *Mr Gilfil's Love Story* the effect of this time scheme is more complicated than at first appears. Its general effect is to increase the charm of the story by muting it; the reminiscent air of narration suits what is, of its nature, a rather tepid story. The one scene in which George Eliot unwisely tries to heighten her tale—the scene of Caterina rushing to her revenge—is thus given unfortunate prominence by its contrast with the rest of the story. Moreover, the first chapter frames the tale; if we are later to be given Gilfil's brief moment of 'passion and poetry' we are clearly meant to relate this to the aged Gilfil living out the prose of his life. The effect of this is two-fold; scratch the surface, George Eliot implies, and you will find unsuspected and interesting depths even in the simplest seeming of men. Moreover, the prosaic frame serves to give a valid air to the romantic picture set within it; this is not *mere* romance, though these things *do* happen, we should not exaggerate them or exploit them for the purposes of sensational fiction. The love story is carefully kept below the tragic level and the double remove in time acts as a damper; it creates the right, balanced perspective for the reader. So much is made explicit in the first chapter where George Eliot, dilating on Gilfil's fondness for gin-and-water, takes the opportunity of addressing the reader:

Allow me to plead that gin-and-water, like obesity, or baldness, or the gout, does not exclude a vast amount of antecedent romance, any more than the neatly executed 'fronts' which you may someday wear, will exclude your present possession of less expensive braids. Alas, alas! we poor mortals are often little better than wood-ashes— there is small sign of the sap and the leafy freshness, and the bursting buds that were once there; but wherever we see wood-ashes, we know that all the early fullness of life must have been.

This natural image is taken up and expanded in the Epilogue which completes the framing effect of the first chapter:

But it is with men as with trees: if you lop off their finest branches, into which they were pouring their young life-juice, the wounds will be healed over with some rough boss, some odd excrescence; and what might have been a grand tree expanding into liberal shade, is but a whimsical misshapen trunk.

It is a measure of the story's promise of things to come that we feel this metaphor to be fully justified; it corresponds exactly with the sense of both change and continuity in Gilfil which is structurally enforced by the device of the time-frame. We are given the pathos of loss and change, of poetry turning into prose, and yet at the same time we feel that the young Gilfil always has within him the latent possibilities which are in fact realized in old age.

If this were all that could be said about the control of time in *Mr Gilfil's Love Story* we could hardly object. Unfortunately, George Eliot complicates things by giving us a story within a story; I mean Chapter 3, which relates the history of Caterina's childhood and of her adoption by the Cheverels. The first two chapters have already imposed enough time-shifts upon us, and we cannot but feel that this further extension in time is an irritating check to the main story for which we are by now becoming impatient.

The clumsiness of this contrasts with the similar device in *Daniel Deronda* whereby we learn of Mirah's early life; but there the greater scope of the novel allows George Eliot much greater freedom in the placing of the flashback. Nor, I think, do we feel such irritation at the similar flashback in Chapter 6 of *Felix Holt*, in which we learn the truth, or part of the truth, about Esther. For one thing, the narrative is here well under way and we are already aware that the plot of *Felix Holt* is going to be extremely complicated. In fact, it is the most involved of all George Eliot's plots; consequently one of her chief tasks in the novel is to subdue in us as much as possible the sense of contrivance. We must not be *too* mystified; there are sufficient revelations to come at the end of the book and were we held in ignorance of Esther's history we should probably feel a sense of mere ingenuity operating on a novelettish level of incident and intrigue.

Felix Holt, with its introductory chapter of solid description and social analysis, is a good example of the characteristic way in which George Eliot takes care to establish a stable temporal relationship between the present and the past world which is generally her subject. Only two exceptions need be mentioned. The first, which I have already discussed in Chapter III, is the fireside reverie that opens *The Mill On The Floss*, an index of the unusually autobiographical nature of that novel. The second—and more complex—instance is the opening of *Romola*, where George Eliot faces the problems posed by the historical novel. The opening paragraphs make explicit one of the main points of the novel—the essential continuities that, beneath the accidents of historical change, link past and present in one common humanity. The earth abides; the sun of 1492 'saw the same great mountain shadows on the same valleys he has seen today', and the continuity of landscape points by analogical extension the continuity of man. 'The great river-courses which have shaped the lives of men have hardly changed, and those other streams, the life-currents that ebb and flow in human hearts, pulsate to the same great needs, the same great loves and terrors.' But George Eliot is not content with this natural metaphor; she conjures up the spirit of a cinquecento Florentine to survey the city four hundred years after his death, so that his viewpoint, his notation of change and continuity, supplements the historical imagination of the author. The bridge between the past and present carries a kind of two-way traffic; it is an ingenious device but not altogether happy in its effect, perhaps because of George Eliot's self-conscious handling of it which results in references to 'our resuscitated spirit' and the like. The proem ends with her lecturing the Florentine spirit on the theme of continuity, a theme which by then has been given an interesting twist. For the ghost, meditating on change, wonders of his own age, 'How has it all turned out?' In a sense, of course, the reader who is gifted with historical hindsight does know how it all turned out. Thus the function of the proem is not merely to emphasize the continuity of past and present but also to encourage us to view the action in a large historical perspective so that the characters, living in their dramatic present and unaware of what the future holds, are fixed for us in an ironic temporal frame. When we encounter Savonarola or the young Machiavelli we cannot but view their present actions against the background of their future destinies; the historical view thus bestows its own kind of omniscience.

Both these points, continuity and perspective, are taken up and continued throughout the novel. The continuity of past and present appears, unfortunately, in the guide-book

H

element which is so obtrusive in *Romola*; 'the inlaid marbles were then fresher in their pink, and white, and purple, than they are now' or 'surmounted by what may be called a roofed terrace, or loggia, of which there are many examples still to be seen in the venerable city'. But occasionally George Eliot uses this device more elaborately as, for instance, in this ironic comment on a fifteenth-century variety of utilitarianism: 'Such intervals of a fiesta are precisely the moments when the vaguely active animal spirits of a crowd are likely to be the most petulant and most ready to sacrifice a stray individual to the greater happiness of the greater number.' There are several other points in the novel where we feel that Renaissance Florence is simply embodying the problems and preoccupations of a nineteenth-century intellectual.

George Eliot's control of historical perspective is more complex and interesting. Generally in her novels, temporal irony results from her placing the dramatic present against the past, but here, probably because *Romola* is a historical novel, she varies her practice. Instead she places the dramatic present against the future of which the characters are necessarily unaware. It is not the past that suddenly resurrects itself; it is the future that yawns like a trap ahead of the characters. She speaks, for instance, in this case non-ironically, of 'that young painter who had lately surpassed himself in his fresco of the divine child on the wall of the Frate's bare cell—unconscious yet that he would one day himself wear the tonsure and the cowl, and be called Fra Bartolommeo'. Again, when Francesco Valari signs the death warrant of the five Medicean conspirators he is in effect signing his own death warrant since the tide of political power will soon turn against him. This kind of historic irony is muted but constant throughout *Romola*, serving to give the novel a kind of temporal depth or density which in her other novels is achieved by stressing the pressure of the past on the present.

Nothing that has been said so far about George Eliot's treatment of her narrative chronology is, in any important sense, central to her achievement. But it can be shown, I think, not only that her treatment of time is less simple and straightforward than it appears but also that time is an important structural agent in her work. We may see this better if we examine one novel in some detail; I choose for this purpose *Adam Bede*, since in one way it has the least complicated time-scheme of all George Eliot's novels and yet it is remarkable for its precise and varied use of narrative chronology.

Two of the most recent critics of *Adam Bede*, Mrs Van Ghent and Mr Maurice Hussey, have both stressed the importance of time in the novel.[1] Both of them, quite rightly, consider time as it manifests itself in those natural rhythms governing the rural community of Hayslope; both of them, in Mrs Van Ghent's words, consider 'the types of material that in *Adam Bede* present themselves with the patient rhythm of day and night, of the seasons, of planting and harvest, of the generations of men, and of the thoughts of simple people who are bound by deep tradition to soil and to community'. But the case is more complex than this; time manifests itself in many ways in *Adam Bede* and each of these has some particular function or some bearing upon the structure and themes of the novel.

Mr Hussey remarks that '*Adam Bede* has a most explicit time scheme; one wonders if the chronology is so detailed in any previous novel'. Patient labour is all that is needed to support his surmise; it is not difficult, by a close reading of the novel, to construct a chronological chart of the novel's action in which events can generally be allocated not only to particular days and dates but even to particular hours and minutes. The time scheme is generally characterized by its clarity and detailed precision; it is also simple and straightforward in its advance, with one exception we shall later examine in detail.*

[1] Van Ghent, *The English Novel, Form and Function*, pp. 171-181; M. Hussey, 'Structure and Imagery in *Adam Bede*', *Nineteenth Century Fiction*, 10, 1955, pp. 115-29.
* See p. 248.

We have already seen in Chapter 3 how carefully George Eliot establishes her status within the novel so that through her we, too, are firmly and clearly related to the fictional world of the book. We examined in particular Chapter 17, in which George Eliot imagines herself as providing an audience for the now aged and reminiscent Adam Bede. What we should notice here is that this provides a double time-shift akin to that in *Mr Gilfil's Love Story*. George Eliot tells us a tale which was told to her a long time ago and which actually happened a long time before it was told to her. Why should this be so, and why is it so important?

One reason concerns the nature of George Eliot's talent. Critics have often noticed that her novels are generally weakest when she fails in objectivity and allows a wrong kind of personal emotion to invade her work. The novels then become a form of therapy, an outlet for the tensions of her own life without the transmuting intervention of the creative artist. The result is either an idealization of a character (e.g. Maggie Tulliver, Will Ladislaw, Daniel Deronda) or the presence in the work of an unjustified hostility (e.g. the treatment of Hetty Sorrel in the first two-thirds of *Adam Bede*). In brief, George Eliot sometimes fails to achieve an adequate distancing of her experience; the woman who suffers, to adapt Mr Eliot's formulation, is not sufficiently separate from the artist who creates. Were there not this removal in time, I believe George Eliot would have failed much more in that steadiness and clarity of vision so necessary to the success of her art.

Moreover, this time-shift helps the reader to achieve a stable relationship to the novel. Indeed the reader must be able to count upon a stable point of view if he is to encompass the manifold, complex and changing experience offered to him for contemplation and moral judgment. It is precisely because of this need for a stable relationship between reader and novel that the most infuriating lapse in George Eliot's handling of the omniscient author convention is precisely her juggling with time, her disconcerting switch into the historic present at climactic moments in the novel. This annoys because it is unnecessary; George Eliot can render her subject sufficiently vivid without the help of a trick like this. But more fundamentally it is a flaw because it disturbs the reader-novel relationship which the double remove in time has so firmly established; for a moment our vision of the novel shifts and wobbles as we are distracted from our proper task by the need to adjust ourselves to a sudden alteration in the author's technique. This technique is not the proper object of our contemplation; it is a means to an end and should not usurp our attention.

Generally however, George Eliot's technique, in so far as it concerns the control of time, is successfully unobtrusive. This may be the reason why one of the most interesting and important aspects of time in *Adam Bede* has, so far as I am aware, gone completely unnoticed. This is the part George Eliot's control of time plays in the structure—moral and aesthetic—of the novel. The theme of the novel, with its strong sense of nemesis, its emphasis on consequences rather than motives, clearly demands the heavy stress on temporal evolution that is reflected in the precision of the narrative chronology. But a study of that chronology soon shows that the art of the novel, no less than its distinctive moral theme, is fundamentally concerned with temporal processes.

The art of narrative, at its lowest, implies a simple sequential interest; this happened and then that and then that. George Eliot's moral emphasis infuses simple sequential interest with a strong element of causality; this happened because of that. Beyond this we concern ourselves with those properties that provoke a spatial approach; a narrative pattern based on juxtaposition, parallelism, contrast, anticipation, recollection and the rest. George Eliot's typical method of interweaving concurrent stories lends itself readily to the establishing of such a pattern of interest. This pattern is the subject of my next chapter; I anticipate it here only to point out what should be obvious, that in such a pattern the author's control of time must play an important part.

Consider, for example, the relationship of Hetty and Dinah, one of the main sources in the novel of this kind of spatial pattern. The parallels and contrasts between the two are enforced in a number of ways which I shall discuss in the next chapter; but in the network of connections between the two girls, time is important. For example, Dinah leaves the Bedes' cottage, returning from her errand of mercy (Chapter 14), at exactly the same time as Hetty parts from Arthur on the first stage of her downfall (Chapter 13). Hetty's good angel, Dinah, leaves for Snowfield (Chapter 11) at about the same time as her bad angel, Arthur, leaves for Eagledale (Chapter 16). It is in November that Adam becomes betrothed to Hetty, it is in the following November that he marries Dinah. Dinah leaves Snowfield for Leeds on the same day that Hetty, pretending to visit her at Snowfield, sets out to find Arthur at Windsor. And so on—I have only quoted a few instances.

One of the main emotional effects of this kind of pattern is clearly that dominant kind of irony we find in George Eliot's novels; the reader perceives what the characters do not, precisely because he can make connections of this kind of which they are necessarily unaware. The most interesting example of this is in that section which is least straightforward in its chronology, Book V. As we read this part, we encounter first Adam's unavailing search for Hetty (which is caused by and which balances Hetty's unavailing search for Arthur), we hear of her arrest and witness her trial. It is only through the evidence given at the trial and through Hetty's subsequent confession to Dinah that we learn what happened to Hetty after her return from Windsor. Meanwhile Arthur, hearing of the old Squire's death, has been journeying homewards, pleasantly anticipating the future and little knowing what the future really holds in store for him. Apart from the obvious irony directed at Arthur, one other ironical stroke of fate emerges with appalling clarity from the disordered chronology; in Chapter 39, Adam, not yet aware of Hetty's arrest, tells Irwine:

'You was t'ha' married me and Hetty Sorrel, you know,
sir, o' the 15th o' this month.'

The 15th of March is, in fact, the date fixed for Hetty's
execution; Adam spends the previous night with Bartle
Massey:

> Sometimes he would burst out into vehement speech—
> 'If I could ha' done anything to save her—if my bear-
> ing anything would ha' done any good . . . but t'have to
> sit still, and know it, and do nothing . . . it's hard for a
> man to bear . . . and to think o' what might ha' been now,
> if it hadn't been for *him*. . . . O God, it's the very day we
> should ha' been married.'

This is surely emphatic enough. What I wish to stress at
this point are the submerged parallels and the unemphatic
ironies. If one clarifies the chronology of the events related
in Chapters 38 and 43, one perceives clearly what the
arrangement of the narrative tends to conceal. One sees, for
example, how nearly the paths of Adam and Hetty cross,
how nearly he saves her from her fate. George Eliot herself
must have been aware of this; the unique detail and precision
of time in the novel and its careful construction make this
clear. Why, then, did she conceal this crossing of Adam's
path with Hetty's, or rather, why did she not choose to draw
the reader's attention to it? We can imagine what Hardy
would have done with such a situation, the bitter irony he
would have extracted from a contemplation of the two frustrated searchers almost, but not quite meeting; the tragedy,
nearly, but not quite being averted.

In fact, the reference to Hardy may help us towards
answering the question why George Eliot did not exploit the
possibilities latent in the situation. The sense we derive
from, say, *Tess of the D'Urbervilles*, which Hardy sums up in
his famous final paragraph about the President of the Im-
mortals at his sport, is precisely the sense that George Eliot
wishes to avoid in her novels. Her work, as we have seen,
does exhibit a variety of determinism, does rigorously share

the workings of Nemesis, but these workings are rarely made so explicit by her as they are by Hardy; they are not obtruded or advanced as a philosophy of life but are thoroughly submerged beneath the surface of the novel's action. To draw attention to the facts which I have elicited by rearranging the chronology would be to convert the novel into another, and possibly lower, form of art. These coincidences, these criss-crossings of individual destinies are more potent if left unremarked, working beneath the level of conscious attention and only indirectly contributing to our sense of a remorseless destiny inexorably working itself out in consequence of man's moral blindness and his egoistic refusal to face the facts of his life. These consequences, this destiny, represents perhaps the deepest, most intimate connection of the basic themes of the novel with the temporal process through which, of necessity, they must work themselves out. The working out makes in itself a sufficiently powerful impact on the reader; there is no need for the author to call these processes to our attention by an over-conscious manipulation of the novel's chronology.

In one sense, of course, every aspect of time in the novel is functional. Thus George Eliot's stress on the natural background and on the rhythm of the seasons—so much emphasized by other critics—is a basic part of her vision of life and the most important way of establishing her narrative in a larger temporal context. Beginning and end in the strict Aristotelian sense *Adam Bede* does not possess; rather we feel that the story has been taken from a larger continuum of time which envelops it and to which it looks both backwards and forwards. This is achieved in a number of ways; memory, especially the memory of old men like Martin Poyser, is an important agent here. Or again, we have at the outset of the novel the sense of other lives and other stories which impinge only briefly and tangentially on this life, this story. The history of the Bede family, and especially Adam's relationship with his father, is one instance. Here, for a moment, a shaft of light is thrown back in time on a set of human relationships that we never actually see in the novel, except obliquely in their effect on the character of Adam. Moreover, the particular stories with which we are concerned are already under way when the novel opens; Dinah, for instance has not just arrived in Hayslope—in fact, she is shortly to depart; the affair between Arthur and Hetty has already started, though as yet so imperceptibly that they are not really aware of it. Many more cases could be cited; all through the book we are similarly made aware of contiguous and contingent lives—such awareness is, indeed, a necessary part of George Eliot's naturalistic technique. But this sense of the continuum of time and of many interconnected lives all leading off into other uncharted histories is combined with a keen sense of form. Many tributaries flow into the mainstream of the novel; there are many quiet and enticing backwaters, but we are not allowed to stop and explore them, so firmly does George Eliot guide us on our journey. All that she asks of us is that we should be aware of these tributaries and backwaters; this is part of the characteristic solidity and density of the life portrayed in her novels and part, too, of that technique of ever-widening perspectives I have tried to describe in an earlier chapter.

It should be stressed that *Adam Bede* differs from the rest of George Eliot's fiction only in degree, not in kind. None of the other novels exhibits the same astonishing chronological detail, but all of them are equally rewarding when analysed in this way. I will quote only two examples of functional time by way of justifying this generalization. In *Daniel Deronda* we have not only the characteristic interweaving of different narrative strands but also a complicated temporal pattern which begins in the dramatic present and then makes a series of excursions into the past histories of Gwendolen and Deronda, always returning to the same present. Clearly such a pattern is a fruitful source of those temporal parallels and contrasts I have mentioned; the one I would isolate here occurs if we compare Chapter 10 with Chapter 17; Gwendolen meets Grandcourt at about the same time as Deronda saves Mirah from committing suicide. The interacting destinies of these two couples, if we charted them on a graph, would share the same starting-point in time; this cannot be coincidence.

My second example is taken from *Silas Marner*; the symbolic connection between the miser's love of his gold and his discovery of the golden-haired Eppie has frequently been remarked. What has not been generally noticed is that this symbolic balance is reinforced by a careful temporal symmetry. In Chapter 1 we are told that it is fifteen years since Silas appeared in Raveloe; in Chapter 16 (the opening chapter of Part II), we jump forward sixteen years in time. Allowing for the time taken up by the narrative action of Part I, this jump forward in time almost exactly equals the initial flashback; in other words, the period of Silas's miserdom and exile from society is neatly balanced by the period of his redemption and gradual reintegration into the community.

Many more examples could be cited, but these should suffice to show that the method of *Adam Bede* is representative of George Eliot's novels. *Romola* and *The Lifted Veil* are the two exceptions; apart from these, George Eliot's distinctive talent is intimately linked with a full sense of time in all its complexities. It is no accident that George Eliot looks back in so many ways to Wordsworth, nor is it a coincidence that Proust should have found her so great a novelist. *Adam Bede* shows us as clearly as anything in Proust the interaction of temporal and spatial modes; time itself is used to help us to perceive extra-temporal relationships. But before I deal with the spatial aspects of the novel I should say something about what I have called the reader's chronology.

Perhaps the most important governing factor in this chronology is tempo and by this I mean the rate at which the reader's grasp of the full experience of the novel expands. Very often the rate of the expansion will differ radically from the tempo of the narrative chronology; for example, an extremely fast moving sequence of incidents which may be mechanically necessary to the narrative structure of a novel may contribute remarkably little to the reader's sense of what the novel is, in the fullest sense, about. But generally in George Eliot's novels these two rates of progress tend to coincide. The typical tempo of her novels seems at first straightforward, steady and monotonous, the even, onward march of the narrative reflecting her moral concerns and particularly the train of consequences following inexorably from any act. One might perhaps generalize and say that careful manipulation of tempo is of supreme importance only to the comic novelist; certainly the steadily increasing speed of, say, *Tom Jones* has a point and a relevance not shared by those novels of George Eliot, like *The Mill On The Floss*, which gather momentum towards the end. The variation of tempo in this case is not designed to underline the catastrophe; rather it is the result of George Eliot's failure to plan adequately the overall structure of her novel.

We know from her letters that she always had trouble with the conclusions of her novels; she is quite explicit about *The Mill On The Floss*; she writes to Blackwood that 'the third volume has the material of a novel compressed into it', and a little later she comments on Bulwer-Lytton's criticism that 'the tragedy is not adequately prepared. This is a defect which I felt even while writing the third volume, and have felt ever since the MS left me. The *epische Breite* into which I was beguiled by love of my subject in the first two volumes, caused a want of proportionate fulness in the treatment of the third, which I shall always regret.' (*Haight*, III, p. 317)

I shall discuss the end of *The Mill On The Floss* in greater detail later, but it seems to me that its failure is not so much due to the idealization of Maggie as Dr Leavis thinks, but rather—as George Eliot herself suggests—to a simple structural disproportion. It is not the fact that Stephen is the object of Maggie's infatuation that worries me, nor the emotional intensity of the relationship; worthless popinjays no doubt frequently arouse intense emotions. The trouble is that even as a worthless popinjay Stephen isn't adequately realized, he isn't really there as a force in the novel at all. It is not the fact that he is a shallow dandy, an unworthy object of Maggie's passion, that is at fault; rather it is the fact that aesthetically he simply isn't substantiated. Stephen as an overdressed dummy of a man would be acceptable, but there is all the difference in the world between a full picture of a character who is in fact shallowly egoistical (witness Rosamund Vincy) and an inadequate sketch of such a picture. Stephen is only a sketch; he is gestured at, not portrayed; certainly he is insufficiently elaborated to make the relationship convincing. And the simple truth of the matter is that George Eliot had no *time* to portray him; given the space left at her disposal, she could do no more than sketch in a few gestures. It is not, then, the difference in the quality of Maggie's and Stephen's character, but the difference in the realization of them which is the true cause of the book's disharmony.

Given this disproportion—Maggie fully and leisurely portrayed, Stephen hastily sketched in—we can see the increasing tempo of the book as indicating not the natural crescendo of the catastrophe but rather the breathless rush to finish things off within the limits of the conventional three-decker novel. This is particularly apparent in the device which George Eliot uses to reach her conclusion, a fully premeditated conclusion as we learn from a letter to D'Albert Durade:

> To my feeling, there is more thought and a profounder veracity in 'The Mill' than in 'Adam'; but 'Adam' is more complete, and better balanced. My love of the childhood scenes made me linger over them; so that I could not develop as fully as I wished the concluding 'Book' in which the tragedy occurs, and which I had looked forward to with much attention and premeditation from the beginning. (*Haight*, III, p. 374)

As George Eliot realized, there remains a gap between intention and achievement, a failure which is brought out if we contrast the end of *The Mill On The Floss* with the end of

The Awkward Age. Both James and George Eliot use the
same device, a series of climactic interviews whereby the
relationship of the protagonist to the more important of the
other characters is summed up. But whereas Nanda Brook-
enham's interviews are in perfectly decorous relation to the
highly dramatic nature of the rest of *The Awkward Age*, we
cannot but feel that Maggie's comparable series is stagey
and contrived. This is because the method of compression
and concentration enforced by such a device contrasts too
radically with the leisurely narrative of the rest of the novel;
we are switched from one mode of fiction to another and we
cannot but feel the jerk as the gears change and the novel
accelerates.

Maggie has to be brought into a final relationship with
Philip, Lucy, Stephen and Tom, in that order. Philip and
Stephen appear by proxy in the form of letters, Lucy and
Tom appear in person. Breaking this sequence is Maggie's
interview with Dr Kenn which articulates the main moral
themes of the book, which are thus summed up and disposed
of so that the novel can end on a personal and not a didactic
note. This sequence begins in Book VII, Chapter 3, with
Philip's letter which is clearly meant to contrast with
Stephen's letter in Book VII, Chapter 5. Philip's letter again
sounds the vibrant chord of renunciation, forgiveness and
sympathy, something taken up again by Maggie's final
encounter with Lucy; Stephen's letter by contrast has the
clang and clatter of a shallow and self-satisfied, because
essentially uncomprehending, egoism—'Maggie! whose
pain can have been like mine? Whose injury like mine?'—
mine, me, my, I, the personal pronouns repeat insistently;
Stephen is simply incapable of understanding Maggie's
moral crisis; his offer of reunion belongs to the rejected
world of romantic day-dream. Romance, though still tempting, is again and finally rejected, and Maggie in agony falls
on her knees in prayer:

'Oh God, if my life is to be long, let me live to bless
and comfort—'

At that moment, Maggie felt a startling sensation of sudden cold about her knees and feet; it was water flowing under her. She started up; the stream was flowing under the door that led into the passage. She was not bewildered for an instant—she knew it was the flood!

At this climactic moment one cannot but feel that the novel comes perilously close to the ludicrous, so promptly is Maggie's prayer answered, so pat upon its cue does the river enter. And the disquiet we feel here is mainly the result of enforced speed. This over-compression may also give rise to more serious doubts; to the view, for instance, that the catastrophe is really an evasion by George Eliot of the moral problems she has posed in the rest of the book, rather than a true and satisfying conclusion.

The counterpart of the rushed and crowded ending is the over-leisurely beginning; George Eliot only slowly learned the art of exposition and the technique of introducing her characters at the right time and in the right sequence. Her openings tend sometimes to be indigestible lumps of information; this is most noticeable in *Scenes of Clerical Life*, partly because this is a novice's work and partly because the shortness of the form demands a stricter compression than the full-scale novel—as Lewes remarks to Blackwood of *Janet's Repentance*:

> One feels the want of a larger canvas so as to bring out those admirable figures—old Mr Jerome—the Linnets— and the rest; but that is the drawback of all short stories. (*Haight*, II, p. 378)

Blackwood was an acute critic of these early tales; it was on his advice that George Eliot simplified the distressing death-bed scene in *Amos Barton*, cutting out a good many details about the children. Again, we find Blackwood commenting on the first four chapters of *Janet's Repentance*:

> The glimpse at the end shows that a powerful and pathetic story is coming and I rather wish you had plunged sooner into it instead of expending so much

humour in the delineation of characters who do not seem likely to assist materially in the movement of the Story and who are not in themselves interesting. (*Haight*, II, p. 344)

George Eliot's reply, 'The descriptions of character are not so alien to the drama as they possibly appear to you at present,' is not very convincing.

There are, then, two main defects in George Eliot's handling of the early stages of her narrative; large chunks of description and information, and the introduction of too many characters who tend to clutter up the story and confuse the reader. The first of these is best illustrated by the second chapter of *Mr Gilfil's Love Story* in which we are given several pages describing in far too great detail the beauties of Cheverel Manor, a method which George Eliot consciously assimilates to that of the landscape painter. The second defect is most clearly seen in the opening chapters of *Janet's Repentance*. Here we have in Chapter 2 not only a long chunk of social analysis of a familiar kind, but flanking it, in Chapters 1 and 3, two kinds of chorus which contrast with each other, a common feature of George Eliot's later stories. Dempster and his cronies in the bar of the Red Lion balance the good ladies of Miss Linnet's parlour; and although this contrast foreshadows the main social conflict of the story we feel nevertheless that too much time is spent elaborating for their own sakes minor characters who do not in fact perform a truly choric function and who at this stage in the story only impede the action. Thus Chapter 3 is clearly present in the story largely for its comic possibilities, though these are never exploited later in the tale. If we contrast *Janet's Repentance* with *Silas Marner* the difference is obvious. In *Silas Marner*, too, the male chorus of the Rainbow Inn (Chapter 6) is later balanced by the female chorus preparing for the great dance at the Red House (Chapter 11). But in this case the minor characters are advanced only so far as they throw light on the community as it is involved with the particular story being told; they are delightful in themselves but they fit in with the rest of the book in a much more assured manner than the comparable characters of *Janet's Repentance*.

There are, I think, three causes of the defect I have just described. The first is George Eliot's concern to place her characters in a detailed social context and to give her protagonists depth and perspective by having them move and act within a group of less fully realized characters. This is essential to the nature of her art and she quickly learnt the ways of achieving it. Basically only a few techniques are involved; firstly, the successful handling and placing of the chorus as, for example, in *Silas Marner*. Secondly there is the careful infiltration into the novel of passages of social analysis either by dispersing this into the body of the action so that it is taken for granted by the reader (for example, the birthday celebrations in *Adam Bede*) or by placing it in deliberate isolation from the rest of the novel (for example, the preface to *Felix Holt*) or else by placing it at some natural break in the novel's action, where the reader will naturally tend to pause and take stock. Thirdly there is the problem of the careful placing of the more important characters, of introducing them at sufficiently wide intervals so that each of them has the chance of establishing himself in the reader's memory and imagination. Even George Eliot's first novel, *Adam Bede*, reveals what an advance she has made in this respect over *Scenes of Clerical Life*. Finally there is the problem of contriving a smooth and easy transition between an individual and his social milieu or between one group of characters and another group. In *Scenes of Clerical Life* these transitions are often arbitrary and abrupt; the reader's attention is jerked from one focus to another like a badly handled spotlight.

By contrast, to show how skilful George Eliot became in her handling of this aspect of her art, we may examine Chapter 10 of *Middlemarch* which marks the first change of focus from Dorothea and Casaubon to Lydgate and Rosamund. Since it is the *first* transition of this kind it is a crucial one, for if we do not accept it we are liable to reject the whole fabric of interwoven stories which makes up *Middlemarch*. We should notice first of all that the book is well advanced before George Eliot makes the transition; Dorothea, Celia, Brooke and Casaubon are by this time firmly placed in our minds; there is no danger of confusing them or forgetting them as we switch our attention elsewhere.

With this much established we are ready for an expansion of interest. Towards the end of Chapter 10 we encounter a number of new characters at 'a dinner-party that day, the last of the parties which were held at the Grange as proper preliminaries to the wedding' of Dorothea and Casaubon. The company is more mixed and miscellaneous than usual; 'there was the newly elected mayor of Middlemarch,who happened to be a manufacturer; the philanthropic banker his brother-in-law, who predominated so much in the town that some called him a Methodist, others a hypocrite, according to the resources of their vocabulary, and there were various professional men'. In such a casual manner are Vincy and Bulstrode introduced to us. We have here, in dramatic form, a microcosm of Middlemarch society, of town mingling with county, the sense—subdued now but explicit in the next chapter—of social change, of growth and process. The characters we meet and the conversations we hear have various functions. The first of these is to forward a change in the narrative; since these narrative changes frequently involve and depend upon social changes it is appropriate that this first transition should be accomplished by means of a social occasion. The minor characters who briefly occupy the stage help to give us the sense of Middlemarch society in depth; they are carefully placed for us, socially and economically, so that their relativity of viewpoint, the different opinions they express about the major characters, help to give solidity and extension to the protagonists we already know. This is one function of gossip in this chapter, and in the novel generally; another function is to offer us an oblique or anticipatory introduction to major

I

characters who have not yet directly appeared on the scene. This is neatly contrived in Chapter 10. The men, naturally enough, talk about the women and in doing so unobtrusively direct our attention to the major structural balance between Dorothea and Rosamund. Thus Mr Chichely says, 'Between ourselves, the mayor's daughter is more to my taste than Miss Brooke or Miss Celia either. If I were a marrying man I should choose Miss Vincy before either of them.' This male chorus is carefully, almost symmetrically, balanced by its female counterpart. If the men discuss women, the women, equally naturally, discuss sickness and so direct our attention to the presence of Lydgate at the dinner-party. George Eliot carefully keeps Lydgate in the background; his conversation is reported but not presented, and we are not shown his first meeting with Dorothea although his reactions to her are stated:

> Mr Lydgate, of course, was out of hearing. He had quitted the party early, and would have thought it altogether tedious but for the novelty of certain introductions, especially the introduction to Miss Brooke, whose youthful bloom, with her approaching marriage to that faded scholar and her interest in matters socially useful, gave her the piquancy of an unusual combination.
>
> 'She is a good creature—that fine girl—but a little too earnest,' he thought. 'It is troublesome to talk to such women. They are always wanting reasons, yet they are too ignorant to understand the merits of any question, and usually fall back on their moral sense to settle things after their own taste.'

This looks back to Mr Chichely's observations and forward to Lydgate's opinions as stated at the opening of the next chapter—one notices the clearly implied parallelism:

> 'He had seen Miss Vincy above his horizon almost as long as it had taken Mr Casaubon to become engaged and married.'

The narrative transition and the expansion of interest is completed in Chapter 11 by a detailed analysis of Middlemarch society, which because of the immediately preceding dramatic presentation of that society does not seem external or artificially contrived; by the time the chapter finishes we are firmly placed within the Vincy family and are hearing of other groups and characters still to come—the Garth family and Featherstone.

This is George Eliot at her best and it is a far remove from the novice work of *Scenes of Clerical Life*. If I may return to that work for a moment I should like to isolate two other reasons for George Eliot's clumsy handling of her narrative structure, factors which we might expect to find in the early work of most novelists. Both spring from the author's natural initial mistrust of her creative powers, a mistrust which could only be overcome by experience and success. The first is an over-reliance on memory, on actual facts and situations already known to the novelist. It is significant that those interested in the local history behind George Eliot's fiction find their richest source in *Scenes of Clerical Life* rather than in the most personal of her novels, *The Mill On The Floss*. George Eliot can describe Cheverel Manor in such lengthy and elaborate detail because she is remembering Arbury Park, the home of the Newdegates. Description rather than creation is, indeed, the keynote of this first volume. She is, of course, always concerned to make the background of her novels as accurate as possible; she will look up almanacs for details of floods for *The Mill On The Floss*, she will read *The Times* reports of the 1832 election for *Felix Holt*, she will do an immense amount of historical research for *Romola*. But in none of these—not even in *Romola*—does she depend so heavily on remembered or re-constructed detail as she does in *Scenes of Clerical Life*.

I have already touched on the other reason when I said that Chapter 3 of *Janet's Repentance* contains comic possibilities which are never in fact realized. The inexperienced novelist will often tend to fear that he may dry up before he reaches the end of his story; consequently he will lay down reserves of material in his novel that he never actually draws upon. We can sometimes recognize the seed of a plot that never germinates, the embryo of a character that never develops. Such a novel may sometimes develop a trajectory that leads nowhere; it will arouse in us expectations which, if we remember them, are disappointed because the novelist no longer needs or no longer has time to fulfil the latent possibilities he has so carefully prepared. I am not thinking here of absurdly contrived plot mechanisms like the mysterious horseman who in Chapter 2 of *Adam Bede* listens to Dinah preaching on the village green and who at the end of the novel turns out to be the governor of the prison in which Hetty is confined. Nor am I thinking of cumbrous and uneconomic plot complications like the chain of incidents in Chapters 12-14 of *Felix Holt*, a clumsy sequence of coincidences whereby Christian's pocket-book, stolen by Scales as a joke, is found by Felix Holt and passed on to Rufus Lyon, who then thinks that Christian may be Esther's father. Such complication is unnecessary in an already involved plot since it actually leads nowhere; its only result is to put Lyon in a position where he can challenge the Reverend Debarry to a debate. The whole episode is a piece of artistic indiscipline rare at this stage of George Eliot's career.

If we think of the main narrative thread of the novel as a river, there often exist a number of tributaries which seem promising and inviting but which ultimately peter out or wind back upon themselves. We must distinguish these from the other kind of tributaries I mentioned earlier in this chapter, those oblique and unexplored relationships which give the sense of a particular life and history merging into other adjacent lives and histories. These are controlled and calculated; they are deliberately subdued and muted, not accidentally left unexplored because the author had no time or need to use them. Three brief examples should be enough to clarify my point.

In Chapter 32 of *Adam Bede* the company of the Donnithorne Arms is excited by the rumour that the Squire intends to hire a new bailiff. Gossip is substantiated when the Squire visits the Poysers to discuss certain changes in their lease; as a result of Mrs Poyser's temper they are threatened with eviction when their lease expires. Subsequent events of course preclude the realization of this threat, but the whole episode is oddly isolated from the main stream of the novel. The chapter does have certain advantages; it allows George Eliot to exploit Mrs Poyser's comic qualities to the full and it serves as a bridge-passage, as a necessary interposition between Hetty's disillusionment about Arthur and her subsequent acceptance of Adam, which otherwise would seem too abrupt. It can even, with a little ingenuity, be related to the main strands of the book; the comic possibility of eviction which here faces the Poysers is later changed into a tragic possibility of voluntary removal in the face of Hetty's public disgrace. It looks for a moment as if Mr Poyser's statement of one of the main themes of the novel—'We should leave our roots behind us, I doubt, and niver thrive again'—is to be ironically fulfilled.

But when all these allowances have been made, the episode remains distinct and insufficiently assimilated to the rest of the novel; it is an example of a plot complication which is never properly worked out. In *The Mill On The Floss* it is not a single episode but a pattern of relationships which is hinted at but not explored. In Book VI, Chapter 4, Bob Jakin suggests to Maggie that Tom is in love with Lucy; this is the reason why he sits 'by himself so glumpish, a-knittin' his brow, and a-lookin' at the fire of a night'. It seems likely that George Eliot contemplated turning the Maggie-Stephen-Lucy triangle into an emotional parallelogram by the addition of Tom, but the situation is not in fact developed; perhaps she felt that to do so would be to make the symmetry of the pattern too obvious and certainly she had neither time nor space at the end of the book to allow for this possible subsidiary relationship.

My final example is from *Felix Holt* and illustrates the way in which our expectations are aroused and then disappointed as we follow the line of the story only to come to an un-

expected gap. As we have seen, the complicated history of
Christian's pocket-book enables Rufus Lyon to challenge
the Reverend Debarry to a debate. Debarry prudently dele-
gates this task to his curate, Mr Sherlock. All the evidence
points to the fact that George Eliot was working towards a
grand comic set piece which would display Lyon's rhetoric
to its best advantage and which should also act as a kind of
comic parallel to the political theme dominating this part of
the novel. We are told, indeed, in Chapter 24 that 'the
feminine world of Treby Magna was much more agitated by
the prospect than by that of any candidate's speech.' Yet in
this same chapter we learn that the wretched Sherlock has
defaulted with the result that the debate never in fact takes
place. This, while comic in itself, cannot but be anti-clim-
actic in view of the elaborate preparations leading up to the
scene. Why George Eliot should have decided not to give us
this debate must remain conjectural, though there are several
possible reasons. Possibly she felt, no doubt rightly, that
Lyon's rhetoric, comic though it is in small doses, would
become merely tedious if indulged in to the extent demanded
by a debate. Perhaps she felt that the scene would detract
from the political comedy or that it would distract the reader
from the complications of the plot. But whatever the reason,
one feels that she has here led us into a cul-de-sac; our
expectations are thwarted, a great deal of elaborate preparation leads to virtually nothing at all.

At the same time it must be said that *Felix Holt* is one of
the most interesting of George Eliot's novels from the point
of view of the reader's chronology. Sometimes we are told
the truth—or part of the truth—in advance, but equally
often we are held in suspense and our gradual enlightenment
goes hand in hand with that of the characters in the novel.
George Eliot has often to show us a character being over-
taken by his past—Bulstrode is the obvious example—but
generally she does not contrive this in any striking or original
way. But in *Felix Holt* both the legal complications of the
plot and our gradual realization of the truth about Jermyn's

relationship with Harold and Mrs Transome are masterfully handled; this is the nearest George Eliot approaches to the same gradual process of painful enlightenment that forms the basis of *The Portrait of A Lady* and it is certainly superior to the hero's realization of his true nature and origin in *Daniel Deronda*.

George Eliot's treatment of time, then, is not so unremarkable as it may appear at first glance. Indeed, as I have tried to show with *Adam Bede*, its very unobtrusiveness can enhance the effectiveness of its function. There are many flaws in her handling of time, particularly in her early work. But I hope I have also shown that a consideration of her novels as temporal works—temporal both in the sense of the plot's construction and in the sense of an unfolding experience in the reader's mind—reveals a profound concern on George Eliot's part with formal qualities of her art that far transcend those of the mere story-teller. These formal qualities are the aesthetic counterparts of an equally profound concern with the processes of moral growth and decay.

CHAPTER VI

Structure III
Architecture

I n an earlier chapter I tried to define what is meant by
the spatial pattern of a novel and what happens to our
reading when we are engaged in discovering these
patterns. The simplest disturbance of a straightforward
narrative chronology which provokes such critical activity is
explicit foreshadowing by the novelist of what is to come.
This may be achieved by comment and exposition or by the
interaction of character. Thus when in *Silas Marner* Godfrey
Cass sees the face of his dead wife and George Eliot comments:

> He cast only one glance at the dead face on the pillow,
> which Dolly had smoothed with decent care; but he remem-
> bered that last look at his unhappy hated wife so well,
> that at the end of sixteen years every line in the worn face
> was present to him when he told the full story of this
> night. (13)

We are immediately alerted to the possibility of the way in
which the story will end. Similarly, even if we are reading
The Mill On The Floss for the first time, we can hardly ignore
the hint offered us when Phillip attacks Maggie's passion
for renunciation:

> It is mere cowardice to seek safety in negations. No
> character becomes strong in that way. You will be thrown
> into the world some day, and then every rational satisfac-
> tion of your nature that you deny now, will assault you
> like a savage appetite. (V, 3)

This explicit foreshadowing is only the most obvious
example of an intricate network of anticipation and recollec-

tion, transcending the narrative chronology, which is clearly the result of George Eliot's major moral concerns—Nemesis, the complex chain of effects deriving from a single cause, moral growth and decay, the narrowness or breadth of the individual moral life (which includes narrowness or breadth in time, the ability to learn from the past and to weigh future consequences), the determining pressures of one's past life, and so on. Take, for example, one of the larger structural balances of *The Mill On The Floss*, the gathering of the Dodson clan in Book I, Chapter 7 and Book III, Chapter 3. The meeting of the constituent families has several functions, the simplest of which is obviously the production of a good deal of local comedy. But it also serves to illuminate the major contrast of characters—Tom and Maggie—and to give a sense of social solidity. George Eliot can no longer show the whole community in action, as she did on several occasions in *Adam Bede*—the society of St Oggs is now too large and complex for that. Nevertheless, the cramping and thwarting pressures of the community are vitally important and must therefore be imaged in small by the device of the family, the collective voice of the St Oggs' ethos. But finally, and most relevant to George Eliot's moral concern, the family scene in III. 3 is the direct result of the gathering in I. 13. In the later chapter the family are met to see if they can salvage anything from Tulliver's catastrophic bankruptcy—but the seeds of this catastrophe were sown at the first family gathering, when Tulliver, having quarrelled with Mrs Glegg, had to borrow five hundred pounds from one of Wakem's clients (I. 13) in order to repay her loan. Thus his ruin is caused not only by discord within the community at large (his litigation over the river) but also by discord within the smaller community of the family. The first scene thus anticipates the second in the most direct way possible; the one causes the other. A comparable case, though the connections here are more devious, is the similar structural balance in *Adam Bede*, the two meetings of Adam and Arthur in the Grove.

Often, however, there is no causal or narrative link between these balancing masses; the reader has to make the
connections for himself, and in doing so he creates a perspective within which the characters are seen in an ironic or
foreboding light. Such is the implicit contrast between the
opening chapter of Book VI of *The Mill On The Floss* with
its ironical title, 'A Duet In Paradise', reinforced within the
chapter by references to 'The Creation', part of which Lucy
plays. The reader, when he comes to this, cannot but re-
collect the other paradise in the book, the Eden of childhood
from which, at the very end of the second Book, Tom and
Maggie are expelled.

> The two slight youthful figures soon grew indistinct on
> the distant road—were soon lost behind the projecting
> hedgerow.
> They had gone forth together into their new life of
> sorrow, and they would never more see the sunshine un-
> dimmed by remembered cares. They had entered the
> thorny wilderness and the golden gates of their childhood
> had for ever closed behind them.

Such a recollection will strengthen the reader's impression
—derived from a view of the innocent Lucy and the sophisticated Stephen—that this second paradise is also a very
precarious state, that the whole situation is delicately poised
before the forthcoming visit of Maggie. The sense of poise,
of imminent change, does something to prepare us for the
speed and violence of events in this part of the novel.

Similarly, irony may be the result when anticipation is
unconscious on the part of the character. Thus when in
Book I, Chapter 7, Mr Tulliver boasts of his son's education:

> 'But then, you know, it's an investment; Tom's eddica-
> tion 'ull be so much capital to him.'
> 'Ay, there's something in that,' said Mr Glegg. 'Well,
> well, neighbour Tulliver, you may be right, you may be
> right:
> > When land is gone and money's spent,
> > Then learning is most excellent.'

We must see irony not only in Mr Glegg's unconscious prognostication of ruin but also in the complete worthlessness of Tom's education, of which Mr Tulliver is so proud, in face of that ruin.

There are many modes of anticipation apart from those we have just mentioned. One device is the apparently casual but in fact significant conversation; thus, for example, the conversation between Irwine and Arthur in Chapter 16 of *Adam Bede* clearly propounds some of the major moral themes of the book—and this without any sense of strain or contrivance. In this it may be contrasted with the conversation between Arthur and Adam earlier in the same chapter which foreshadows their fight in the Grove and which doesn't arise quite naturally out of the situation and their previous conversation.

Such a device is fairly extended and formal; but at the other end of the scale anticipation may be introduced in a very devious or oblique manner. Chapter 2 of *Silas Marner* is a good example. Early in the chapter Silas Marner's attitude to religion is defined:

> A weaver who finds hard words in his hymn-book knows nothing of abstractions; as the little child knows nothing of parental love, but only knows one face and one lap towards which its stretches its arms for refuge and nurture.

Here the vehicle of the comparison clearly looks forward to a state of affairs which will actually develop in the story; the image is soon converted into literal fact. Similarly the close symbolic connection between the golden-haired Eppie and the miser's hoard is hinted at towards the end of this chapter when Marner thinks 'fondly of the guineas that were only half earned by the work in this loom, as if they had been unborn children'.

Anticipation, then, may manifest itself in the novels in anything from large balancing masses and contrasts down to the details of the most casual image. In this it differs from another device, juxtaposition. Juxtaposition on a small scale

may complicate our attitude by introducing overtones ranging from gentle humour to downright malice. I mean, for
example, the local force of the phrasing in this description
of Grandcourt:

> It was to be supposed of him that he would put up with
> nothing less than the best in outward equipment, wife
> included; and the bride was what he might have been
> expected to choose. (35)

But juxtaposition on a large scale is necessary if the mere
fact of contiguity is to force us to make connections between
the contiguous parts which will transcend and outlast their
merely temporal sequence. Within these limits George Eliot
uses the device fairly frequently and extremely effectively.
Thus in *Adam Bede*, Chapters 4, 5 and 6 present us with
three contrasting ways of life by putting together the Bede,
Irwine and Poyser households, thereby fulfilling the humble
function of introducing us to many of the most important
characters and also of giving us a sense of the different social
strata within the apparently narrow and isolated community
of Hayslope. Dinah's spiritual failure with Hetty in Chapter
15 is immediately followed by Irwine's similar failure with
Arthur in Chapter 16, while Chapters 36 and 37 contrast
formally Hetty's two journeys, of hope and despair. The
effect of these juxtapositions is to throw into greater relief
the likeness or unlikeness existing between characters and
relationships. Most of the structural devices in George
Eliot's novels that we could term spatial are directed to
the creation of parallels and contrasts or, more subtly, of
areas of human character and behaviour within which similarity and dissimilarity are inextricably mixed. The perception of this network of relationships is, as I have said, the
major end of the novels and the methods of creating it the
determining factor in their formal properties.

These relationships are rarely simple or single. Thus the
contrast of Dinah and Hetty is only the most important of a
whole range of interlocking parallels and oppositions. We

have already seen how important the temporal qualities of
the novel are in creating this contrast, but it is enforced in
many other ways. Dinah is the blood-niece of Mrs Poyser as
Hetty is of Mr Poyser, and they are both like Arthur in that
their parents died early. It is as if George Eliot is saying,
'This is what they share at the outset, yet look how different
their final destinies.' This is a favourite trick of hers, the
effect of displaying the various possibilities of life by having
different individuals diverge fan-wise from a common starting-point. In Chapters 7 and 8 Arthur and Hetty are
formally paired off as against Dinah and Irwine; profane is
balanced against sacred. At the end of Chapter 8 the two
girls are carefully contrasted by their reactions to the death
of Adam's father. In Chapter 11 they are brought together
for the first time, carefully and explicitly, as an object for
comparison in Adam's mind. The whole of Chapter 15 is
well-nigh taken up with an extended comparison; Dinah
looking outwards in meditation over the landscape, Hetty
peering into the blotched mirror that serves—as with
Gwendolen Harleth—as an apt image of her self-enclosed
egoism. In Chapter 20 Hetty emerges as a kind of parody
of Dinah:

> The little minx had found a black gown of her aunt's,
> and pinned it close round her neck to look like Dinah's,
> had made her hair as flat as she could, and had tied on one
> of Dinah's high-crowned borderless net-caps. The thought
> of Dinah's pale grave face and mild grey eyes, which the
> sight of the gown and cap brought with it, made it a
> laughable surprise to see them replaced by Hetty's round
> rosy cheeks and coquettish dark eyes.

And so on—there is no need to labour the point. But
beside this we must place the fact that the Dinah-Hetty
relationship illuminates and is illuminated by the other
relationships in the novel; Hetty-Adam, Hetty-Arthur,
Adam-Arthur, Dinah-Irwine, Dinah-Adam, Dinah-Mrs
Poyser; all of these criss-cross and intersect or else meet and
run parallel for a while before diverging. And this network

is further complicated and supported by the minor characters—Lisbeth Bede, Seth Bede, Bartle Massey, even Bessy
Cranage.

It would be superfluous to repeat this kind of analysis
with all the novels; it is something that any reader easily does
for himself. Indeed, the danger is not that the novels will be
found deficient in this respect but that such analysis will
tend to overemphasize their formal characteristics and make
them too schematic, each part neatly and precisely interlocking with the rest. Sometimes George Eliot *is* too neat;
I have in mind the kind of thing exemplified by Farebrother's
love for Mary Garth in *Middlemarch*. This creates a neat
subsidiary triangle, but it does not ring true; it shows too
obviously the contriving and manipulating hand of the artist
anxious to inject a little drama into even the most subsidiary
of her situations. Elsewhere George Eliot avoids the trap;
thus she decides not to make Esther Lyon a Transome; she
does not wish 'to adopt this additional coincidence. Setting
it aside, the story is in the track of ordinary probability'
(*Haight*, IV, p. 231). But the problem is not merely one of
coincidence; it is a question of reconciling the blurred edges
and loose ends of the naturalistic surface of life with the kind
and degree of formal organization required of a work of art.
It is a question which constantly confronts the naturalistic
writer. On the one hand the writer must avoid the naturalistic fallacy that art should or can directly render the quality
of real life; on the other hand he must not impose too schematic a moral pattern upon his material. As with the writer,
so with the reader. The reader must beware of applying
moral criteria to the novel as though it were merely evidence,
a transcript of what actually happens. But it is the opposite
danger which most confronts the reader in an age of great
critical sophistication, the danger that by neatly smoothing
away the blurred edges and tying up all the loose ends he
may convert the novel into a precise pattern, a beautifully
articulated jigsaw which is yet unfaithful to the vision of
life inherent in the novel. The reader must follow George

Eliot in steering between the Scylla of naturalism and the Charybdis of formalism.

With this in mind let us return for a moment to James's review of *Middlemarch*. This, like most of his criticism of George Eliot, reflects the mixed feelings I tried to analyse in my opening chapter. On the one hand he tries once again to shape the formal structure of the book around one central figure, faulting it because naturally it refuses to conform to this pattern. 'And yet, nominally,' he writes, '*Middlemarch* has a definite subject—the subject indicated in the eloquent preface. . . . Dorothea's career is, however, but an episode, and though doubtless in intention, not distinctly enough in fact, the central one.'

What we know of the history of *Middlemarch's* creation is evidence enough for supporting that James has mistaken George Eliot's intention. But even taking the novel in isolation, we should surely not allow the impression of the preface (in itself unfortunate) to overrule or to predetermine the impression derived from the novel as a whole.

'It is not compact, doubtless, but when was a panorama compact?' James's ambivalent attitude, his mixture of admiration and exasperation, comes out in this question. But the question itself conceals a view of the novel which is at best only half true. Certainly *Middlemarch* is, in one sense, panoramic; that is to say, if one wants to find a unifying centre, one does better to locate it in a society, in Middlemarch itself, rather than in any one individual. And yet, one must insist in the face of James, the novel *is* extraordinarily compact; it is remarkable how little one can cut out or reduce in scale without vitally impairing its essential achievement— certainly much less than in *Adam Bede* or *The Mill On The Floss*. Fortunately James has given us an idea of what, he thinks, could have been excised.

The greatest minds have the defects of their qualities, and as George Eliot's mind is preeminently contemplative and analytic, nothing is more natural than that her manner should be discursive and expansive. 'Concentration' would doubtless have deprived us of many of the best things in the book—of Peter Featherstone's grotesquely expectant legatees, of Lydgate's medical rivals, and of Mary Garth's delightful family. . . . Mr Farebrother and his 'delightful womankind' belong to a large group of figures begotten of the superabundance of the author's creative instinct. At times they seem to encumber the stage and to produce a rather ponderous mass of dialogue; but they add to the reader's impression of having walked in the Middlemarch lanes and listened to the Middlemarch accent. To but one of these accessory episodes—that of Mr Bulstrode, with its multiplex ramifications, do we take exception. It has a slightly artificial cast, a melodramatic tinge, unfriendly to the richly natural colouring of the whole. Bulstrode himself—with the history of whose troubled conscience the author has taken great pains—is, to our sense, too diffusely treated; he never grasps the reader's attention.

James, in part, answers his own objection. The minor characters do cumulatively create that sense of social density from which the protagonists derive so much of their strength, without which they would be unimaginable. Granted that a large part of Lydgate's solidity of specification lies in his professional life and granted that his tragedy lies in the corrosion of his ambition by social forces, how could we do without a picture of his medical colleagues? Confronted with James's criticism of Bulstrode, one can only assert the contrary; he is, surely, one of the book's great successes, with a certain grasp of 'the reader's attention'. He is one of the book's finest end-products; with his equals he provides us with the best possible reason for reading the novel. We may grant that the 'multiplex ramifications' of his story can be criticized. Not so much, I think, the Raffles-Rigg part of the plot mechanism; George Eliot persuades us of the paradoxical naturalness of chance and coincidence in a quite remarkable way. The weak point, rather, is the linking of Bulstrode's past history with that of Ladislaw; this is the wrong kind of coincidence and it does have 'a slightly artificial cast, a melodramatic tinge'.

What of the centres of interest represented in the novel by Featherstone and the Garth family? That the Featherstone episodes provide locally a good deal of grotesque comedy is true but is not a sufficient reason for their presence in the novel. We may also discount the fact that Featherstone's death starts in motion the Rigg-Raffles chain of events which leads to Bulstrode's downfall—some other device of plot could easily have been made to produce the same results. But, of course, Featherstone relates also to Casaubon and to Bulstrode. The novel does not—must not —make the relationship overt, but we are surely led to connect the effect of Featherstone's will on Fred and Mary with the effect of Casaubon's will on Dorothea and Ladislaw. The connecting element is just strong enough, the results sufficiently diverse, for us to feel that effect of unity in variety which is so important a part of George Eliot's sense of the quality of life. And if we assimilate these two instances, seeing them as particular examples of the dead hand of the past controlling the living present, then we can contrast these two cases with Bulstrode. The dead hand of Featherstone or Casaubon paradoxically liberates and re-vivifies those whom it was meant to govern or thwart; Bulstrode's past, which he thought dead and buried, springs to life and destroys him. Bulstrode is in many ways close to Featherstone; for both of them—for Featherstone crudely, for Bulstrode subtly—money is power. This is Featherstone:

> He loved money, but he also loved to spend it in gratifying his peculiar tastes, and perhaps he loved it best of all as a means of making others feel his power more or less uncomfortably. (34)

Set him beside Bulstrode:

> His private minor loans were numerous, but he would inquire strictly into the circumstances both before and after. In this way a man gathers a domain in his neighbours' hope and fear as well as gratitude; and power, when once it has got into that subtle region, propagates itself, spreading out of all proportion to its external means. (16)

K

It is no wonder that Featherstone, in one of those anti-cipatory hints we discussed earlier, sees so clearly into Bulstrode's heart, diagnosing so acutely the tangled strands of money and religion:

> And what's he?—he's got no land hereabout that ever I heard tell of. A speckilating fellow! He may come down any day, when the devil leaves off backing him. And that's what his religion means: he wants God A'mighty to come in. (12)

It is entirely appropriate that Stone Court should pass from Featherstone to Bulstrode. If Featherstone were re-moved from the novel, two of its main centres (although, for James, Bulstrode himself is only accessory) would be con-siderably weakened.

The role of the Garth family is more complex. Again, I discount their own intrinsic interest, their function in the plot and their role in composing part of the social strata of Middlemarch—though these, in themselves, might be thought sufficient reasons for their presence in the novel. We must examine their other structural functions. Caleb Garth is an embodiment—like Farebrother—of a moral norm, of the good life; as such he is much more successful than George Eliot's similar attempts in her other novels. His integrity is clear when, having heard the truth from Raffles about Bulstrode, he refuses to work for him any longer,

> 'I would injure no man if I could help it,' said Caleb; 'even if I thought God winked at it.' (69)

In the one sentence he puts straight all that is perverted in Bulstrode himself, for Bulstrode lives under the special Providence of a God who conveniently looks the other way. In his integrity, his refusal to be involved or compromised, Garth contrasts in this and succeeding chapters with Lyd-gate. (Incidentally, Garth's real poverty throws Lydgate's financial worries into relief.)

The Garths are the one solidly happy family in the book

and as such provide a standard whereby the failings of the
other marriages can be measured. Apart from the devious
contrasts with the Casaubons and the Lydgates, the Garths
relate especially—because of Fred—to the Vincy household.
The different relationships of parents to children is especially
well illustrated in Chapter 25 while the different reactions of
Mrs Garth and Mrs Vincy to the news of Fred's decision to
work for Caleb illustrate George Eliot's mature control over
that difficult and complex area of human experience where
likeness and unlikeness merge into each other. Comparison
and contrast always involve a fine sense of psychological and
moral discrimination.

Mary Garth most obviously throws Rosamund into relief;
Chapter 12 is a fine illustration of this. Mary is at this stage
a kind of deputy for Dorothea so far as this particular
relationship is concerned. She is used here so that the direct
contrast of Rosamund and Dorothea—they have already
been linked in Lydgate's mind—need not be introduced too
early in the novel but can be reserved for later climactic
moments. But Mary is in many ways a minor analogue to
Dorothea; she is very much to Fred (and Featherstone) what
Dorothea is to Will (and Casaubon). Her refusal to burn
Featherstone's will is very like Dorothea's delay in agreeing
to Casaubon's final request.

Of course, Mary cannot be treated adequately without
reference to Fred. I will notice here only two minor points.
Just as Fred serves to illuminate more important characters
—generally Will and Lydgate—so he in turn is illuminated
by an even lesser character, by the visit to the Garth home of
this favourite and successful son, Christy. The smallest roles,
the most fragmentary appearances have their function.
Secondly the novel ends not with any great climax, but
quietly, in the Garth family. This casts further doubt
on James's views of George Eliot's intention concerning
Dorothea. George Eliot does allow Dorothea her climactic
moment and she prepares for it by a device which she also
used in *The Mill On The Floss* (and of which James also was

very fond); the mounting series of interviews—Dorothea and Lydgate, Dorothea and Rosamund, Dorothea and Will. But the quiet close reminds us that the story is not Dorothea's alone; it contributes to that peculiarly open effect in George Eliot's novels, that sense of life spreading out and continuing in time. It is for this reason primarily that we can accept the Epilogue as something more than an awkward convention.

Mary Garth leads us to Fred Vincy and Fred, if we had time to deal with him properly, would lead us to larger and still larger characters and issues until we had encompassed the whole novel. It is in this sense of connection, of relationship, that the true form and unity of *Middlemarch* is to be discovered.

Clearly the kind of approach I have outlined in this chapter has certain dangers. One may too easily forget that such analysis does not in itself provide sufficient grounds for a final judgment. It may help towards such judgment, but the care with which a work yields to our technical examination is no safe guide to its quality. Technical finesse all too often beguiles the critic into applauding not the work but his own skill. Nevertheless, when all qualifications have been made, such an approach is useful. Even as ordinary readers we cannot avoid a simple kind of spatial analysis if we are to appreciate the network of relationships, the sequence of ever-widening perspectives which bestows on us that increase in sympathy and understanding, that moral enlargement which is the end to which all George Eliot's aesthetic means are directed. It is mainly by such an approach that we can realize with all the novels James's comment on the best of them:

A work of the liberal scope of *Middlemarch* contains a multitude of artistic intentions, some of the finest of which become clear only in the meditative after-taste of perusal.

CHAPTER VII

Character I
The Background

APART from the investigation of image-patterns, the effect of Shakespearian criticism on the criticism of the novel has nowhere been greater than in our changing concept of character. Every self-respecting undergraduate has been taught to regard the characters of a Shakespearian play not as autonomous entities, living lives of their own, but as elements in the total imaginative configuration of the work. That this change in outlook has been accomplished by an increasing emphasis on the primary importance of the poetry in Shakespearian drama can be seen from even a casual reading of, say, Professor Knights's *How Many Children Had Lady Macbeth?* And because the poetic use of language is so obviously a central fact, this change in our view of Shakespearian characters has undoubtedly marked a genuine and valuable advance. But this new emphasis, when transferred to the novel, has been less happy in its results, partly because the novel is texturally less interesting than the poetic play, partly because it is a more expansive, leisurely form, and partly because it often aims at the kind of naturalism which blinds and blinkers us if we try to discover it in Shakespearian drama. Moreover, this new approach can easily dwindle into a perfunctorily mechanical and jargon-ridden routine in which the merely fashionable replaces the genuinely perceptive.

This change in outlook—its value and some of its limitations—can be seen in an extract from a recent article by Professor Leo Kirschbaum, which is fairly representative of a broad sector of modern criticism:

It is no longer the fashion for criticism to regard a Shakespeare play as a kind of D.N.B. volume of life-portraits. We now recognize that he wrote poetic drama, and that such drama is necessarily governed by pattern or design. Character, event, language, theme and image are now seen as parts of a complex architecture. Moreover we are beginning to recognize that such poetic design enforces a non-naturalistic mode the recognition of which must ultimately affect our view of character and characterization. . . . F. P. Wilson writes, 'In *Macbeth*, many characters are brought in with no attempt to make them individual; the sergeant, the messenger, the doctor, the waiting-woman, the murderers, the Old Man, and we may add Ross, Angus and Lennox. The core of the play's experience is expressed through Macbeth, and these characters are without personality, as much as characters in a morality play. They act as chorus to the "swelling act of the imperial theme!" ' (*Elizabethan and Jacobean*, 1945, p. 122). But neither *chorus* nor *symbol* is a completely satisfactory term. The first tends to disallow both those touches of individualism in which the lavish Shakespeare excels, and also any involvement of the character in the action; the second implies *unity* of significance and hence cannot cover a character who possesses little realistic unity and yet has a multiplicity of 'ideational purposes'. I prefer the term *function*, looser as it is.[1]

Clearly this viewpoint must be modified considerably if we are to discuss George Eliot in these terms. She is not faced, like Shakespeare, with the urgent demands of compression and concentration, and her avowed aims involve a fair degree of naturalism. She is not a poet and she is not concerned, as Shakespeare so often is, with extreme and special cases, but with the humdrum, the usual and the mediocre. The gap between the unique, particular instance and the general state of things is much narrower in her than in Shakespeare—as we have seen, the omniscient author convention is here one important bridging agent. The kind of universality she attains is not that of Shakespeare, in

[1] L. Kirschbaum, 'Banquo and Edgar: Character or Function', *Essays in Criticism*, 7, 1957, pp. 1-21.

which we are compelled to acknowledge that life, wrought
to such a pitch and lived with such intensity, *could* be like
this; if she is at all to be assimilated to poetry, her kind of
achievement is much more like that of Gray's *Elegy* which,
as Johnson says, 'abounds with images which find a mirror
in every mind and with sentiments to which every bosom
returns an echo'. Nevertheless, we should do well to recognize in George Eliot's novels characters whose role in the
'complex architecture' of her work is primarily functional.

Some characters, indeed, are elaborated so little that their
individuality is completely subordinated to that functional
role. These characters tend to fall into three groups. There
are those who play some minor but necessary part in the plot
of the novel, mechanisms rather than persons. Or they may
exist to state in its most explicit form some moral norm or
positive—they are voices rather than persons; Dr Kenn in
The Mill On The Floss is perhaps the best example of this.
Or they are voices of another kind, voices not of the individual but of the community, part of a background or a
chorus which if it were differentiated or individualized,
would obtrude and distract our attention.

Once we advance beyond these simple categories, however, our difficulties begin. At the opposite extreme of these
agents or voices are the protagonists whose characters col-
lectively form the area in which the moral struggles of the
book are played out. In a sense these characters are ends in
themselves, not functions or means to an end; the novels
exist to reveal their moral dilemmas and conflicts. As I have
said, George Eliot's characteristic method is to have several
of these moral centres interacting and competing for our
attention and sympathy; the structural correlative of this is
her typical interweaving of concurrent stories. (There are,
of course, other links—often complex and subtle—between
these centres of interest, but these connections operate at
deeper levels than the purely narrative, levels which engage
not merely our interest but our deepest powers of understanding, sympathy and moral sensitivity.) Consequently it

is useless to search in George Eliot's novels for a *disponible* in the Jamesian sense of the word; the one possible exception is Maggie in *The Mill On The Floss*, but even Maggie is not the commanding centre that Isabel Archer is in *The Portrait of A Lady*. We must look, then, for pattern or design, but we must realize too that this pattern may be composed of characters who are not merely functions in the pattern but also ends in themselves. Too much emphasis on the functional aspects of characterization may easily lead to critical distortion. It is surely true that a concern with character-as-function comes through the critical filter more easily than a concern with character-as-an-end-in-itself. To deal with the functional aspects of a character, to analyse its place in the total imaginative configuration of the novel is perhaps a more satisfying critical process because it is more definite and clear-cut, and because it is more easily verified by reference to the actual work of art. But such an emphasis may lead us unawares into evading the challenge of the novel to our deepest, most mature comprehension of the quality of life embodied in it.

I do not wish to underestimate the value of such an approach nor to deny that it is impelled by anything but the most respectable of motives—on the one hand, the determination that what Professor Kirschbaum calls the 'D.N.B.' approach shall never occur again, and on the other hand a proper fear lest the moral burden of the novels be distorted into an ethical treatise. But I think that if we are honest with ourselves we shall find that in our effort to discover and analyse this or that aspect of technique, we sometimes fob off the challenge to judge the qualitative content of the novels with a reference to 'moral vision' or to 'thematic unity'. Nowadays we frequently have insights, perceptions, but I feel that these have often little to do with the demand for wisdom that the work of art makes of us.

The stress on 'thematic unity' is so heavy, I suppose, because such a concept is more inclusive than traditional concepts like plot and character. Moreover, it is a very flexible concept. It may be dealt with broadly and briefly in that opening or concluding paragraph which is the critic's face-saving gesture of recognition that his analytical concern does not, of course, encompass the whole of the work with which he is dealing. It may be related to plot and character, frequently with the assertion that it controls and disciplines these things; it may be dealt with by narrowing down the focus of attention to deal with particular details of language. All of this gives the critic the satisfying feeling that he is getting close to the heart of the novel. And, indeed, the inclusiveness and flexibility of the thematic approach should not be underestimated. But it is, I think, liable to two chief dangers.

Other approaches, of course, may have their dangers too. If one is dealing with a novel in terms of plot, one may not get very far unless one complicates the concept as, for example, Professor R. S. Crane does when dealing with *Tom Jones* in an essay in which *plot* ends up as synonymous with the unifying 'idea' of the total work.[2] Again, with character as one's central concept, one may tend to substitute one's own creations for the realities of the book or to view those of the book as autonomous beings. But the filter of the critical intellect may distort the idea of theme no less than those of plot and character, by its inevitable translation of an imaginative into an intellectual mode. Unless we are very careful, a thematic approach may lead to even greater abstraction than the traditional concepts; we may see at the heart of the book our own general and satisfying—because self-formulated—statement, instead of the complex and sometimes annoyingly muddled particulars which actually compose the work.

Consider, for instance, the theme of vocation in *Middlemarch*. In one sense it is clearly central and yet it is not the theme as such that makes its impact but rather the tangle of differentiated and yet connected destinies, individually

---

[2] R. S. Crane, 'The Plot of *Tom Jones*', in *Critics and Criticism*, pp. 616-48. University of Chicago Press, 1952.

worked out through the various characters. It is to these individual destinies that we should primarily attend, not to the theme of vocation which, strictly speaking, has no separate existence apart from them, although the ease with which it is formulated and handled in critical terms may lead us to suppose that it *is* the centre. In fact, it is a lowest common denominator, a reduction we make—purely for convenience—from a number of very different histories.

Of these, the stories of Lydgate and Dorothea are obviously the most important. Their destinies are sufficiently alike for us to draw parallels between them and these are certainly an important part of the novel's structure. Both have a similar brand of idealism operating in the different spheres of social reform and scientific research. Both are similarly 'placed'; Dorothea is to St Theresa as Lydgate is to Vesalius. Both are frustrated in their vocation by a combination of milieu and individual failings—in Lydgate's case his 'spots of commonness', in Dorothea's her 'too theoretical nature'. Further comparisons between the two could be drawn without much ingenuity, but I doubt whether we should be tempted by these into leaping the gap between two individual characters and a generalized theme called 'vocation'. The differences between Lydgate and Dorothea are, after all, more important than the similarities, differences both in conception and in the degree of success with which they are realized by George Eliot. Henry James has finely summed this up:

> Each is a tale of matrimonial infelicity, but the conditions in each one are so different and the circumstances so broadly opposed that the mind passes from one to the other with that supreme sense of the vastness and variety of human life, under aspects apparently similar, which it belongs only to the greatest novels to produce.[3]

Around these two cluster other characters, any of whom might be enlisted in the interests of our vocational theme;

[3] In his review of *Middlemarch*.

Casaubon, whose perversion of scholarship ends in a sterile parody of the real thing; Fred Vincy, urged to take holy orders but who avoided choosing a vocation that would be the wrong one for him; the Reverend Farebrother, who has done what Fred avoids doing but who, nevertheless, makes a decent job of his wrong choice and who, therefore, is pre-eminently the man to advise Fred; Will Ladislaw, the man with no real vocation at all, who dwindles from being a dilettante artist into a political journalist and who ends up, unconvincingly, as a philanthropist. Many more examples could be cited; the point I wish to make is that when we read the novel we are concerned primarily with the relationship of each of these characters to the others, not with the rela-tionship of all of them to an imaginary thematic centre, labelled vocation. Such a concern could only properly take first place if we were dealing with a *roman à thèse*, and what-ever failings George Eliot's novels exhibit, they are not of this order of art. It is dangerous, then, to discuss *Middle-march* simply from a thematic point of view, since what emerges is not so much a theme as a set of variations and it is not in any abstract statement but in a richly depicted and subtly discriminated body of life that the strength of the novel lies.

In any case the implied antithesis between character-as-function and character-as-an-end-in-itself is a false one since many of George Eliot's characters are obviously and simul-taneously both. Most nineteenth-century novelists, in fact, take delighted advantage of the scope and plasticity of their medium to elaborate and portray characters for their own sake; in many cases we should only begin to apply the kind of criteria based on a functional view when a character grows to such proportions or bursts out in such local exuberance that it threatens to disrupt the overall structure of the book. Our experience of *The Portrait Of A Lady*, for instance, would surely be diminished if we took too austere a view of James's distinction between *ficelle* and *disponible*, if we were to deny our simple enjoyment of Miss Stackpole's primacy over our perception of her function in relation to Isabel Archer. And it is the figures in George Eliot's novels with roughly the same status as Miss Stackpole who present the purest instances of characters at once functional and a source of delight in themselves. These are the characters who occupy, so to speak, the middleground of George Eliot's human landscapes, mediating between the protagonists of the novels and that host of background figures who act as chorus or who give substance to our sense of a community in action. We may take Mrs Poyser as fairly representing this class of characters.

These middleground characters are generally exploited for their comic possibilities and we may well pause to ask why this should be so. The obvious reason is that George Eliot had a strong sense of humour which can rarely be allowed full play in the main plots and characters; therefore it tends to find its natural outlet in secondary characters and subsidiary episodes. This humour, however, is rarely used as comic relief in the normal sense of the term, though as we saw in Chapter 4, in the case of Mrs Poyser's interview with the Squire, it can be used to fill up a gap in the main narrative sequence or to modulate from one theme to another. But the comedy rarely serves as mere contrast or emotional relaxation; in the total spectrum of feeling presented by George Eliot, one mood shades off into another so that it is difficult and misleading to break up the wholeness of vision into its constituent elements. The other chief reason why comedy flourishes chiefly among the secondary characters is that these are, in the main, less disciplined to the overall structure of the book; they carry less of the moral burden than the protagonists and George Eliot has therefore greater room for manœuvre, greater freedom to elaborate them for their own sake.

But this elaboration, this simple delight in idiosyncratic exuberance, is rarely uneconomic. It is not difficult to discover the functional aspects of Mrs Poyser's role in the book. Comedy for its own sake is reconciled with comedy for the novel's sake. Take, for example, this scene from Chapter 53, part of the Harvest Supper at the Poyser household:

> 'Ah!' said Bartle, sneeringly, 'the women are quick enough—they're quick enough. They know the rights of a story before they hear it, and can tell a man what his thoughts are before he knows 'em himself.'
>
> 'Like enough,' said Mrs Poyser, 'for the men are mostly so slow, their thoughts overrun 'em, an' they can only catch 'em by the tail. I can count a stocking-top while a man's getting's tongue ready; and when he outs wi' his speech at last, there's little broth to be made on't. It's your dead chicks take the longest hatchin'. Howiver, I'm not denying the women are foolish; God Almighty made 'em to match the men.'

This comic clash of the sexes is a traditional, time-hallowed and public joke; Mrs Poyser and Bartle Massey are only playing the parts their delighted audience expects of them. It is a kind of comic ceremonial, translating into fun impulses and tensions which could lead to tragedy—the kind of tragedy that is, in fact, played out in *Adam Bede*. And that this comic ritual can now be fully and wholeheartedly performed is a sign of health and reassurance; the catastrophe has worked itself out and the community is now back to normal; the course of nature has been reestablished.

The pithiness and pungency of Mrs Poyser's speech, its profusion of homely metaphor attaining at times an almost proverbial status, points to another of her functions. Irwine underlines the point:

> 'Sharp! Yes, her tongue is like a new-set razor. She's quite original in her talk, too; one of the untaught wits that help to stock a country with proverbs.'

She is the mouthpiece of the community, the articulation of a way of life. Into her witty aphorisms are compressed the wisdom of a tradition, a compassion, honesty and an acceptance of all the facts of life, so that we are not really surprised when she is so quick to forgive Hetty. Hers is a limited way of life but it is a good one.

This way of life, as embodied in Mrs Poyser—natural, robust, earthy, common-sensical—is set against the way of life represented by Dinah. The one obliquely comments on the other. In the first description she gives us of Mrs Poyser, George Eliot sets the key-note for this contrast:

> The family likeness between her and her niece Dinah Morris, with the contrast between her keenness and Dinah's seraphic gentleness of expression, might have served a painter as an excellent suggestion for a Martha and Mary. (6)

There is much to be said for both Martha and Mary in this world. In so far as Dinah escapes being idealized by George Eliot—clearly it is not a complete escape—this is because her dedication is constantly qualified by the shrewd worldliness of Mrs Poyser. One example, from many in the book, will suffice:

> 'Yes, and the Bible too, for that matter,' Mrs Poyser rejoined, rather sharply; 'else why shouldn't them as know best what's in the Bible—the parsons and people as have got nothing to do but learn it—do the same as you? But, for the matter o' that, if everybody was to do like you, the world must come to a standstill; for if everybody tried to do without house and home, and with poor eating and drinking, and was always talking as we must despise the things o' the world, as you say, I should like to know where the pick o' the stock, and the corn, and the best new-milk cheeses 'ud have to go. Everybody 'ud be wanting bread made o' tail ends, and everybody 'ud be running after everybody else to preach to 'em, stead o' bringing up their families, and laying by against a bad harvest. It stands to sense as that can't be the right religion. (6)

We know that this is a mistaken and partial viewpoint; it is the voice of lush Loamshire which knows nothing of the world of Stonyshire, that speaks here; yet so attractive is the speaker, so vividly and exuberantly is she realized, that the weight of our sympathy is with her rather than with Dinah. This use of secondary characters to create an ironic frame which qualifies our response to the protagonists is a constant and important feature of George Eliot's novels.

Characters like Mrs Poyser also provide a kind of relief analogous to comic relief. These characters are generally fixities and definites, 'flat' in E. M. Forster's terminology. We come to know them thoroughly after a short acquaintance and we can depend upon them to remain much the same throughout the novel. Because they are in this sense static they provide opportunities for a relaxation of tension by allowing us to rest our attention on what is familiar and well-known instead of expanding our attention to take in what is new or developing. Moreover, their fixity acts as a point of reference whereby we can measure the development of the protagonists. By viewing X, who changes, in relation to Y, who is static, at different points in the novel, we can get a measure of the amount and kind of change in X. Mrs Cadwallader does not change in *Middlemarch*, but we can estimate the alteration in Dorothea's character by noting that she is much more vulnerable to Mrs Cadwallader's criticisms at the beginning of the novel than at the end.

But to return to Mrs Poyser, I would end where I began by insisting that she is not to be resolved into a bundle of functions and that our primary response to her, our primary sense of what constitutes her character, is a local interest and delight in her speech and actions, and that the satisfaction we derive from perceiving her function within the total work is a subsequent act of critical rationalization. Indeed, without the primary enjoyment we should hardly bother to rationalize.

This view must, however, be modified. To say simply that perception of function or of the relationship of the part to the whole is a subsequent critical act would by itself be misleading since this act, in a rudimentary way, enters into even the initial stages of our reading. This is so because all novels, and especially those founded on the kind of moral and aesthetic basis I have outlined in Chapter II, compel us to see a pattern of human relationships, the configuration of which in large part makes up our perception of the total work. So much is obvious and trite, but the point may be taken a little further. Our perception of those character relationships constitutes in large measure our awareness of what any one character, considered in isolation, truly is. Surely, for example, one of the most important differences between Lydgate and Dorothea which prevents us from relating them too easily to a single thematic centre is simply the fact that Lydgate marries Rosamund and Dorothea marries Will. It is not merely that the difference in their choice differentiates them; the fact that Rosamund is aesthetically a finely and strongly drawn character in herself lends strength and fineness to the depiction of Lydgate since the relationship between the two is an important part of the character of each. By contrast, Dorothea is weakened by the weakness in George Eliot's presentation of Will. It cannot be an accident that we feel happier about Dorothea, that we feel she is in some sense more of a 'real' person when she is married to Casaubon, another subtle and deeply felt creation.

This sense of character-as-relationship is only one of a complex scale of elements which together make up our sense of what constitutes a character in George Eliot's novels. And since we are so frequently told that she describes her characters rather than presents them, it is worth while insisting on her command of the simpler and more obvious constituents of characterisation. One is her command of the dramatically revealing possibilities of speech and dialogue; her characters are sometimes distinguished and enlivened by the kind of imagery that is distinctively theirs. But George Eliot's control of speech does not merely consist of vividness, variety and fidelity; it can also be subtly discriminating. Consider, for example, these three varieties of pompousness from *Middlemarch*; the first two come respectively from

Casaubon and Bulstrode while the third, a kind of comic echo of them, belongs to Mr Trumbull.

(*a*) 'I have little leisure for such literature just now. I have been using up my eyesight on old characters lately; the fact is, I want a reader for my evenings; but I am fastidious in voices, and I cannot endure listening to an imperfect reader. It is a misfortune in some senses; I feed too much on the inward sources; I live too much with the dead. My mind is something like the ghost of an ancient, wandering about the world and trying mentally to construct it as it used to be, in spite of ruin and confusing changes. But I find it necessary to use the utmost caution about my eyesight.' (2)

(*b*) 'I shall rejoice to furnish your zeal with fuller opportunities,' Mr Bulstrode answered, 'I mean by confiding to you the superintendence of my new hospital, should a maturer knowledge favour that issue, for I am determined that so great an object shall not be shackled by our two physicians. Indeed, I am encouraged to consider your advent to this town as a gracious indication that a more manifest blessing is now to be awarded to my efforts which have hitherto been much withstood.' (13)

(*c*) 'Oh yes, anybody may ask,' said Mr Trumbull with loud and good-humoured though cutting sarcasm, 'Anybody may interrogate. And one may give their remarks an interrogative turn,' he continued, his sonorousness rising with his style. 'This is constantly done by good speakers, even when they anticipate no answer. It is what we call a figure of speech—speech at a high figure, as one may say.' The eloquent auctioneer smiled at his own ingenuity. (32)

The last passage would be easy to spot since the obvious and underlined comedy—hence the descriptive comments— are appropriate to the simple character of Mr Trumbull. In the case of the first two passages, although it would not be easy for analysis to yield all the reasons, it is clear that the quality of the prose points to something which Casaubon and Bulstrode have in common and yet, while revealing this

L

shared area of humanity, also subtly discriminates between them. In Bulstrode's case the distinguishing factor is primarily a matter of diction, the religious flavour of the language; with Casaubon it is, I think, mainly a question of rhythm and of rhetorical balance; he talks like a book and this is entirely in keeping with his character. What the prose shares is something derived from the egoism common to both men and also from a simultaneous though obliquely ironic view of that egoism. There is a felicity, of which Casaubon is unaware, in his saying that he feeds too much on his inward sources when we know how arid and stultifying his inner life really is; in a very real though unintended sense, he does 'live too much with the dead'. With Bulstrode the irony springs from his assurance that he lives by a special kind of providence, an irony which is finally and brutally brought home to him and us later, in Chapter 53, when after a fine key analysis of his spiritual state, he is suddenly confronted with Raffles:

> Five minutes before, the expanse of his life had been submerged in its evening sunshine which shone backward to its remembered morning; sin seemed to be a question of doctrine and inward penitence, humiliation an exercise of the closet, the bearing of his deeds a matter of private vision adjusted solely by spiritual relations and conceptions of the divine purposes. And now, as if by some hideous magic, this loud red figure had risen before him in unmanageable solidity—an incorporate past which had not entered into his imagination of chastisements.

And Raffles, twisting the knife as he drives it home, insists that their meeting, too, is part of that providential plan which Bulstrode has so egoistically interpreted—'But you see I was sent to you, Nick—perhaps for a blessing to both of us.' It is a masterstroke of irony since it strikes to the core of Bulstrode's variety of religious egoism; the same irony is there, I think, muted but potent, in the speech of Bulstrode to Lydgate that I have already quoted.

Dramatic speech shades naturally into dramatic dialogue,

and here again *Middlemarch* is George Eliot's masterpiece. The particular triumph of *Middlemarch* lies in its first book, especially in the various conversations of Dorothea and Celia. There are many other examples, however, and it is noticeable —though this is a severely limiting judgment—that George Eliot is best at dialogue when sexual or romantic relationships are not in question. Thus I would instance the wonderfully sure and revealing perception of family relationships in the interchange between Rosamund, Fred and their mother in Chapter 11, in which the essential vulgarity of Rosamund is unconsciously expressed through her rebuke of her mother's honest vulgarity. Better still, I would point to the wonderful cut and thrust of the dialogue between Rosamund and Mary Garth in Chapter 12.* This is too long to quote, but it is masterly; speech at once natural and stylized, as witty as anything in, say, Miss Compton-Burnett—wittier, in fact, since it springs from a solidity of human life quite beyond the vacuum through which the dialectic of Miss Compton-Burnett leaps and crackles.

No one, reading such passages, could surely deny George Eliot a very high degree of dramatic representation. That she has so often been denied just this is probably due to the presence in her novels of long passages of character analysis. I have already tried to show, when discussing George Eliot's omniscient techniques, what an essential part such analysis plays in her novels, especially when she is primarily concerned with the moral life of her characters. I must insist again that such analysis often has a wonderful immediacy and concreteness, that it is in fact the substructure of her richness of characterization, that there is rarely any gap between it and the dramatic representation that flowers from it, and that it is the most economic way of placing her characters in the moral dimension so necessary to their realization. Moreover, it gives us, surely and unobtrusively, the means of viewing them in a wide ironic perspective which increases rather than excludes compassion and which leads

* See p. 248.

us to the desired state of understanding and sympathy. None of George Eliot's most successful characters—Rosamund, Lydgate, Bulstrode, Casaubon, Gwendolen Harleth and the rest—could conceivably exist without this element of analysis. These are obvious examples; for more detailed discussion I will take an earlier creation and one misunderstood, I think, by many critics, including Dr Leavis. Leavis, it seems to me, does less than justice to *Adam Bede*. He begins by judging—a disputable judgment but one with which I shall not here argue—that 'the book is too much the sum of its specifiable attractions to be among the great novels—that it is too resolvable into the separate interests that we can see the author to have started with'.[4] On the first of these interests, Mrs Poyser, I agree with him; on Adam and Dinah I feel that he is too easily satisfied, that their limitations are more potent than he allows. Then follows the crucial passage which seems to me to misplace its emphasis on the kind of success achieved by the book as a whole:

Mrs Poyser, Dinah and Adam—these three represent interests that George Eliot wanted to use in a novel. To make a novel out of them she had to provide something else. The Dinah theme entails the scene in prison, and so there had to be a love-story and a seduction. George Eliot works them into her given material with convincing skill; the entanglement of Arthur Donnithorne with Hetty Sorrel—the first casual self-indulgence, the progressive yielding to temptation, the inexorable Nemesis—involves a favourite moral-psychological theme of hers, and she handles it in a personal way. And yet—does one want ever to read that large part of the book again? does it gain by re-reading? doesn't this only confirm one's feeling that, while as Victorian fiction—a means of passing the time— the love story must be granted its distinction, yet, judged by the expectations with which one approaches a great novelist, it offers nothing proportionate to the time it takes (even if we cut the large amount of general reflection)?[5]

4 F. R. Leavis, *The Great Tradition*, p. 36. London: Chatto and Windus, 1948.
5 Leavis, *op. cit.*, p. 37.

To answer, first of all, Dr Leavis's questions as bluntly as possible I should say, 'Yes, I *do* want to read that part of the book again and it *does* gain by re-reading.' It is not simply a way of passing the time nor merely part of the necessary machinery of the novel; rather it is the source of one of George Eliot's central and distinctive achievements. In other words, I see the moral-psychological theme as existing vitally at the heart of the novel. This theme, moreover, is embodied almost entirely in Arthur Donnithorne. It is irrelevant to the kind of charm represented by Mrs Poyser; Dinah and Adam are insufficiently realized to bear much of its weight while Hetty for most of the novel is necessarily too inarticulate to share in it. The portrait of Arthur Donnithorne seems to me one of the essential triumphs of the book, a triumph achieved mainly, though not entirely, by analysis of a quite different sort than that suggested by Leavis's phrase, 'general reflection'. Moreover, as soon as we explore Arthur's character we realize that he is so much more than mere machinery, and that the kind of interest he represents is not easily detached from the 'sum of specifiable attractions' presented in the total work.

We first meet Arthur when, with Irwine, he visits the Poyser's farm. In other words, George Eliot is careful to establish him in a dramatic scene before offering any analysis of him. From this scene we learn a good deal both about him and about other things necessary to the novel—the awe in which the gentry are held, for example, which is so necessary to the kind of tragedy which later develops. On the one hand, this awe contributes to Hetty's romantic dreams while on the other, it establishes a necessary ignorance about the villagers on the part of the gentry. It is, in fact, Irwine who suggests that Hetty will make a good wife for Craig and that Adam is destined to marry Mary Burge. Arthur only learns about Adam's feelings for Hetty when it is too late. In this first scene, too, the relationship between Arthur and Hetty is set in motion while one important facet of Arthur's character is firmly established. This is what one might call the public part of his personality—his desire to be liked, to cut a fine figure in society, to be a good squire. His tragedy is in part caused by this desire; the misguided perception within himself of a reflection of what he thinks the world sees in him prevents true self-knowledge and thus perverts and obscures true moral judgment. It is also part of his tragedy that his desires should be frustrated at the very moment when, having inherited the estate, he has the chance of realizing them; Chapter 44 wrings all the possible irony out of this situation. What this desire—potentially a genuine and valuable one—amounts to, is seen in this opening scene; all his good qualities are somehow twisted by his anxiety for the good opinion of the world; his natural courtesy and goodwill dwindle into traditional but empty gestures, into giving sixpences to little Totty. Arthur must learn that some things cannot be bought and that other things can never be paid for. Gestures, promises to himself, blank cheques drawn on the future—these constitute a large part of Arthur's moral life and George Eliot's subsequent analytical comment underlines the impression of these first scenes.

> We don't inquire too closely into character in the case of a handsome generous young fellow who will have property enough to support numerous pecadilloes—who, if he should unfortunately break a man's legs in his rash driving, will be able to pension him handsomely; or if he should happen to spoil a woman's existence for her, will make up to her with expensive *bon-bons*, packed up and directed by his own hand. (12)

This deceptive public persona which he creates and which is, by and large, accepted at its face value by the other characters, is insisted on throughout the book. But it is not only firmly set in perspective for us by the author's comments; sometimes Arthur's balloon of self-esteem is deflated by another character, by Irwine, for example, in this passage:

> 'I mean to announce the appointment to them and ask them to drink Adam's health. It's a little drama I've got

up in honour of my friend Adam. He's a fine fellow and I like the opportunity of letting people know that I think so.'

'A drama in which friend Arthur piques himself on having a pretty part to play,' said Mr Irwine smiling. (22)

George Eliot also allows us to make our own judgments; judgments we arrive at, for instance, by contrasting Hetty's romantic dreams with the worldly, social tone of Irwine and Arthur as they ride away from the Poyser's farm. Arthur possesses a moral dimension lacking in Hetty; whereas she lives in a narrow and stunted present, 'he felt the situation acutely; felt the sorrow of the dear thing in the present, and thought with a darker anxiety of the tenacity which her feelings might have in the future'. (29)

The dimensions of Arthur's moral life are limited, however, by the social perspective in which he views things, all part and parcel of the public persona he creates for himself. Thus Hetty's dreams are sharply and ironically corrected by Arthur's reflections:

> To flirt with Hetty was a very different affair from flirting with a pretty girl of his own station; that was understood to be an amusement on both sides; or, if it became serious, there was no obstacle to marriage. But this little thing would be spoken ill of directly, if she happened to be seen walking with him; and then those excellent people, the Poysers, to whom a good name was as precious as if they had the best blood in the land in their veins—he should hate himself if he made a scandal of that sort, on the estate that was to be his own some day, and among tenants by whom he liked, above all, to be respected. (13)

But this social view is not supported by any real sense of social responsibility. Instead we have a moral vacuum which is masked but not filled by a graceful observance of traditional forms and by lavish promises to the future. Arthur's weakness at the core is revealed when he has to come to terms with a personal issue and the burden of this revelation is carried largely by passages of analytical comment. These define with remarkable precision the evasive twists and turns of Arthur's mind, dominated as it is by 'hopeful self-persuasion'. The first extended instance of this, in Chapter 12, shows, typically, Arthur's decision to be really an evasion of the issues to be decided, a trait which clearly links up with the easy rationalization of guilt in the scene in which he determines to break with Hetty:

> It was an unfortunate business altogether, but there was no use in making it worse than it was by imaginary exaggerations and forebodings of evil that might never come. The temporary sadness for Hetty was the worst consequence; he resolutely turned his eyes away from any bad consequence that was not demonstrably inevitable. But—but Hetty might have had the trouble in some other way if not in this. And perhaps hereafter he might be able to do a great deal for her, and make up to her for all the tears she would shed about him. She would owe the advantage of his care for her in future years to the sorrow she had incurred now. *So* good comes out of evil. Such is the beautiful arrangement of things! (29)

This is a line of thought which is contradicted by the whole moral bias of the book; Arthur himself realizes as much at the very end when he says to Adam:

> 'I could never do anything for her, Adam—she lived long enough for all the suffering—and I'd thought so of the time when I might do something for her. But you told me the truth when you said to me once, "There's a sort of wrong that can never be made up for." ' (*Epilogue*)

Arthur's irresponsibility, his easy optimism, his evasion of guilt and his sense that the future can be bribed with good intentions all derive from a familiar aspect of George Eliot's egoists—one that is most fully developed later, in Bulstrode, but which is present from the very beginning:

> Arthur told himself, that he did not deserve that things should turn out badly—he had never meant beforehand

to do anything his conscience disapproved—he had been led on by circumstances. There was a sort of implicit confidence in him that he was really such a good fellow at bottom, Providence would not treat him harshly.

This, like several of the other comments I have just quoted, comes from Chapter 29, the final and key-analysis of Arthur. This analysis is strategically placed and balances the similar analyses of Hetty; but whereas Hetty has to be analysed because she is by nature so inarticulate, Arthur is thus treated at this point because he is about to be removed from the action for a considerable time and it is therefore important that our impressions of him should be fixed and clinched before he disappears. I think we feel happier about this treatment of him than we do about Hetty, partly because George Eliot is not here so personally involved and partly because this analysis is backed up by a greater body of dramatic demonstration, whereas Hetty's big scenes are still to come. This treatment of Arthur seems to me both central and successful. It is not difficult to see from the passages I have quoted how his role in the total work is far more important and integral than Leavis suggests. Granted the enclosed world of Hayslope and granted Arthur's dreams of what he might do for the community, private tragedy merges into public tragedy just as the public persona Arthur creates for himself is a very real part of his private character. Thus the seduction of Hetty is not just an unfortunate domestic affair but a blow against the nature of things, against the long-established hierarchy of Hayslope life. The community must suffer as well as the individual; the Poysers feel themselves disgraced even to the point of uprooting themselves and moving elsewhere while the whole village loses, with the departure of Arthur for the wars, somebody who might well have grown into the good squire that he imagines himself to be. The title of Chapter 40, *The Bitter Waters Spread*, sums up this sense of the diffusiveness of evil consequences.

This brief analysis of Arthur Donnithorne should serve

to re-emphasize the tremendous functional importance of those background and secondary characters I have already mentioned. We see the protagonists in depth because we see them against a varying range of characters whose status differs from that of a mere voice to that of an individual with sufficient vitality and elaboration to make its own demands on our attention and interest. If we leave aside the shorter tales and *Silas Marner*, where the community is in itself one of the main protagonists, there seems a clear correlation between the success of the whole book and the success with which George Eliot achieves her declared intention, 'It is the habit of my imagination to strive after as full a vision of the medium in which a character moves as of the character itself' (*Haight*, IV, p. 97). This is written in defence of *Romola* and it is no accident that however much she strives to give us the sense of the community of Florence—and the novel abounds in set scenes which have no other function—the protagonists of the novel, and particularly Romola herself, are brought into insufficient relation to the background so elaborately contrived. The effort of historical imagination, however detailed and minutely faithful its results, does not 'discountenance the idea of a Romance being the product of an Encyclopaedia' (*Haight*, III, p. 474). Similarly, it is no accident that the weakest main character in *Middlemarch*, Will Ladislaw, has no real relation to the provincial society depicted in the novel. The same holds true of Mordecai in *Daniel Deronda*. The 'medium in which a character moves' is not merely a question of natural setting, historical background, or social and economic analysis, though it includes all these things—George Eliot, for example, is one of the few great novelists to place an important emphasis on the importance of a man's work in his life. But primarily this medium is a human medium, a network of characters and relationships which provides a significant and life-giving context for the protagonists. The relationship of protagonist to medium is, of course, extremely complex and may be of very different kinds. Sometimes the medium will act as part

of the machinery of the novel—witness the function of
gossip in *Middlemarch*. Sometimes the main issues are
broken up and refracted, with more or less distortion, in
secondary characters and minor groupings—for example,
the Featherstone episodes in the same novel. Sometimes the
lesser characters embody a kind of normal, ordinary human
behaviour against which both the ardours and the excesses
of the protagonists can be measured—as we have seen, this
is one of the functions of Mrs Poyser. Sometimes the very
discrepancy between protagonist and medium provides a
fruitful source of irony; there is a fine example of this in
Middlemarch. Lydgate orders that Raffles shall not be allowed
liquor; in this he is in advance of the current medical practice
of his time. When Bulstrode, contrary to Lydgate's orders,
allows Raffles alcohol and he dies, the other doctors of
Middlemarch have to give their reluctant support to Lydgate
since Bulstrode's quasi-murderous action is in fact in line
with their own practice. Thus the backwardness of Middlemarch which elsewhere impedes the reformist Lydgate, here
ironically serves him.

And these examples underline the general truth that while
secondary characters may be the proper object of considerable elaboration, generally for comic effects, they do at the
same time play an immensely important part in the spinning
of that web of human and social relationships which at once
governs the narrative construction of the novels and also
provides the most elaborate metaphor for George Eliot's
moral vision of society, her deepest sense of the interdependence of things. From this tangle of relationships which constitutes so much of George Eliot's medium I wish now to
isolate two subordinate functions of the secondary character
—those of providing ironic commentaries on, and ironic
analogies to, the main issues.

The simplest way in which central issues are reflected and
refracted in the medium is by providing comic parallels or
analogies to the actions and natures of the main characters.
We should expect this in any extended or complex work of

art; Don Quixote has his Sancho Panza, Tom Jones his
Partridge. Perhaps the clearest instance of this function is to
be found in Shakespeare's clowns; Lance apostrophizing his
dog provides a suitable comment on the amorous habits of
the gentlemen of Verona; the lamentable history of Pyramus
and Thisbe glances at the midsummer madness of lovers.
Moreover, as we know, the Shakespearian fool is often wise
in his folly; such, as we shall see, is often the case in George
Eliot's novels. But I shall take first an early and simple
example which I mentioned in a previous chapter; the role
of Bessy Cranage in *Adam Bede*.

She at once parallels and contrasts with Hetty. We meet
her first when Dinah is preaching on the village green; she is
a particular object of compassion for the Methodists 'because her hair, being turned back under a cap which was set
at the top of her head, exposed to view an ornament of which
she was much prouder than of her red cheeks—namely, a
pair of large round ear-rings with false garnets in them' (2).
This surely foreshadows Hetty in her bedroom pathetically
parading before the blotched and tarnished mirror her gimcrack adornments which are the exactly right material
correlative of her limited, romantic dreams:

> It was an old scarf, full of rents, but it would make a
> becoming border round her shoulders, and set off the
> whiteness of her upper arm. And she would take out the
> little earrings she had in her ears—oh, how her aunt had
> scolded her for having her ears bored!—and put in those
> large ones; they were but coloured glass and gilding;
> but if you didn't know what they were made of, they
> looked just as well as what the ladies wore. (15)

The effect of Dinah's preaching is to make Bessy repent in
terror, but this is short-lived; as soon as Dinah leaves the
district, Bessy reverts to her former ways. In this she contrasts with Hetty; initially Dinah has far less effect on Hetty
than on Bessy, but in the long run far more; thus the scene on
the village green foreshadows in different ways both the

bedroom scene in Chapter 15 and the scene in the prison cell. George Eliot picks Bessy out of the communal background on one other occasion, during the festivities celebrating Arthur's coming of age. Bessy is here bitterly disappointed by the gentry. She hopes for a grand prize in the race she has won and instead is offered 'an excellent grogram gown and a piece of flannel'. Her disillusionment is surely a parody of Hetty's treatment at the hands of the gentry; indeed, it is at this point that George Eliot makes most explicit the parallel between the two girls:

> Bessy had taken to her earrings again since Dinah's departure, and was otherwise decked out in such small finery as she could muster. Any one who could have looked into poor Bessy's heart would have seen a striking resemblance between her little hopes and anxieties and Hetty's. (25)

Bessy is part of the village community of Hayslope and hardly emerges as an individual character; she represents a common type and that is enough for the purposes of the novel. For a rather more elaborate instance of the same functional relationship we must turn to *Felix Holt*. The contrast between Harold Transome and Felix Holt is one of central importance and George Eliot places them side by side early on in the novel when she is discussing the interaction of private and public lives:

> It was through these conditions that a young man named Felix Holt made a considerable difference in the life of Harold Transome, though nature and fortune seemed to have done what they could to keep the lots of the two men quite aloof from each other. Felix was heir to nothing better than a quack medicine; his mother lived up a back street in Treby Magna, and her sitting-room was ornamented with her best tea-tray and several framed testimonials to the virtues of Holt's Cathartic Lozenges and Holt's Restorative Elixir. There could hardly have been a lot less like Harold Transome's than this of the

quack doctor's son, except in the superficial facts that he called himself a Radical, that he was the only son of his mother, and that he had lately returned to his home with ideas and resolves not a little disturbing to that mother's mind. (3)

These facts, of course, turn out to be anything but superficial; one notices here, however, that George Eliot is careful to avoid any suggestion of stage-manipulation by asserting the unlikeness rather than the likeness of the two men. It is precisely upon such points of difference that the whole novel turns and these differences underlie the apparent similarities —thus Felix's radicalism turns out to be very different from that of Harold. But it is the relation of son to mother that I would stress here; when, a little later, we hear Mrs Holt pouring out her maternal troubles to Rufus Lyon we cannot but realize that this is a comic echo of the silent and constricting anxieties of Mrs Transome. As with private relationships, so with public; we have already seen that the proposed debate between Lyon and Mr Sherlock is a comic parallel to the political theme of the novel.

Most of these echoes or analogues involve a secondary character in relation to a protagonist and it is from the secondary characters, also, that most of George Eliot's ironic commentators are drawn. Such characters become commentators because to them is given, often casually and unemphatically, some truth or insight which is basic to the major themes of the novel. Sometimes these truths are in themselves non-ironic; for instance, Luke's 'Things out of nature never thrive' in *The Mill On The Floss* or Caleb Garth's 'Things hang together' in *Middlemarch*. But generally such commentators are ironic in two senses; their remarks, rather than expressing in a gnomic way some central theme, cast a qualifying light on some particular character or situation—such, as we have seen, is Mrs Poyser's relation to Dinah. Secondly, it is often limited or even decidedly foolish characters who speak the truth although they do not perceive it as such; their wisdom only becomes wisdom when the reader perceives it in a context larger than the character's comprehension.

From this point of view, as from most others, *Middlemarch* is incomparably the richest of George Eliot's novels. Frequently the same truth is approached from different angles by various characters; thus Mr Garth's 'Things hang together' links up with Mr Trumbull's 'Trifles make the sum of human things—nothing more important than trifles', with Will Ladislaw's 'The little waves make the big ones' and even with Brooke's electioneering sentiments, 'We're all one family you know—it's all one cupboard'. All these are variants of an insight which is close to the heart of the moral vision of the novel.

Mr Brooke is the richest source of those ironic glances at the protagonists. The kind of comedy he represents, unconsciously self-revealing, is handled by George Eliot with a deftness and lightness of touch that belies her reputation for elephantine gravity; in many ways it anticipates, as Dr Leavis has pointed out, the happiest effects of E. M. Forster. Thus Brooke's opinion of Ladislaw:

> Ladislaw's sentiments in every way I am sure are good —indeed, we were talking a great deal together last night. But he has some sort of enthusiasm for liberty, freedom, enthusiasm—a fine thing under guidance—under guidance, you know.

This is of the same order as Mr Pembroke's:

> 'It is true that I vote conservative. . . . But why? Because the Conservatives, rather than the Liberals, stand for progress. One must not be misled by catchwords.

It is the unconscious humour of Brooke's remarks that in part constitutes their irony. They reveal him in all his limitations and foolishness, yet at the same time they contain a grain of shrewdness. The hopeless muddle of his short-lived enthusiasms is in effect a parody of Casaubon's sterile pedantry; we are meant to be reminded of this when he remarks to Casaubon that he hopes Ladislaw 'will stay with me a long while and we shall make something of my documents'. From this comic analogy derives the irony of his remarks on Casaubon such as this:

> 'I overdid it at one time'—Mr Brooke still held Dorothea's hand, but had turned his face to Mr Casaubon —'about topography, ruins, temples,—I thought I had a clue, but I saw it would carry me too far, and nothing might come of it. You may go any length in that sort of thing, and nothing may come of it, you know.' (28)

Casaubon's key to the Mythologies shrivels up in such a context. Mr Brooke speaks truer than he knows. Most of his remarks—and also those of his fellow-commentators—are, however, concerned with Dorothea herself. Cumulatively they qualify our views of her, acting as a check on any tendency to idealize her. It is to this question of idealization, in which the ironic commentator plays an important role, that we must now turn.

CHAPTER VIII

Character II
The Protagonists

IT is important at the outset to have firstly clearly in mind what is meant by the term 'idealization'. Obviously there is very little of the merely romantic or the pretty-pretty in George Eliot's novels. One might perhaps expect a tendency to moral idealization, to the depiction of characters not as they are but as they ought to be, of which the extreme instance is the character who is too good to be true. As we have seen in Chapter II this tendency runs completely counter to George Eliot's avowed moral aims and to her naturalistic techniques. And when we look at the novels themselves we find that there is remarkably little idealization of a didactic kind. They key passage for a full understanding of the term occurs in George Eliot's reply to a letter from Frederic Harrison, dated July 19, 1866, in which he advocates the retailing in fiction of a positivist programme. He declares that:

> Positivism is a conception of society with all the old elements reknit and recast. In it society and men exist under the old relations reharmonized. Its dogma is vast, abstract, unpopular. The social and human form is eminently sympathetic, capable of idealization, and popular. Comte designed to close his life by the work of moulding the normal state into an ideal in a great comprehensive poem—a task he would never have accomplished and did not begin. But some one will one day. In the meantime the idealization of certain normal relations is eminently the task of all art.

To the Positivist, he continues:

> It seems that the great elements of society and human life can even now be treated with completeness in their normal

M

forms with conscious relation to the complete ideal of Comte. There is not any one, there never has been any one but yourself to whom we could look for this. (*Haight*, IV, p. 286)

George Eliot was clearly reluctant to enlist her fiction in the cause of any creed or dogma and she tactfully but firmly declined to convert herself into the fictional oracle of Positivism; on August 15, she wrote to Harrison:

That is a tremendously difficult problem which you have laid before me, and I think you see its difficulties, though they can hardly press upon you as they do on me, who have gone through again and again the severe effort of trying to make certain ideas thoroughly incarnate, as if they had revealed themselves to me first in the flesh and not in the spirit. I think aesthetic teaching is the highest of all teaching because it deals with life in its highest complexity. But if it ceases to be purely aesthetic—if it lapses anywhere from the picture to the diagram—it becomes the most offensive of all teaching. (*Haight*, IV, p. 300)

Such a passage might seem to lend weight to Henry James's assertion that:

We feel in her, always, that she proceeds from the abstract to the concrete; that her figures and situations are evolved, as the phrase is, from the moral consciousness, and are only indirectly the products of observation.[1]

This is not so likely to be true of the secondary characters who bear a much more direct relation to observation and who issue from a generally less disciplined play of invention. But in so far as we feel James's remark to be just when we are considering the protagonists we are confronted by idealization as I should wish to define it. Idealization, then, results from George Eliot's failure to make her vision thoroughly incarnate; we sense the abstract behind the concrete, the diagram behind the picture. What I mean by idealization,

---

[1] From his review of the *Life* by Cross.

therefore, is a simplification of character which is not dictated by the necessity of the novel, a certain abstraction or
reduction of a full body of human life, of the various tensions
and conflicts, the interplay of attitudes, the processes of
change and growth, and of the kind of irony which results
from the relation of a necessarily limited character to a wider
and more inclusive context.

Clearly the conditions in which idealization may occur are
varied and complex and no clear cut categories are possible.
But with this qualification I should say that in general idealization results from one or more of the following conditions:

(1) When a character is too static or is insufficiently
elaborated.

(2) When a character is too isolated.

(3) When a character remains theoretic.

(4) When a character cannot bear the weight of value or
significance attached to him.

(5) When the author is too emotionally involved in his
characters.

(6) When the author evades certain problems or areas of
experience necessary to the full realization of a character.

Of course, these are not the only possible conditions of
idealization, but, as I have said, George Eliot avoids on the
whole the simpler romantic, sentimental or didactic crudities.
Granted these rough categories, we may now look at some
examples.

We may begin with Dinah in *Adam Bede*. We can best
approach her by differentiating what she represents from the
kind of success George Eliot achieves with Adam Bede himself. Here, again, it seems to me that Leavis oversimplifies
when he maintains that 'she is idealized as Adam is idealized;
they are in keeping'. We surely feel less uneasy about Adam
than about Dinah; this for the reason that he develops more
as the book progresses. He undergoes a process common to
many of George Eliot's characters, a kind of education
through suffering by which he is brought to realize that his
initially-held rules and moral categories are too rigid and are

inadequate to the complex facts of experience which success-
ively confront him. It is, of course, a process which culminates in his disillusionment over Hetty, but it has started
much earlier in the novel with his father's death; thus at the
funeral:

> 'Ah! I was always too hard,' Adam said to himself.
> 'It's a sore fault in me as I'm so hot and out o' patience
> with people when they do wrong and my heart gets shuts
> up against 'em, so as I can't bring myself to forgive 'em. I see
> clear enough there's more pride nor love in my soul, for
> I would sooner make a thousand strokes with th' hammer
> for my father than bring myself to say a kind word to him.
> ... It seems to me now, if I was to find father at home to-
> night, I should behave different, but there's no knowing—
> perhaps nothing 'ud be a lesson to us if it didn't come too
> late. It's well we should feel as life's a reckoning we
> can't make twice over; there's no real making amends in
> this world, any more nor you can mend a wrong sub-
> traction by doing your addition right.' (18)

The tone of this is appropriate both to Adam's moralizing
nature in general, and to the solemn occasion in particular,
while its relevance to the main issues of the book, particularly to the Arthur-Hetty relationship, is obvious. But Dinah
being what she is, cannot participate in this process. Her
character, as it reveals itself to us, is essentially static; this,
I think, is the primary reason for our disquiet at the last
Book and the marriage of Dinah and Adam. It is not the
suddenness of this but its arbitrariness which causes dis-
comfort; Dinah does not develop in this last Book, she
simply changes and George Eliot cannot quite gloss over
the psychological discontinuity which results. The latent
conflict between a religious vocation and a desire for marriage
which might have given Dinah greater psychological solidity is gestured at earlier in the novel, but clearly George
Eliot had to keep this theme muted and subsidiary; it is
inherently so strong a theme that had it been developed it
would have disrupted the whole novel. But the fact that it

has to be played down adds to the air of contrivance which mars the last Book.

Dinah is not only static; she is simply not on the scene of action long enough for George Eliot to elaborate her in any detail. She is kept in mind by other characters referring to her and by devices like the letters to Seth, but George Eliot cannot allow her time or room enough to gain a very firm grasp on our imaginations. Moreover, George Eliot does not successfully solve the problem of the special religious language which is Dinah's natural idiom; such an idiom quickly changes and time has made Dinah more remote than ever. She is always more convincing in what she does rather than what she says.

Nevertheless, George Eliot does attempt to check the idealization of Dinah. There is, for example the discrepancy between Dinah's precept and example and the results she achieves; she fails, not only with Bessy Cranage, but also with Hetty—a failure which is neatly balanced, as we have seen, by Irwine's similar failure with Arthur. The world of Hayslope is so vivid and attractive that it cannot but put the values of Stonyshire into some sort of perspective. As we have seen, Mrs Poyser is the main representative of this world, and as such, implicitly qualifies and criticizes Dinah's position. She is not alone in this. Lisbeth Bede (a small masterpiece of characterization) does much the same sort of thing. When Dinah declares for the dedicated life, she retorts:

'That's very well for ye to talk, as looks welly like the snow-drop—flowers as ha' lived for days an' days when I'n gathered 'em, wi' nothing but a drop o' water an' a peep o' daylight; but th' hungry foulks had better leave th' hungry country. It makes less mouths for the scant cake.' (11)

This kind of thing, however, is only intermittent and not very noticeable; certainly it is insufficient to establish the kind of tension between the values of Hayslope and the values represented by Dinah that would force us to take

Dinah more seriously than we do. I say 'the values represented by Dinah' since one does feel a gap between these
values and the character as it engages us; this is a clear
instance of George Eliot failing to make 'certain ideas
thoroughly incarnate'.

If Dinah is absent too long in *Adam Bede*, then Romola is
the best example of a character who, while more or less continuously soliciting our attention, is inadequately placed in
any real contact with the network of other characters in the
novel. In other words, in the range of elements making up
Romola as an individual, the element I have termed character-as-relationship is deficient. That George Eliot herself
felt something to be wrong can be seen from her letters. To
R. H. Hutton she expressed her dissatisfaction with the character of Romola (August 8, 1863), while in the crucial letter
to Harrison from which I have already quoted, she writes:

> Consider the sort of agonizing labour to an English-fed
> imagination to make art a sufficiently real back-ground,
> for the desired picture, to get breathing, individual forms,
> and group them in the needful relations, so that the pre-
> sentation will lay hold on the emotions as human experi-
> ence—will, as you say, 'flash' conviction on the world by
> means of aroused sympathy.
> I took unspeakable pains in preparing to write Romola
> —neglecting nothing I could find that would help me to
> what I may call the 'Idiom' of Florence in the largest
> sense one could stretch the word to. And there I was only
> trying to give *some* out of the normal relations. I felt that
> the necessary idealization could only be attained by adopt-
> ing the clothing of the past. (*Haight*, IV, pp. 300-1)

I feel that the failure of *Romola* lies deeper than anything
George Eliot could diagnose. It is not simply a failure to
recreate the 'Idiom' of Florence, not merely a matter of life
being swamped by the products of historical research. That,
as we have seen, was Henry James's view. But if it were
merely that, we should be hard put to it to account for the
comparative success of Tito, the most thorough-going repre-

sentative of the process of moral degeneration in all of
George Eliot's novels. In her letter to Harrison George
Eliot talks of using her novels to urge the 'human sanctities';
one feels a radical disbalance in the character of Romola;
there is too much of the sanctity and too little of the human.
This, I feel, is because she is basically aloof from the life
created around her; her efforts, for example, to serve her
community in times of trouble and pestilence remain entirely impersonal. There is no intimately human context in
which she can figure; if I had to differentiate, I should say
that she is more successfully realized in relation to her father
than to her husband, but the difference is not great. In
relation to Tito she remains a person who illuminates and
realizes others without being realized or illuminated herself.
If one takes her relationship to Cousin Brigida, the nearest
thing in the book to a Florentine Mrs Poyser, and compares
it with Dinah's relation to the actual Mrs Poyser, or if one
compares Romola-Tessa with Dinah-Hetty, the difference
is obvious. Again, take this passage which is representative
of the best things in the book; it comes from the end of
Chapter 12 in which Tito declares his love for Romola:

> If the subtle mixture of good and evil prepares suffering
> for human truth and purity, there is also suffering pre-
> pared for the wrong-doer by the same mingled conditions.
> As Tito kissed Romola on their parting that evening, the
> very strength of the thrill that moved his whole being at
> the sense that this woman, whose beauty it was hardly
> possible to think of as anything but the necessary conse-
> quence of her noble nature, loved him with all the
> tenderness that spoke in her clear eyes, brought a strong
> reaction of regret that he had not kept himself free from
> that first deceit which had dragged him into the danger of
> being disgraced before her. There was a spring of bitter-
> ness mingling with that fountain of sweets.

Even here there is something obscurely but potently
wrong with the language, something stilted, something close
to cliché. But what strength the passage has is drawn from

the vicious circle within which Tito is imprisoned; his real love for Romola prevents him from confession, his failure to confess will poison the real love that he feels for her at this moment. The point is, that it is Tito who is the main centre of interest; Romola serves to focus his dilemma, but nothing in him reciprocates the process. Romola remains merely one factor in the complex equation which constitutes Tito's moral decay.

Mordecai in *Daniel Deronda* represents tendencies in both Dinah and Romola pushed to an extreme. He is the purest example in George Eliot's work of an almost entirely theoretical character, whose individuality is completely subordinated to his functional purpose. He shares with Dinah the difficulties that a special rhetoric impose; we find it hard, in the context of the novel, to adjust ourselves to this kind of thing:

> 'That is a truth,' said Mordecai. 'Woe to the men who see no place for resistance in this generation! I believe in a growth, a passage, and a new unfolding of life, whereof the seed is more perfect, more charged with the elements that are pregnant with diviner form. The life of a people grows, it is knit together and yet expanded, in joy and sorrow, in thought and action; it absorbs the thought of other nations into its own forms, and gives back the thought as new wealth to the world; it is a power and an organ in the great body of the nations.' (42)

This, for Mordecai, is comparatively subdued. One notices that it is a public mode of address. Mordecai exists almost entirely on this level; he rarely speaks, he makes speeches. He is a mouthpiece though not, like Mrs Poyser, the voice of a community. We do not feel the Jewishness of Mordecai since to be realized as a Jew he must first be realized as a human being and for that we have to go to the charming and acute picture of the Cohen family. Mordecai is rather the mouthpiece of a vision, a doctrine, something essentially abstract. His lack of depth is partly due to the fact that, like Romola, he is seen in insufficient relation to the other characters of the novel, but it is more than that; he is the simplification of fanaticism. George Eliot, indeed, anticipates this response and tries to explain it away.

'I don't think that you will find that Mordecai obtrudes any preaching,' said Deronda. 'He is not what I should call fanatical. I call a man fanatical when his enthusiasm is narrow and hoodwinked, so that he has no sense of proportions, and becomes unjust and unsympathetic to men who are out of his own track. Mordecai is an enthusiast; I should like to keep that word for the highest order of minds—those who care supremely for grand and general benefits to mankind.' (46)

But Deronda's testimony and distinction count for little here; fanatic or enthusiast—whatever the word, Mordecai is drastically reduced from the status of a human being realized in all his complexity. It would be possible, though extremely difficult, to give a full and naturalistic picture of a fanatic; it would involve placing him firmly in a larger human context; he would, if he were to retain our sympathy, have to be seen from many different points of view, seen with all his faults and failings. George Eliot does attempt something of the kind with Savonarola though she is not very successful. Here she does not even make the attempt. Mordecai is intrinsically a special and extreme case and as such not amenable to the natural bias of George Eliot's talent, but she makes little effort to bring him into contact with the ordinary, the humdrum and the mediocre which is preeminently her main area of strength.

If, in Mordecai, the man is swamped by the mission, then Will Ladislaw is perhaps the clearest case of a character who crumples under the weight of the symbolic value with which he is laden. As Casaubon is associated with images of gloom, autumn, closed rooms, tombs and prisons, so Will is by contrast associated with sunlight, the open air, spiritual refreshment. Thus, for Dorothea:

The mere chance of seeing Will occasionally was like a lunette opened in the wall of her prison, giving her a glimpse of the sunny air. . . . Will sat down opposite her at two yards' distance, the light falling on his bright curls and delicate but rather petulant profile, with its defiant curves of lip and chin. (37)

This line of imagery culminates in something very rare in George Eliot—certainly there is not another example of equal explicitness. This is her use of a classical myth not far below the surface of the naturalistic prose; in this case, the myth of Dorothea as Euridyce caught between an Orphic Will and a Plutonic Casaubon:

> She longed for work which would be directly beneficent like the sunshine and the rain, and it now appeared that she was to live more and more in a virtual tomb, where there was the apparatus of a ghastly labour producing what would never see the light. To-day she had stood at the door of the tomb and seen Will Ladislaw receding into the distant world of warm activity and fellowship—turning his face towards her as he went. (48)

But my main point is that while the gloomy and claustro-phobic images clustering about Casaubon blend with and reinforce everything else that we know about him, the oppos-ing light images assigned to Will assert a meaning which is discontinuous with the rest of his character. Will, in so far as he is realized as a human being, is simply not strong enough or interesting enough to bear the values which Dorothea—and George Eliot—find in him. Naturalism and symbolism here contradict and cancel each other out.

So far in our discussion of idealization we have seen that in many cases the tendency to idealize is checked or qualified in various ways—by omniscient analysis, by the comments of other characters, by the clash of opposing values or by the interaction of the individual with a larger human context. (It is nearly always a *human* context; man is rarely rebuked or diminished by nature in George Eliot's novels.) This is also true to some extent of Maggie Tulliver, my example of that kind of idealization which results from the author being in some illegitimate way emotionally involved in her fiction.

The important question is, to what extent? It has been most cogently posed by Leavis. After noting that 'we feel an urgency, a resonance, a personal vibration, adverting us of the poignantly immediate presence of the author', he continues, discussing Maggie's spiritual nature:

> That part of Maggie's make-up is done convincingly enough; it is done from the inside. One's criticism is that it is done too purely from the inside. Maggie's emotional and spiritual stresses, her exaltations and renunciations, exhibit, naturally, all the marks of immaturity; they involve confusions and immature valuations; they belong to a stage of development at which the capacity to make some essential distinctions has not yet been arrived at—at which the poised impersonality that is one of the conditions of being able to make them can't be achieved. There is nothing against George Eliot's presenting this immaturity with tender sympathy; but we ask, and ought to ask, of a great novelist something more. 'Sympathy and understanding' is the common formula of praise, but understanding, in any strict sense, is just what she doesn't show. To understand immaturity would be to 'place' it, with however subtle an implication, by relating it to mature experience. But when George Eliot touches on these given intensities of Maggie's inner life the valuation comes directly and simply from the novelist, precluding the presence of a maturer intelligence than Maggie's own. It is in these places that we are most likely to make with conscious critical intent that comment that in George Eliot's presentment of Maggie there is an element of self-idealization. The criticism sharpens itself when we say that with the self-idealization there goes an element of self-pity. George Eliot's attitude to her own immaturity as represented by Maggie is the reverse of a mature one.[2]

Can we, in the face of this, say anything in defence of Maggie or George Eliot? Something, I think, but not very much; certainly not enough to demolish Leavis's diagnosis

[2] Leavis, *op. cit.*, pp. 41-2.

completely. One should notice, however, that an intermittent attempt is made to 'place' Maggie by the comments and views of other characters, notably Philip and Tom. But it is significant, granted the intimately personal nature of the book, that George Eliot's main effort at qualification by referring immaturity to mature experience is by way of omniscient analysis. I wish to deal in some detail with one example of this, which occurs during one of Maggie's great spiritual crises—her first attempt at renunciation as described in Book IV, Chapter 3.

The chapter begins with Bob Jakin bringing Maggie a bundle of books; after relating her misguided attempts at self-education it describes how she began to read Thomas à Kempis:

> Maggie drew a long breath and pushed her heavy hair back, as if to see a sudden vision more clearly. Here, then, was a secret of life that would enable her to renounce all other secrets—here was a sublime height to be reached without the help of outward things—here was insight and strength, and conquest, to be won by means entirely within her own soul, where a supreme Teacher was waiting to be heard. . . . With all the hurry of an imagination that could never rest in the present, she sat in the deepening twilight forming plans of self-humiliation and entire devotedness; and, in the ardour of first discovery, renunciation seemed to her the entrance into that satisfaction which she had so long been craving in vain. She had not perceived—how could she until she had lived longer?—the inmost truth of the old monk's outpourings, that renunciation remains sorrow, though a sorrow borne willingly. Maggie was still panting for happiness, and was in ecstasy because she had found the key to it.

Here, surely, there are overtones that could not result from an immature attitude to Maggie's intensities? The subtle egoism beneath the renunciation is there (*satisfaction*); there is a cool recognition of Maggie's naïveté (*forming plans*) and of her inexperience (*how could she until she had lived longer*); the spiritual *ardour* dwindles very quickly into *panting for happiness*; the *ecstasy* is an adolescent vulgarization of that spiritual state which results from long discipline. The prose itself carries its own qualifications without the need of any overt comment.

George Eliot then broadens her description of Maggie's reactions into an extended passage of social analysis:

> But good society, floated on gossamer wings of light irony, is of very expensive production; requiring nothing less than a wide and arduous national life condensed in unfragrant deafening factories, grinding, hammering, weaving under more or less oppression of carbonic acid— or else, spread over sheepwalks, and scattered in lonely houses and huts on the clayey or chalky cornlands, where the rainy days look dreary. . . . Under such circumstances there are many among its myriads of souls who have absolutely needed an emphatic belief. . . . Some have an emphatic belief in alcohol, and seek their *ekstasis* or outside standing-ground in gin; but the rest require something that good society calls 'enthusiasm'.

The focus then narrows down again to the individual case of Maggie:

> From what you know of her, you will not be surprised that she threw some exaggeration and wilfulness, some pride and impetuosity, even into her self-renunciation; her own life was still a drama for her, in which she demanded of herself that her part should be played with intensity. And so it came to pass that she often lost the spirit of humility by being excessive in the outward act; she often strove after too high a flight and came down with her poor little half-fledged wings dabbled in the mud.

Thus what is hinted at in the texture of the prose is reinforced by social analysis and finally made explicit by omniscient comment. All of this is clearly the result of George Eliot trying to view her heroine objectively; Maggie is seen as one instance of a general tendency of a social class and the immaturity and egoism underlying her renunciation are again clearly stressed. I would underline only two points; whenever George Eliot speaks of a character as creating or enacting a drama we should nearly always look for a critical or qualifying attitude—some process of moral self-deception is generally at work. So it is here. Moreover, Maggie's supposition that she has found the key to happiness takes on a resonance in the context of the whole novel, since part of the book's main moral drift is to insist that there are no such keys; so much is made explicit at the end of Book VII, Chapter 2:

> The great problem of the shifting relation between passion and duty is clear to no man who is capable of apprehending it; the question whether the moment has come in which a man has fallen below the possibility of a renunciation that will carry any efficacy, and must accept the sway of a passion against which he had struggled as a trespass, is one for which we have no master-key that will fit all cases.

This chapter, then, does strike me as an instance in which George Eliot is relating immature to mature experience; there seems little self-idealization or self-pity here. As such it does go some way towards meeting Leavis's criticism. But it must be said that such instances are only intermittent and that George Eliot does not generally maintain this steadiness of view towards Maggie. Thus I would modify Leavis's diagnosis to this extent—that instead of agreeing *tout court* that George Eliot's attitude to Maggie is the reverse of mature, I would prefer to view the novel as in itself a struggle towards maturity, towards an impersonal working-out of very personal dilemmas and crises. It is by no means a completely successful struggle, but it does result in more than mere immaturity. This may seem an academic quibble, but it is important since Leavis tends to see other instances of the same process in George Eliot's work, instances which are less justifiably diagnosed in his terms. One of these instances—and I am not forgetting Leavis's own qualifications

—is Dorothea; here again, he maintains, 'we have the confusions represented by the exalted vagueness of Maggie's
soul-hunger; we have the unacceptable valuations and the
day-dream self-indulgence'.[3]

We must take Dorothea and Will together since it is
primarily her relation to Will that points to what is wrong
with George Eliot's conception of Dorothea. This weakness
develops late in the book; one must disagree with Leavis's
judgment that Dorothea is maturely treated only in the first
few chapters; I find myself that I can accept her with very
little qualification at least up to the death of Casaubon.
Nevertheless it is true that she is most finely and firmly
treated in the first Book of the novel and if we examine
George Eliot's mechanism of ironic placing in some detail
here we shall find, I think, that it is more subtle, complex
and lasting than Leavis allows.

We may start with the most obvious device—comment
and analysis which ranges from considerable elaboration:

> Her mind was theoretic and yearned by its nature after
> some lofty conception of the world which might frankly
> include the parish of Tipton and her own rule of conduct
> there; she was ennamoured of intensity and greatness and
> rash in embracing whatever seemed to her to have these
> aspects; likely to seek martyrdom, to make retractions,
> and then to incur martyrdom after all in a quarter where
> she had not sought it. (1)

At the other end of the scale there is the sly but illumin-
ating notation of her reaction to Mr Tucker's assurance that
there was little vice or misery in the parish of Lowick:

> In the next few minutes her mind had glanced over the
> possibility, which she would have preferred, of finding
> that her home would be in a parish which had a larger
> share of the world's misery, so that she might have had
> more active duties in it. (9).

Contrasting with such comment is the revelation offered

[3] Leavis, *op. cit.*, p. 77.

by the fully dramatic scene of which the finest example is the discussion by Celia and Dorothea about their mother's jewels:

> 'How beautiful these gems are!' said Dorothea, under a new current of feeling, as sudden as the gleam. 'It is strange how deeply colours seem to penetrate one, like scent. I suppose that is the reason why gems are used as spiritual emblems in the Revelation of St John. They look like fragments of heaven.' . . . All the while her thought was trying to justify her delight in the colours by merging them in her mystic religious joy. (1)

This rationalization of intensity strikes one as unhealthy and one is content to rest in the worldy-wise Celia's view, to whom jewels are simply jewels and need no spiritual justification.

Between these extremes of comment and drama there is a complex spectrum of illumination; Dorothea, for instance, often unconsciously reveals her own limitations and immaturities; such is her view of Casaubon which ironically contains a truth other than the one she intends:

> Almost everything he had said seemed like a specimen from a mine, or the inscription on the door of a museum. (3)

Or again, her attitude to art, taken up in her first conversation with Will and later developed in her reactions to Rome, reveals a certain priggishness in her nature (a note stressed in other ways—her discussion on pets with Sir James, for example):

> To poor Dorothea these severe classical nudities and smirking Renaissance-Correggiosities were painfully inexplicable, staring into the midst of her Puritanic conceptions; she had never been taught how she would bring them into any sort of relevance with her life. (9)

Finally, and perhaps most important, there is the impression we derive from the interaction of Dorothea with the other characters and the comments of these other characters

on her. These range from the kind stupidity of Sir James—
'You seem to have the power of discrimination,' he tells her,
when we know that this is precisely what she lacks at the
moment—through the shrewd asperities of Mrs Cadwallader
to the purring, kittenish, 'negative wisdom' of Celia, a minor
but very accomplished creation. Celia's view of Dorothea is
limited but just; Celia hates 'notions', to her Dorothea's
reforming plans are just a fad, she doesn't think 'it can be
nice to marry a man with a great soul'. But the most important of these ironic commentators is Mr Brooke—we have
already seen his function in relation to Casaubon; he throws
a similar light on Dorothea. To her he can say, and we supply
the implied criticism, 'I thought you liked your own opinion
—liked it you know,' or he can quietly deflate a typical piece
of Dorothea's gush.

> 'No; but music of that sort I should enjoy,' said
> Dorothea. 'When we were coming home from Lausanne
> my uncle took us to hear the great organ at Freiburg, and
> it made me sob.'
> 'That kind of thing is not healthy, my dear,' said
> Mr Brooke. (7)

All this cumulatively amounts to a rich and firmly controlled human context in which Dorothea's value is not
denied but is seen in an ironic perspective of greater maturity
than anything she herself can comprehend. George Eliot
achieves continuously here what is only intermittent in her
treatment of Maggie, and in doing so draws on much richer
and more varied resources. These resources are supple-
mented by one other device of ironic placing which is not
confined to Dorothea or to Book I and which is exploited in
Middlemarch to a much greater degree than in any of the
other novels. It is a device akin to that of mock-heroic,
though local in its effects and perhaps more subtle. When
Prufrock grants that he is not Prince Hamlet nor was meant
to be, the justness of the comparison derives from our recognition of simultaneous points of likeness and unlikeness

N

within it. Its main effect is to make Prufrock dwindle under the ironic pressure of the collocation. George Eliot frequently exploits this kind of thing in *Middlemarch*. We do not need, for example, to argue about the relation of Casaubon to Mark Pattison to recognize that within the very name itself lies a satiric dissimilarity between George Eliot's pedant and the great Renaissance scholar. For Dorothea marrying Casaubon would be like marrying Pascal, to Mrs Cadwallader he is our 'Lowick Cicero', Will nicknames him Thomas Aquinas. Casaubon shrivels beneath such names. There are many other examples of this, all having the same diminishing effect. Thus when Mr Brooke says of Will, 'Well, you know, he may turn out a Byron, a Chatterton, a Churchill—that sort of thing—there's no knowing,' the comedy lies not only in the heterogeneity of Mr Brooke's list but also in the inappropriateness of his reference to what we actually know of Will's amateurish artistic inclinations. Brooke does this again later when he compares Will—this time in his role of secretary—to Hobbes, Milton or Swift.

Granted that this is a conscious and consistent device, can we place Dorothea in the same kind of ironic cultural context? When Lydgate leaves her, thinking of her as a kind of Virgin Mary, I am not sure that we are meant in any way to endorse his evaluation; he is, after all, a creature of limited insight and this parallel is better taken as an index of his limitations rather than as attaching a positive value to Dorothea. Of course, the largest, most inclusive of these cultural placings is the comparison of Dorothea to St Theresa. How are we to take this—as a straight comparison or as an ironic perception of similarity within dissimilarity akin to Prufrock-Hamlet? It is worth pointing out that St Theresa herself is treated in the Prelude with a gentle irony. One notices, too, that when in Chapter 5 Dorothea is explicitly criticized, the ironic comparison contains a religious term:

> It was this which made Dorothea so childlike, and, according to some judges, so stupid, with all her reputed

cleverness; as, for example, in the present case of throwing
herself, metaphorically speaking, at Mr Casaubon's feet,
and kissing his unfashionable shoe-ties as if he were a
Protestant Pope.

But Dorothea's status, within this context, remains for me
ambiguous, and this ambiguity, which results from a tension
between George Eliot's impulse to idealize her and her concurrent impulse to view her ironically, remains unresolved
at the very heart of the book.

We have already seen that Will is laden with a quite
unacceptable weight of symbolic value, but it is also worth
noticing that he is, much more than Leavis allows, viewed
ironically. Apart from the device of ironic cultural placing,
he is also deflated by other characters; Dorothea herself
occasionally pricks the balloon of his artistic pretensions
while he is also subject to his share of comment; I think the
opening of Chapter 10 is a good example or, rather more
subtly, this from the end of Chapter 19:

> He was conscious of being irritated by ridiculously
> small causes, which were half of his own creation. Why
> was he making any fuss about Mrs Casaubon? And yet
> he felt as if something had happened to him with regard
> to her. There are characters which are continually creating
> collisions and nodes for themselves in dramas which
> nobody is prepared to act with them. Their susceptibilities
> will clash against objects that remain innocently quiet.

Indeed the whole of Will's progress, his dwindling down
from the romance of the arts to the prose of political journal-
ism, can bear some ironic weight. Yet when all is said and
done, he remains a radically unsatisfactory character, the
weakest thing in the novel, and Dorothea, in so far as she is
involved with him, shares that weakness. But in so far as her
moral development can be viewed apart from their relationship—as it can, to some extent, even in the later parts of the
book—then Dorothea is a much stronger figure than is
generally allowed. Take this passage, for example, from the

end of Chapter 80 which describes her night of crisis after finding Will and Rosamund together:

It has taken long for her to come to that question, and there was light piercing into the room. She opened her curtains and looked out towards the bit of road that lay in view, with fields beyond outside the entrance-gates. On the road there was a man with a bundle on his back and a woman carrying her baby; in the field she could see figures moving—perhaps the shepherd with his dog. Far off in the bending sky was the pearly light; and she felt the largeness of the world and the manifold wakings of men to labour and endurance. She was a part of that voluntary, palpitating life, and could neither look out on it from her luxurious shelter as a mere spectator, nor hide her eyes in selfish complaining.

That, in context, seems to me very moving and just; the passage has transcended its occasion—her relationship with Will—and the emphasis is on a new kind of moral insight and acceptance very different from the blind devotion and easy desire to serve and reform from which she started out. Within the whole novel the passage is supported by a cluster of opposing claustrophobic-expansive images which have persistently attached themselves to Lowick Manor; symbolism here reinforces and does not, as with Will, contradict. One grants validity to this scene and this moral decision because Dorothea has struggled towards it through much painful experience; as George Eliot says, 'all this vivid sympathetic experience returned to her now as a power; it asserted itself as acquired knowledge asserts itself and will not let us see as we saw in the day of our ignorance'.

If what I have said is true, then it follows that we cannot explain any doubts or qualifications we may have about Dorothea simply in terms of self-idealizing impulses on the part of George Eliot, as we might do in the case of Maggie Tulliver. Why, then, is the Dorothea-Will relationship so unsatisfactory? The answer, I believe, is simpler than any suggested by Leavis although it throws the limitations of

George Eliot's maturity into equal or even stronger relief. It is simply that there are some areas of human experience that George Eliot was unwilling or unable to treat fully and properly, the most important of these being romantic or passionate love between two adults. When Leavis concludes of George Eliot that 'her best work has a Tolstoyan depth and reality', one agrees, with the qualification that it does not have a Tolstoyan range. One cannot imagine George Eliot encompassing either Levin's simple joy at being alive and in love or the complex intensities of Anna Karenina's passion. George Eliot is best at portraying the relationship which is more than friendship but not yet love (Janet and Mr Tryan), or the relation which excludes sexual feeling (Maggie and Tom, Romola and her father), or marriages which are based on a faulty and incomplete relationship (Rosamund and Lydgate, Dorothea and Casaubon); Daniel's relationship with Gwendolen is stronger than with Mirah; Mrs Transome's with Jermyn stronger than Felix Holt's with Esther. But the Will-Dorothea affair is at the centre of the book and George Eliot cannot evade or diminish the issue. Her failure is not catastrophic; she does as well here with this theme as anywhere else in her novels. But this is not to say very much, and one certainly feels that compared with the richness and density of the rest of the novel this part of it is insubstantial and uncertainly grasped.

By dealing at such length with the question of idealization I have clearly excluded from consideration George Eliot's distinctive and assured successes—Bulstrode, Casaubon, Lydgate, Rosamund, Gwendolen, Grandcourt and the rest. I have deliberately been concerned to probe the weak spots, the blurs, the partial failures; some of my examples—Mordecai, for instance—are beyond rescue, but I hope that I have shown that for others, for Maggie and Dorothea, there is more to be said than some critics will allow. I have ignored the obvious successes because the central nature of George Eliot's achievement here has been amply stressed by other critics. Granted that these successful creations move primarily in a moral dimension, I would only underline the point that George Eliot is no mere analyst, that she writes great novels and not ethical treatises, that analytical insight and detachment go hand in hand with great understanding and compassion, and that she often has the effortless power to move us deeply. One has only to think of Mrs Bulstrode bidding her ruined husband to look up or this scene from Chapter 42 of *Middlemarch* in which Dorothea has painfully suppressed her emotional rebellion:

> If he did not come soon she thought she would go down and even risk incurring another pang. She would never again expect anything else. But she did hear the library door open, and slowly the light advanced up the staircase without noise from the footsteps on the carpet. When her husband stood opposite to her, she saw that his face was more haggard. He started slightly on seeing her, and she looked up at him beseechingly, without speaking.
>
> 'Dorothea!' he said, with a gentle surprise in his tone. 'Were you waiting for me?'
>
> 'Yes, I did not like to disturb you.'
>
> 'Come, my dear, come. You are young and need not to extend your life by watching.'
>
> When the kind quiet melancholy of that speech fell on Dorothea's ears, she felt something like the thankfulness that might well up in us if we had narrowly escaped hurting a lamed creature. She put her hand into her husband's and they went along the broad corridor together.

That, in itself, is very simple; whatever complexity it has derives from its relation to the rest of the novel. Confronted by it, the critic can do little more than gratefully accept it; he can only note that this power to move the reader deeply and immediately is at once the necessary pre-condition and the fine result of George Eliot's creative genius.

CHAPTER IX

Diction, Imagery and Rhetoric

Iɴ this chapter I shall be mainly concerned with George
Eliot's images, not as they reveal themselves in recurrent
and significant patterns, but individually, examining
certain instances of odd and eccentric usage to see what light
they throw on the strength and weakness of George Eliot's
art.

To view the subject clearly we must first deal with one
general critical problem we have already encountered in
different forms. This is the problem of determining the
degree of the novelist's self-awareness, of discovering how
far she was exploiting, deliberately and dramatically, material
and attitudes which we might otherwise mistakenly locate in
her own imperfectly objectified interests, desires and fears.
On the largest scale this is the question I discussed at the end
of the previous chapter, the question of how far characters
like Maggie and Dorothea are *deliberate* studies in idealization and how far they derive from idealizing impulses in the
author's own personality. The question may be tackled by
considering the large-scale imaginative structures within the
novel; alternatively it may be studied, as here, by examining
quite minute and local details of language.

George Eliot shows certain overt signs of self-awareness
and of conscious control of the material she is handling. Her
philosophical interests make her well aware of the nature of
metaphor, its potentialities and dangers; more than once she
uses this awareness for her own ironic purposes. Of Mr
Stelling's teaching, for instance, she writes in *The Mill On
The Floss*:

It is astonishing what a different result one gets by
changing the metaphor! Once call the brain an intellectual

stomach and one's ingenious conception of the classics and geometry as ploughs and harrows seems to settle nothing. (II. 1)

Again, in *Felix Holt*, she exploits her insight into the absurdities of political rhetoric. A more extended instance of such self-awareness can be seen in a minor but interesting sequence in *Middlemarch*. In general, as one would expect, this self-awareness grows as she comes to artistic maturity, and in *Middlemarch* one can observe her deliberately exploiting her consciousness of the techniques she has evolved. This particular sequence starts with a passage of amorous rhetoric from Casaubon, followed by the comment that:

> No speech could have been more thoroughly honest in its intention; the frigid rhetoric at the end was as sincere as the bark of a dog or the cawing of an amorous rook. Would it not be rash to conclude that there was no passion behind those sonnets to Delia which strike us as the thin music of a mandolin? (5)

It can be argued that if George Eliot had had complete confidence in her stylistic resources, Casaubon's speech would not have needed such a comment. Indeed, as I tried to show in the previous chapter, George Eliot does exploit elsewhere the full possibilities of unconscious and dramatic self-revelation through speech and dialogue without feeling the need to interpose such stage directions. What I wish to stress, here, however, is the reference to the Elizabethan sonneteers, a form of cultural reference related to the ironic use of names noticed in the last chapter. This particular allusion is taken up a little later and applied to Sir James, though modified here to discriminate between his blunt, common-sensical ordinariness and the frigidity of Casaubon. Sir James 'was not one of those gentlemen who languish after the unattainable Sappho's apple that laughs from the topmost bough . . . he had no sonnets to write' (6). This cultural context is used several times in *Middlemarch*; in each case we are sufficiently warned that the style is sophisti-

cated and does not proceed from a naïve outpouring on the
part of the author.

As I have said, George Eliot is frequently content to rest
in the self-revelatory qualities of speech and dialogue and we
must take into account the particular character and dramatic
situation whenever we are estimating the ironic control of
any rhetorical passage. In this scene, for example, we would
obviously be wrong to see George Eliot as in any way idealizing the character of Ladislaw. Dorothea asks:

> 'I wonder what your vocation will turn out to be;
> perhaps you will be a poet?'
> 'That depends. To be a poet is to have a soul so quick
> to discern that no shade of quality escapes it, and so quick
> to feel, that discernment is but a hand playing with finely
> ordered variety on the chords of emotion—a soul in which
> knowledge passes instantaneously into feeling, and feeling
> flashes back as a new organ of knowledge. One may have
> that condition by fits only.'
> 'But you leave out the poems,' said Dorothea, 'I think
> they are wanted to complete the poet.' (22)

This is clearly Ladislaw in his role of artistic dilettante,
and as such connects with the unconscious irony of Brooke's
enthusiastic references to him as a Byron or a Chatterton.
Just as Ladislaw, on the largest scale is placed ironically by
dwindling into a political journalist, so here he is suitably
pinned down by Dorothea's deflating reply. His aspirations
are assumed, his attitude is posed; they are certainly not here
endorsed by his creator.

This exploitation of rhetoric for such purposes is richest
and most complex in *Middlemarch*, but it is there in a cruder
form from the very beginning; thus in *Janet's Repentance*,
for example, the rhetoric of lawyer Dempster is clearly that
of a dramatically realized character. Again one might instance this comment on Captain Whybrow by the Reverend
Gilfil:

> 'The cursed scoundrel,' he muttered between his teeth,
> as he closed the door behind him. 'If it were not for Sir

Christopher, I should like to pound him into paste to poison puppies like himself.' (9)

One could hardly take this kind of thing at its face value; the excessive alliteration is sufficient warning that George Eliot, by pushing Gilfil's speech into the realms of the ridiculous, is reinforcing the amusing side of his character. There is, then, one clear category of rhetoric which is obviously dramatic in intention and effect, just as there are equally clear examples of what may be called intrusive rhetoric. We should notice that between these two extremes there is a large area of neutral ground where decisions about the aim of any given passage are extremely difficult and delicate but where they may be crucial in helping to decide one's attitude to the whole of which they are only a small part. To revert to *Middlemarch*, what precise value are we to allow this passage, one noticed by Leavis but, I think, too easily dismissed by him? It is a description of Ladislaw's reaction to Rosamund's note telling him that she has enlightened Dorothea as to the true nature of their relationship:

> The effect of these words was not quite all gladness. As Will dwelt on them with excited imagination, he felt his cheeks and ears burning at the thought of what had occurred between Dorothea and Rosamund—at the uncertainty how far Dorothea might still feel her dignity wounded in having an explanation of his conduct offered to her. There might still remain in her mind a changed association with him which made an irremediable difference—a lasting flaw. With active fancy he wrought himself into a state of doubt little more easy than that of the man who has escaped from wreck by night and stands on unknown ground in the darkness. Until that wretched yesterday—except the moment of vexation long ago in the very same room and in the very same presence—*all their vision, all their thought of each other, had been as in a world apart, where the sunshine fell on tall white lilies, where no evil lurked, and no other soul entered.* But now—would Dorothea meet him in that world again? (82)

What status are we to give the touch of rhetoric I have italicized? At a first reading we might assign it to Will's consciousness and see it as a dramatic image, the natural product of his pseudo-poetic soul. The passage mentions, after all, his 'excited imagination', his 'active fancy' and the concluding question might seem to clinch the point. Yet I am not sure that we can be as certain as this; the passage seems to me to hover between dramatic image and comment; it is certainly as the latter that it connects with various other paradisal allusions employed elsewhere in the book, allusions to which Ladislaw has no access. In other words, the distinction between dramatic realization and intrusive comment is here blurred and as such the passage is a small indication of a major ambiguity in George Eliot's attitude to Ladislaw which, as I tried to show in the previous chapter, derives from the insufficiently resolved tension in her mind between the impulse to idealize and the impulse to view ironically.

A subsidiary reason for doubting that this is purely dramatic rhetoric lies in the fact that elsewhere in the book Ladislaw is clearly the object of rhetoric which results from George Eliot's attempt to dignify him, to make him more interesting, a worthier recipient of Dorothea's love. Ultimately this derives from George Eliot's evasion, already noted, of certain areas of human experience. This is only one type of bad rhetoric to be found in her work; I wish now to examine briefly certain other kinds and to assign them possible causes.

The simplest form of bad rhetoric is melodramatic in nature and George Eliot soon outgrows it. In an acute form it crops up in *Mr Gilfil's Love Story*, in Caterina rushing to her revenge, for instance, a passage always quoted by hostile critics of George Eliot. (Her advance can be seen by comparing this passage with Baldesarre's thirst for revenge in *Romola*, though this no doubt is made more plausible both by the more extended treatment allowed it and by the distancing inherent in a historical novel.) A similar local instance is this passage from *Janet's Repentance* (we notice here how the elaboration of the image does not quite conceal its origin in the most threadbare of clichés, 'depths of despair'):

> So she went out into the dewy starlight; and as Mr Tryan turned away from her, he felt a stronger wish than ever that his fragile life might last out for him to see Janet's restoration thoroughly established—to see her no longer fleeing, struggling, clinging up the steep sides of a precipice whence she might be any moment hurled back into the depths of despair, but walking firmly on the level ground of habit. (25)

Similarly the use of the pathetic fallacy as in *Janet's Repentance* ('The wind was very cruel; it tried to push her back from the door where she wanted to go and knock and ask for pity') does not bulk large or persist long. Occasionally we come across a heavy and unacceptable use of circumlocution. Janet's addiction to drink, for instance, is described simply as a 'long-accustomed stimulus'. (This is an odd evasion in view of George Eliot's description of Dempster's attack of *delirium tremens*, though she may have thought that one such passage was sufficient for her tale. But Janet's struggle to recovery is weakened by playing down what she is struggling against.) Sometimes George Eliot exploits this habit for clumsily comic purposes. In *The Mill On The Floss*, for example, Bob Jakin hopes of Stephen Guest that 'he might be in the warmest department of an asylum understood to exist in the other world for gentlemen who are likely to be in fallen circumstances there' (VII. 1). Part of the humour of this no doubt derives from its inappropriate expression of Bob's sentiments; he would express himself more straightforwardly and the kind of wit represented by 'fallen circumstances' is obviously beyond him. But even granted this, the expansion of a simple 'Go to hell' is still laboured and rather coy.

All these instances, however, represent only minor and peripheral categories of rhetoric; what is a central and important flaw is the kind produced by the instability in George Eliot's attitude to her characters that I discussed in Chapter III. She is sometimes too close to her creations and the failure to realize them adequately reveals itself in her style. This instability may be of two kinds; the impulse to idealize or to dignify may be too strong or there may remain obtrusive and unpurged some animus or hostility towards a character. As we saw earlier, the clearest instance of this is Hetty Sorrel in *Adam Bede*. Two examples will suffice.

> It was the same rounded, pouting, childish prettiness, but with all love and belief in love departed from it—the sadder for its beauty, like that wondrous Medusa-face, with the passionate, passionless lips. (37)

The second half of this sentence is simply an attempt to give the first half a more portentous significance, but it remains a merely literary accretion; the gap between the two parts of the sentence is never bridged; 'passionate, passionless' does not really elucidate in any way a paradox about Hetty's nature or appearance; neither word is really appropriate and one feels that the first word has simply bred its alliterative opposite without either coming into contact with the object they are supposed to describe. Or again:

> It is too painful to think that she is a woman, with a woman's destiny before her—a woman spinning in young ignorance a light web of folly and vain hopes which may one day close round her and press upon her, a rancorous poisoned garment, changing all at once her fluttering, trivial butterfly sensations into a life of deep human anguish. (22)

This passage betrays itself not only by the use of the historic present—nearly always a symptom of unease—but also by the wrong kind of mixed metaphor it employs. Both of its constituent images, taken singly, are insistently and appropriately used elsewhere in *Adam Bede*. Indeed the web, as we shall see in the next chapter, is one of George Eliot's

richest metaphors for her sense of the complexity and inter-
relatedness of things. Together, however, the images composing this passage become ridiculous. The web as a garment
is insufficiently realized, while Hetty suffers an inept metamorphosis from spider into butterfly. This sort of thing is
mercifully rare but it is sufficiently present to indicate a
serious flaw in George Eliot's talent. The other uses of
imagery I wish to explore in this chapter are often eccentric
and sometimes bad, but none of them point in quite this way
to such a radical defect in sensibility. Before I turn to them,
however, I wish to notice one or two things about George
Eliot's rhythms and diction.

Rhythmically the narrative staple of George Eliot's prose,
when it is not directed by the colloquial exigencies of dialogue, is not intrinsically very interesting. The syntactical
evolution of her sentences is thoroughly intellectual; the
lengthy and sometimes cumbrous accumulation of parenthesis and qualifying clauses is the correlative of a cerebral
talent concerned to analyse and scrutinize closely the moral
and emotional intricacies of her characters. The prose is
nearly always the product of that contemplative and ironic
attitude I have already tried to describe. It is rarely directly
expressive of any emotional excitement; the rhythms and the
syntax do not participate immediately in the struggle or the
disturbance that may be their subject. Sometimes, however,
the prose is dramatic, enacting what it states. This is especially true of moments of moral climax. The prose, in its
complexity and even in its confusion, is reflective of a character's ambiguity or bewilderment. I have in mind this kind
of thing from *Daniel Deronda* where the hero is in tumult at
the impending revelation of his true parentage. His mind is
at this point a tangle of loyalties, desires, anxieties; his
mother, Mordecai, Mirah and Gwendolen all cross and
tangle themselves in the complex weave of his future. This
is how George Eliot sorts out from the intricate pattern the
thread that is Deronda in relation to Gwendolen; it is a long
passage, but I quote it in full as an example of something

that in a much less extreme form occurs fairly frequently in George Eliot's delineation of complex moral states.

Across these two importunate thoughts, which he resisted as much as one can resist anything in that unstrung condition which belongs to suspense, there came continually an anxiety which he made no effort to banish—dwelling on it rather with a mournfulness, which often seems to us the best atonement we can make to one whose need we have been unable to meet. The anxiety was for Gwendolen. In the wonderful mixtures of our nature there is a feeling distinct from that exclusive passionate love of which some men and women (by no means all) are capable, which yet is not the same with friendship, nor with a merely benevolent regard, whether admiring or compassionate; a man, say—for it is a man who is here concerned—hardly represents to himself this shade of feeling towards a woman more nearly than in the words, 'I should have loved her, if—'; the 'if' covering some prior growth in the inclinations, or else some circumstances which have made an inward prohibitory law as a stay against the emotions ready to quiver out of balance. The 'if' in Deronda's case carried reasons of both kinds; yet he had never throughout his relations with Gwendolen been free from the nervous consciousness that there was something to guard against not only on her account but on his own—some precipitancy in the manifestation of impulsive feeling—some ruinous inroad of what is but momentary on the permanent chosen treasure of the heart—some spoiling of her trust, which wrought upon him now as if it had been the retreating cry of a creature snatched and carried out of his reach by swift horsemen or swifter waves, while his own strength was only a stronger sense of weakness. How could his feeling for Gwendolen ever be exactly like his feeling for other women, even when there was one by whose side he desired to stand apart from them? Strangely her figure entered into the pictures of his present and future; strangely (and now it seemed sadly) their two lots had come in contact, hers narrowly personal, his charged with far-reaching sensibilities, perhaps with durable purposes, which were hardly more present to her than the reasons why men migrate are present to the birds that come as usual for the crumbs and find them no more. (50)

Detailed analysis of prose is often clumsy, but we must risk teasing into a tedious explicitness what is already a rather cumbrous piece of prose. The passage may at first sight seem to exhibit an almost Jamesian labyrinth of convolute qualification, but its overall affect is clearly not Jamesian. Although there is the same concern for minute discrimination in the face of complexity there is none of that delight in nuance and obliquity, no positive engagement in subtlety as a problem for the craftsman to solve, no sense of having brought a particularly difficult feat of legerdemain to an adroit conclusion. To put it bluntly, George Eliot's concern is moral and in no sense aesthetic; there is no sense of *play* in this involved piece of ethical calculus.

There are two closely connected reasons for the kind of complexity which here confronts us. The first is George Eliot's tendency to use her omniscience in order to generalize, to relate the particular predicament of her hero to a general human condition; the passage—witness the pronouns—only gradually struggled free of this tendency. The second reason lies in that aspect of 'the wonderful mixture of our nature' which George Eliot stresses in all of her novels; the interconnection of the private and the public man. Deronda is here inhibited not only by his feelings for Mirah ('some prior growth in his inclinations') but also by his relationship with Mordecai and his growing involvement with some extra-personal destiny (his being 'charged with far-reaching sensibilities, perhaps with durable purposes'). These two—the private and the public—are stressed by George Eliot throughout the passage, yet she does not, perhaps cannot discriminate them with perfect clarity. I am thinking particularly of the sentence beginning 'The "if" in Deronda's case', which I find obscure for several reasons. It is a difficult sentence to refer back to either of the previously mentioned inhibiting causes; one tends naturally to take 'some permanent chosen treasure of the heart' as being personal and relating to Mirah, yet can one be sure in face of those 'durable purposes' which follow a little later? The sentence, moreover, oscillates obscurely between Gwendolen and Deronda, between 'her account' and 'his own', an oscillation reflected in the difficult syntax, especially in the too intrusive parenthesis. But if the two inhibiting causes are here confused—and we should surely be over-sophisticated to take this particular confusion as deliberate, as reflecting Deronda's state of mind—we can surely say that in general it is the public and not the private cause which predominates and which for Deronda culminates in a truth not about himself (for his dilemma is not resolved) but about Gwendolen. This truth is clinched in the fine image contrasting migrant men with migrant birds which surely works far more powerfully in the passage than the equivalent image of 'swift horsemen or swifter waves' which is the emergence into metaphor of the private aspects of Deronda's concern. But this final truth has the kind of ambiguous status I tried to describe earlier in this chapter; can we say with assurance that it belongs dramatically to a process of thought in Deronda's mind rather than to the omniscient generalizing faculty which we have noted at work earlier in this passage?

As I say, this passage is an extreme example and as such is unusually vulnerable to adverse criticism. The dangers risked by such an approach are those of frigidity and a kind of stilted externality—a phrase like 'some prior growth in the inclinations' comes close to this. But when all qualifications have been made, the passage as a whole seems to me successful, and when indulged in more moderately it is remarkable how George Eliot can transform such a technique into an acceptable substitute for the immediacy of dramatic representation. (And granted this, the prose can then be used for purposes beyond the scope of such representation.) Analysis is pushed to the point where it becomes creative; through the grave, heavy measures of meditation we approach the individual, reflecting, hoping, suffering; we

o

feel with remarkable clarity the ebb and flow of a mind
caught up in a particular predicament. Because the prose can
accommodate generalization and a vein of ironic commentary
it is particularly successful in revealing the self-deceptions of
a character, the self-justifications and the rationalizing away
of doubt and guilt. As we have seen, Arthur Donnithorne in
Adam Bede is a particularly good example of this and he is
the prototype of a recurrent character in the novels.

As I noted in an earlier chapter, Dr Leavis's judgment of
Dr Johnson that he was able 'to give his moral declamation
the weight of lived experience and transform his eighteenth-
century generalities into that extraordinary kind of concreteness' can, with suitable modification, be equally well
applied to George Eliot. Her prose—and much of her
sensibility—is surely Johnsonian rather than Jamesian in
its affiliations. There is the same apparent elephantine pon-
derousness which is more apparent than real since it co-exists
with a surprising delicacy and tact of selection and emphasis.
The heavyweight proves astonishingly nimble and light-
footed. The involved syntax, the antitheses, the lengthy
qualifying clauses, are not mere grammatical adornment or
elaboration; they all contribute to a poised judgment—a
judgment which takes careful account of all the facts—and a
fine sense of discrimination. And this is true of the diction
as well as the construction of her prose; the Latinisms, the
apparently pedantic turns of phrase, do more, upon inspec-
tion, than their colloquial equivalents. The language is not
inflated; it has real weight.

Of course, this style has its failures. We are sometimes
left with mere pedantry and sometimes the formidable intellect at work behind the prose acts as a wheel to crush its
butterfly of a subject. When we read this, for instance, we
cannot but feel that the mode of expression is ludicrously
and laboriously inappropriate to what is being said:

> Here should any lady incline to imitate Gwendolen, let
> her consider the set of her head and neck; if the angle
> there had been different, the chin protrusive and the

cervical vertebrae a trifle more curved in their position, ten to one Gwendolen's words would have had a jar in them for the sweet-natured Rex. (7)

This kind of thing generally results from a heavy-handed attempt at humour (we notice as symptomatic both the initial appeal to the reader and the way in which pompousness is followed—and emphasized—by an uneasy attempt at the colloquial); it is deliberate enough but simply falls flat. We must distinguish this kind of failure both from the genuine, unconscious streak of pedantry in George Eliot (which emerges most in *Romola*), and from a similar, and similarly deliberate attempt to derive humorous touches from inflated diction, an attempt saved by the flavour of self-mockery, as though George Eliot is pushing into the realms of the ridiculous a mannerism she sometimes indulges in for quite serious purposes. It is another example of the general critical problem of determining the degree of the novelist's self-awareness. We may find an analogy for this in the poetry of Cowper; frequently he writes straightforwardly and with no ironic intention in that variety of eighteenth-century blank verse which results from blending a sub-Miltonic manner with the material of the *Georgics*. Sometimes, however, the Latinate diction and the pompous inversions are invoked for fun; when Cowper writes in *Yardley Oak*:

> While thus through all the stages thou hast pushed
> Of treeship—first a seedling, hid in grass;
> Then twig; then sapling; and, a century rolled
> Slow after century, a giant bulk
> Of girth enormous, with moss-cushioned root
> Upheaved above the soil, and sides embossed
> With prominent wens globose . . .

it is hard not to feel that in the last line he is indulging in gentle mockery of the literary mode he has adopted. So with George Eliot; we surely react in the same way when we read, for instance, in *Janet's Repentance* that:

> Of the two other Low Church clergymen in the neighbourhood, one was a Welshman of globose figure and

unctuous complexion, and the other a man of atrabiliar aspect, with lank black hair and a redundance of limp cravat. (3)

or in *Amos Barton* that:

> The walls, you are convinced, no lichen will ever effect a settlement on—they are smooth and innutrient as the summit of the Rev. Amos Barton's head, after ten years of baldness and supererogatory soap. (1)

It is noticeable that this trick of style occurs most frequently where one might expect it, in George Eliot's early work, where she has not yet achieved a completely assured manner and where this device acts as a kind of check or defence mechanism, allowing her to convert into ridicule what, taken seriously, would have been a stylistic vice. As she matures she exploits the mannerism in a more subtle and economical way. (The one exception is that tedious tale, *Brother Jacob*, where practically all the humour derives from this trick.) Consider these brief examples, from *Felix Holt*, the novel in which the device is used most often; we shall be able to observe what mutation the mannerism has undergone, and how, in its more sophisticated form, it has a definite if minor ironic function.

> (*a*) 'Mother,' said Felix, who often amused himself and kept good-humoured by giving his mother answers that were unintelligible to her, 'you have an astonishing readiness in the Ciceronian antiphrasis, considering you have never studied oratory.' (22)
> (*b*) Mrs Holt was not given to tears; she was much sustained by conscious unimpeachableness, and by an argumentative tendency which usually checks the too great activity of the lachrymal gland. (4)

The simple quasi-pedantic element has largely disappeared; what we have instead is something analogous to mock-heroic, a disproportion between the elevation or solemnity of the style and the thing being described. This device is akin to that of placing by cultural reference dis-

cussed in the previous chapter or to the radical shift in perspective that occurs when we are invited to see human
activities in the light of some primitive or non-human society.
The method is designed always to ensure that by explicit
analogy or by casual juxtaposition the reader brings into
relation two sets of ideas that would normally be incongruous
or absurd when so related. They *are* incongruous or absurd,
but recognition of this is carefully suppressed by the author;
by taking for normal what is ridiculous she forces us to
react in the desired manner. Here the juxtaposition, the
yoking together of the disparate elements is achieved by the
disproportion between subject and style.

So far I have been chiefly concerned to justify certain
types of rhetoric, certain uses of rhythm and vocabulary
which might at a first reading appear idiosyncratic. I wish
now to turn to certain types of imagery which are definitely
eccentric, though I should point out that many of these are
only exaggerations of a kind of image which when used in
moderation by George Eliot is entirely acceptable. There is
one preliminary consideration that should be mentioned;
when we examine the morphology of any particular image or
class of images we cannot completely divorce it from that
kind of critical concern which deals with patterns of recurrent imagery. An example will clarify the point. Consider
this pair of images, the first from *The Mill On The Floss*, the
second from *Middlemarch*:

(*a*) Phillip felt that he ought to have been thoroughly
happy in that answer of hers; she was as open and transparent as a rock-pool. (VI. 10)
(*b*) In this way, the early months of marriage often are
times of critical tumult—whether that of a shrimp-pool
or of deeper waters—which afterwards subsides into
cheerful peace. (20)

In its context the second example is acceptable in a way in
which the first is not. Context is all-important here; Mrs
Hardy has pointed out how the image of a shrimp-pool is

related to a chain of similar images and is the means of defining the relationship of Dorothea and Casaubon.[1] Indeed, almost on the next page we find George Eliot writing:

> Having once embarked on your marital voyage, it is impossible not to be aware that you make no way and that the sea is not within sight—that, in fact, you are exploring an enclosed basin.

The image of the pool, then, is a variant of those claustrophobic images which help to define the narrow, sterile life of Casaubon. Now there is in *The Mill On The Floss* a very important line of imagery deriving from rivers and water, a pattern which takes its force from the dominant part played in the novel by an actual river. But the simile of the rock-pool does not connect with this main stream of imagery in the way that the shrimp-pool does in *Middlemarch*; it can draw no strength from an intimate relation to a larger whole and thus standing alone strikes us as arbitrary and weak. This isolation is, of course, only one reason for its failure; we can explore its weakness further if we compare it with another similar image, this time from *Romola*:

> It takes very little water to make a perfect pool for a tiny fish, where it will find its world and paradise all in one, and never have a presentiment of the dry bank. (10)

I should say here that when we are discussing the structure of an image we may run into terminological difficulties. There simply are no generally accepted terms. Rather than discuss my examples in terms of tenor and vehicle, I wish to use the words *major* and *minor* to denote the two main parts of the image. Thus our major terms here are Maggie and Tessa, the minor term in each case being that of the pool. Now clearly one requirement of a good image is that the minor term be appropriate (or appropriately inappropriate) to the major. This, I think, is true of the example I have quoted from *Romola*. The image of the tiny fish happily

---

[1] B. Hardy, 'Imagery in George Eliot's Last Novels', *Modern Language Review*, 50, 1955, pp. 6-14.

isolated in its pool fits Tessa as we come to know her; more-over, it is a sufficiently elaborated image for us to make the necessary and right connections between major and minor terms. That suitability and elaboration are lacking in the image describing Maggie; when we read simply that 'she was as open and transparent as a rock-pool' the minor term is insufficiently controlled to discipline our responses, to eliminate from our minds other aspects of a rock-pool which are irrelevant and undesirable at this point. ('A rock-pool is transparent, yes, but what do we see *in* it?') In other words, its arbitrariness is confirmed when we examine it in isolation instead of trying to relate it to a recurrent pattern.

This image, in fact, is one of three main kinds of eccentric image I wish to point to in George Eliot's work. The first of these occurs when the minor term is intrinsically odd or insufficient, or when it allows the wrong cluster of associa-tions to be attracted to it. The second category is caused by over-elaboration of the minor term so that the reader's attention is concentrated on it alone and not on its relation with its major partner; the third is caused by the imaginative gap between major and minor terms being so great that it is never bridged. Clearly these categories are convenient abstractions and we hardly ever find an example falling neatly into one category alone. Combinations of categories one and three, and two and three, are very common; rarer, but still fairly frequent, are combinations of categories one and two; when these occur, of course, the third category is also generally involved. With this proviso, let us look at some examples.

> (*a*) The best part of a woman's love is worship; but it is hard to her to be sent away with her precious spikenard rejected, and her long tresses too, that were let fall ready to soothe the weary feet. (37)
> (*b*) Now, however, it seemed that his inward peace was hardly more stable than that of republican Florence, and his heart no better than the alarm-bell that made work slack and tumult busy. (58)

I choose these two instances to represent my first category because whereas the arbitrariness of the rock-pool image in *The Mill On The Floss* may well result from its brevity and under-elaboration, it is clear that both these images are deliberately chosen and carefully worked out. Example (*b*) (which might also fall into my third category) clearly derives from the residual interests that one had thought fully worked out in *Romola*. Applied to Rex in *Daniel Deronda*, it is completely isolated; there is no longer pattern—say, of images drawn from the body politic—from which it might gain strength. In such isolation the two terms of the image hardly come together to give that particular kind of illumination, that suggestion of deeper strata of meaning, which we expect of a good image. The connections between the two terms are too easily exhausted and George Eliot has attempted to conceal this imaginative poverty by an illegitimate particularization in the minor term. But why *republican Florence* —what does this special reference add by way of suggestion or definition? It suggests a significant precision which isn't really there; the connections between major and minor terms are only—need only—be vague and general. Any alarm bell would do just as well for the minor term and in fact the historical reference draws one's attention from the major-minor relationship into an area of fact and speculation which is here quite irrelevant and distracting.

Example (*a*) is simpler but probably more important. It derives in general from George Eliot's variety of humanism, in particular from her conflation of two versions in the Gospels. While the spikenard comes from Mark xiv. 3, the main allusion is to Luke vii. 37-38:

> And behold, a woman in the city, which was a sinner, when she knew that Jesus sat at meat in the Pharisee's house, brought an alabaster box of ointment, and stood at his feet behind him weeping, and began to wash his feet with tears, and did wipe them with the hairs of her head, and kissed his feet, and anointed them with the ointment.

George Eliot's view of the Gospel story as a supremely moving and heroic but non-supernatural event allowed her the more readily to use it as a source of analogy.* If Christ is seen only in a human dimension the gap between him and the rest of mankind is narrowed to the extent that he becomes a prototype of a class of human beings who repeat on a diminished scale the pattern of experience he supremely embodied. From this view there stems in George Eliot's work a minor stream of biblical reference and quasi-blasphemous analogy, generally in a muted and disguised form; our present example is unusually explicit. As such, it exhibits the lack of controlled association typical of our first category, we cannot allow the woman with the ointment without also allowing the figure of Christ to enter the image. The analogy must be completed; we cannot accept one half of it and reject the other. While to many readers the mere allusion to Christ would make the image unacceptable, it may also be criticized as indecorous on purely literary grounds. Granted that it is a generalized comment, we still cannot divorce it from the particular situation and characters of *Felix Holt* and once we view it thus we see that there is in fact no major term to which it is in any way really appropriate. There are other grounds for criticism—the psychological truth of the general proposition which the image serves to elaborate is open to attack—but viewed simply in terms of its structure the passage can be rejected as rhetoric designed to dignify and ennoble by an illicit use of inappropriate associations.

One example of our second category, from *Felix Holt*, will suffice:

> All life seemed cheapened; as it might seem to a young student who, having believed that to gain a certain degree he must write a thesis in which he would bring his powers to bear with memorable effect, suddenly ascertained that no thesis was expected, but the sum (in English money) of twenty-seven pounds ten shillings and sixpence. (43)

* See p. 248.

This is a fairly simple type of eccentric image; we have here not merely the general oddness of the chosen minor term, but the astonishingly elaborate and particular detail of it. It reads as though George Eliot was here using her knowledge of an actual case; the point, however, is that the minor term creates a kind of little drama of its own which attracts the attention away from the major term to which it is supposed to relate; we get interested in the hopes and frustrations of the student and the connection between the two terms—here, *as it might seem*—is not strong enough to compel the unruly minor term into a proper subordination.

My third category generally exists as a result of the other two, but sometimes the minor term, though in itself controlled, simply fails to make contact with its major; I have in mind things like this description of Gwendolen Harleth's state of mind:

> The one result established for her was, that Deronda had acted simply as a generous benefactor, and the phrase 'reading Hebrew' had fleeted unimpressively across her sense of hearing, as a stray stork might have made its peculiar flight across her landscape without rousing any surprised reflection on its natural history. (48)

Finally, I will quote two passages where all categories break down and merge into each other, the result being extremely eccentric. The first is from *Felix Holt*, a passage in which George Eliot is trying to convey the interdependence of private and public lives. This is one of her favourite themes, but rarely can it have been expressed in so quaint a way:

> Even in that conservatory existence where the fair Camellia is sighed for by the noble young Pine-apple, neither of them needing to care about the frost or rain outside, there is a nether apparatus of hot-water pipes liable to cool down on a strike of the gardeners or a scarcity of coal. And the lives we are about to look back upon do not belong to those conservatory species; they

are rooted in the common earth, having to endure all the ordinary chances of past and present weather. (3)

My second example is from *Daniel Deronda*; the Rector, remembering gossip he has heard about Grandcourt, recalls that he:

> had received hints of former entangling dissipations, and an undue addiction to pleasure, though he had not foreseen that the pleasure which had probably, so to speak, been swept into private rubbish heaps, would ever present itself as an array of live caterpillars, disastrous to the green meat of respectable people. (64)

It would be tedious to expatiate at length on the eccentricity of these two images; I have probably, with the earlier examples, placed too great a burden on comparatively trivial details. The first, if we tease out its implications, suggests that the analogy has perhaps misled George Eliot in the logic of what she wants to say. What she does say is that the hothouse-socialite types, while not dependent on such a diverse range of chances, accidents and external influences as the common-or-garden variety, do depend *much more* on the fewer influences to which they are subject. (Anyway, if we wanted to argue out the analogy we would have to say that the common-or-garden variety is conditioned to its environment in a way that the hothouse species are not.) In fact, few of us, in any ordinary reading of the novel, would bother with the logic; what would immediately strike us— and perhaps repel us—is the grotesqueness of the conceit, the way in which it allows a vein of whimsy to enter which is not at all appropriate. The main reason why my second example is not acceptable is that it is inappropriate to the Rector; when we are considering any image of this kind we have, of course, to consider not only the internal decorum of its terms and the relation of individual image to any larger pattern, but also its dramatic suitability when given to a character. This particular image—and possibly the general feeling behind it—is not here appropriate; moreover, the metamorphosis of the general moral terms of the first half of the passage into the concrete image of the second half is too abrupt and strikes me as vaguely but disturbingly unpleasant.

I invoked just now that familiar safety clause, 'in any ordinary reading of the novel' and I would like to end this chapter by discussing briefly the relevance of the kind of concern manifested in it. With any extended work of art we quite rightly devote our main attention to the larger parts rather than to minute details. This is particularly true of a writer with such range and breadth as George Eliot. She has to be read in bulk if she is to be read rightly. With such a vast canvas confronting us we are properly concerned with major structural effects, with the relative placing of masses, with the overall effect of colour, light and shade. Her effects are largely cumulative, and because of this the tempo of our reading is so adjusted that we do not normally pause from page to page to consider details. Whole chapters and sections are our measure and it is only if we have a special critical purpose that we sharpen our focus to concentrate on the structure of a sentence or the nature of a particular image. What relation, then, does this special and extreme critical scrutiny bear to our normal reading? What interest does it afford or what value acquire?

The interest, as I hope I have shown, is largely symptomatic and negative. Through considering the status of a particular passage we may check a major diagnosis, through a study of aberration we may arrive at a clearer definition of normality. It is part of my main thesis that George Eliot's novels should be regarded as finely integrated works of art; if this is true, then the relation of part to whole—and even of the most minute constituent—should be of interest. We should know how far we can endorse Theodora's enthusiastic judgment in Henry James's dialogue on *Daniel Deronda*; 'The mass is for each detail and each detail is for the mass.' This may not be our main interest, but it is a valid secondary one. By and large, George Eliot's prose is a medium which rarely calls attention to itself. It is a continuum which we generally take for granted. But if the work of art is a truly achieved thing, we should be able to test both its strength and its weakness by a close scrutiny of the medium at any given point. In Chapter II, I tried to analyse one passage in some detail to show how it relates to its enveloping whole and how it reveals a great deal about the nature of George Eliot's talent. So in this chapter, by bringing together examples of certain types of imaginative habit, I hope to have shown how the details of a work may provide us with a check on the total achievement or limitation of George Eliot's art. It is a process of breaking-down and analysis which we do not normally undertake with novels of this kind, but it ought to be both possible and valuable if the total work of art is all that it claims to be.

CHAPTER X

Image and Symbol

THE concern with imagery, and especially with patterns of recurrent images which has been an outstanding feature of Shakespearian criticism during the last thirty years, has naturally infiltrated into the criticism of fiction. Despite the obvious enlightenment afforded by this approach, a primary or exclusive interest in image patterns is open to serious dangers. I discount the statistical analysis of imagery as a source of biographical information; the dangers of a naïve interpretation of such evidence are obvious, and in any case such investigation would be superfluous with George Eliot, whose life is sufficiently well-documented and whose tastes, ideas and moral outlook are amply articulated both within and outside her novels. Even as a purely critical tool, however, image-analysis can easily lead to dangerous excesses. It is liable to precisely the same kind of abstraction as the thematic approach which I discussed in an earlier chapter and it is even more vulnerable to mere ingenuity. It is, in one sense, an easy occupation—at its lowest, not much more than concordance-compiling—and it can easily beguile the critic into believing that it is a sufficient and acceptable substitute for criticism. Above all, it lends itself to a quantitative approach. Clearly, a single striking use of one image may be of far greater importance to the total work than a dozen routine or commonplace uses of another image. Yet the mere fact of recurrence is hypnotic and may mislead us into using a false critical arithmetic in which twelve times nothing amounts to more than one times one. Indeed, one advantage of the kind of minute scrutiny exemplified in the previous chapter is that it directs our attention to the *quality* of particular images. Of course, the routine or commonplace image may, rightly regarded, have

an important function, but the pleasure of recognizing recurrence is, after all, a very elementary criticial procedure.

There is, finally, the danger that by defining imagery in
too strict or formalistic a manner we may isolate one category
from the total range of linguistic patterns used by the novelist. In this way, although we may think that we are dealing
with the heart of the book, the very words which form the
raw material of abstractions like 'plot' or 'character', we shall
make imagery an abstraction just as open to wrong exploitation as these traditional concepts. We must always preserve
a firm sense of the relation of imagery to its total linguistic
context and must realize that the concept of imagery contains a range of different forms, functions and content.

An example from *The Mill On The Floss* will clarify this
concept of a scale of imagistic usage. The river in this novel
is obviously and centrally there as a literal fact; we are never
far way from it and to a large extent it governs the lives and
destinies of all the characters in the novel. It is a source of
Mr Tulliver's ruin; it is a source of Bob Jakin's livelihood.
Related to the river are a large number of images like this,
images consciously recognized as such by the reader:

> Maggie's destiny, then, is at present hidden, and we
> must wait for it to reveal itself like the course of an un-
> mapped river. We only know that the river is full and
> rapid; and that for all rivers there is the same final home.
> (VI. 6)

This kind of image is buttressed by frequent uses of
language like 'flood of emotion', 'current of feeling, 'stream
of vanity'. We should not underestimate these dead or
undeveloped metaphors. Cumulatively and unobtrusively
they may build up in the language a kind of emotional charge
or potential which is only released at some significant point
by the fully developed image. Indeed they are often the
explanation of the mysterious power such images seem to
possess. And these dead metaphors may also allow us to feel
reverberations of greater significance in an apparently

neutral and innocent phrase. When Maggie slips as she is getting into the boat with Stephen or when she tells Tom, 'I was carried too far in the boat to come back on Tuesday', we may feel that the extended non-literal sense of her slipping or her being carried too far is given validity because these phrases occur in a textural context given depth and density by the insistent but unnoticed accretion of these dead or sunken metaphors. This is why I said earlier that the routine or commonplace may have a distinct importance precisely because it is routine, commonplace and therefore unnoticed. There is no need to be conscious of such usages unless we are critically concerned to point out their function; indeed it is probably better that we should not be aware of them since they can generally do their work more effectively below the level of our conscious attention. Nor, of course, is there any need to assume conscious deliberation on the part of the author in order to justify them; this is simply one of the ways in which the creative imagination works.

Granted this, I wish to use the word 'image' very loosely and to discuss it within what I have called the total linguistic context, ranging freely up and down the scale of usage as occasion demands. The dangers of this method, of course, are a lack of clear definition and a greater temptation to ingenious over-reading, but I think that these are compensated for by the greater justice done to the complexity of the actual patterns of language created by the novelist. Similarly, I do not wish to get bogged down by the need for a precise definition of symbolism. Such definitions generally involve long and rather arid stretches of theoretical criticism which often lead us away from whatever particular work we are discussing. Recurrent images may cumulatively attach a symbolic significance to the literal source of those images; thus we should be justified in talking about river-symbolism in *The Mill On The Floss*. But a symbol does not need this imagistic backing; a scene, character or incident may become symbolic simply by the author's treatment of it or by its place in the context of the total work. As such it may be local

or it may be recurrent, pervasive and even basic to the meaning of the novel. Casaubon's house in *Middlemarch* is a
recurrent symbol, the river in *The Mill On The Floss* is
pervasive, the gold in *Silas Marner* is basic; for an example
of the purely local symbol which gains its significance from
its context we may return to *The Mill On The Floss*. In Book
III, Chapter 2, the Tulliver family are ruined; the bailiffs
are in the house and the household goods are to be auctioned.
Mrs Tulliver's concern is for her household linen:

> 'To think o' these cloths as I spun myself,' she went on,
> lifting things out and turning them over with an excite-
> ment all the more strange and piteous because the stout
> blond woman was usually so passive; if she had been
> ruffled before, it was at the surface merely; 'and Job
> Haxey wove 'em, and brought the piece home on his back,
> as I remember standing at the door and seeing him come,
> before I ever thought o' marrying your father! And the
> pattern as I chose myself—and bleached so beautiful, and
> I marked 'em so as nobody ever saw such marking—they
> must cut the cloth to get it out, for its a particular stitch.
> And they're all to be sold—and go into strange people's
> houses, and perhaps be cut with the knives, and wore out
> before I'm dead. You'll never have one of 'em, my boy,'
> she said, looking up at Tom, with her eyes full of tears,
> 'and I meant 'em for you. I wanted you to have all o' this
> pattern. Maggie could have had the large check—it never
> shows so well when the dishes are on it.'

This is both comic and pathetic because Mrs Tulliver has
at once a very imperfect and yet a very real sense of what
their ruin implies. On a naturalistic level it tells us a great
deal about the tangle of human relationships in the Tulliver
family. But it is symbolic in that it bears the full weight of
the materialistic ethos—with all its virtues and its limitations
—that pervades the society of the novel. The whole scene is
an image of what ruin in such a society can mean; behind the
bailiffs in the house and the linen to be scattered and sold to
strangers, we sense the disintegration of normality and a

P

traditional way of life which has held the household together.

This passage underlines one further point that should be
made about imagery and symbolism in the novel. In so far as
this passage can bear the weight of an extended meaning it
is because the scene is strong and true on a literal and
naturalistic level. For a scene or a person to be successfully
exploited as a symbol it must first be realized as a scene or a
person, as something forcefully existing in its own right.
One might add in the case of imagery that the success of any
one image will often depend on its intimate relation to the
whole network of similar images in the novel, though these
in themselves may be of the unobtrusive or routine kind; we
have seen examples of this in the previous chapter. This is
perhaps why so many of George Eliot's scientific images
strike us as arbitrary and unsuccessful; they derive from the
author's attitude to her novel rather than from any body of
life within the novel.

The close interdependence of imagery with its literal
counterpart can be seen from the fact that whereas George
Eliot generally establishes the literal fact or actual presence
—a river, a house, a person—first, and then derives a train
of imagery from it, she sometimes reverses the process and
transforms what has been metaphorically expressed into an
actual event. We have already seen something of the sort at
work in *Silas Marner*. This reversal is often finely exploited
for the purpose of anticipatory irony. Thus in Chapter 15 of
Adam Bede, Dinah is thinking about Hetty:

> Her thoughts became concentrated on Hetty, that
> sweet young thing, with life and all its trials before her—
> the solemn daily duties of the wife and mother—and her
> mind so unprepared for them all; bent merely on little
> foolish, selfish pleasures, like a child hugging its toys in
> the beginning of a long toilsome journey, in which it will
> have to bear hunger and cold and unsheltered darkness.

'The journey of life' is the kind of platitude that naturally
finds its place in Dinah's meditations; it is so commonplace

that we hardly notice it, despite its unusual elaboration. But it is a metaphorical foreshadowing of the actual journey Hetty will make to Windsor and back; life catches up with the metaphor. This interplay of literal and metaphorical need not, however, be primarily ironical. At the end of Chapter 18 we leave Hetty in a disillusioned state, in a 'moment of dull, bare, wintry disappointment and doubt'. This clearly contrasts with Adam's metaphorical vision of Hetty at the beginning of the next chapter:

> It was summer morning in his heart, and he saw Hetty in the sunshine; a sunshine without glare—with slanting rays that tremble between the delicate shadow of the leaves.

In the next chapter this vision is literally fulfilled:

> He could glance at her continually as she bent over the fruit, while the level evening sunbeams stole through the thick apple-tree boughs, and rested on her round cheek and neck as if they too were in love with her.

The way in which such images breed and develop, crossing the boundaries between mental and physical, imagined and actual, literal and metaphorical, is one way of giving depth and richness to the naturalistic substance of the novel without imposing an arbitrary significance on it.

Imagery in George Eliot's novels has several functions. It is, for instance, one means of characterization. Adam Bede sees life in terms of his trade, Mrs Poyser in terms of the farmyard, Bartle Massey in terms of the schoolhouse. But this use of imagery is not so frequent in George Eliot as is sometimes imagined, and the images shared by these three characters are at least as important as the images which differentiate them. What they have in common, of course— what all the characters in *Adam Bede* share—is imagery drawn from nature. Hayslope is a rural community, close to the soil, and thus this kind of imagery derives naturally from the realistic portrayal of the actual processes of life. It is also a kind of language which the characters share with their creator; the language of nature pervades and envelops the whole novel, underlining the community of man with man; of human, animal and inanimate life, stressing the order and continuity of things and reinforcing the awfulness of what is unnatural—of Hetty's murder of her child. This language of nature operates in a complex way, on several levels corresponding to the linguistic scale I described earlier in this chapter. We can only notice two or three of its constituent elements at this point.

The first level, nearest the literal and actual end of the scale, is that of simple description. The weather and the landscape are never described for their own sake in *Adam Bede*; they are always closely linked with human activities, with sowing, hay-making, harvesting. And while they may be described in non-metaphorical terms they often have a function akin to metaphor, in that they image or embody some major theme of the novel. Take, for example, the description of Arthur's birthday:

> Nature seems to make a hot pause just then—all the loveliest flowers are gone, the sweet time of early growth and vague hopes is past; and yet the time of harvest and ingathering is not come, and we tremble at the possible storms that may ruin the precious fruit in the moment of its ripeness. (22)

This reflects exactly the development of human relationships in the story; Arthur and Hetty, too, have reached this point. It is a note which is resumed at the beginning of Chapter 27, an interesting passage which explicitly denies any crude kind of pathetic fallacy but which allows a quasi-metaphorical extension of meaning, the statement of themes seem to be worked out in purely human terms:

> The 18th of August was one of these days, when the sunshine looked brighter in all eyes for the gloom that went before. Grand masses of cloud were hurried across the blue, and the great round hills behind the Chase seemed alive with their flying shadows; the sun was hidden for a moment, and then shone out warm again like

a recovered joy; the leaves, still green, were tossed off the hedgerow trees by the wind; around the farmhouses there was a sound of clapping doors; the apples fell in the orchards; and the stray horses on the green sides of the lanes and on the common had their manes blown about their faces. And yet the wind seemed only part of the general gladness because the sun was shining. A merry day for the children, who ran and shouted to see if they could top the wind with their voices; and the grown-up people, too, were in good spirits, inclined to believe in yet finer days, when the wind had fallen. If only the corn were not ripe enough to be blown out of the husk and scattered as untimely seed!

And yet a day on which a blighting sorrow may fall upon a man. For if it be true that Nature at certain moments seems charged with a presentiment of one individual lot, must it not also be true that she seems unmindful, unconscious of another? For there is no hour that has not its births of gladness and despair, no morning brightness that does not bring new sickness to desolation as well as new forces to genius and love. There are so many of us, and our lots are so different; what wonder that Nature's mood is often in harsh contrast with the great crisis of our lives? We are children of a large family, and must learn, as such children do, not to expect that our hurts will be made much of—to be content with little nurture and caressing, and help each other the more.

There is a great deal to admire here—the easy modulation from description to comment, the local felicity of 'untimely seed' (it is about now that Hetty's child is conceived), the way in which 'blighting sorrow' is revivified by its context and so on. But the important thing about the passage is its function within the total work.

If landscape and weather are closely related to human activities, then man is consistently seen in natural terms. Human life and growth are part of a larger natural process:

We can never recall the joy with which we laid our heads on our mother's bosom or rode on our father's back

in childhood; doubtless that joy is wrought up into our
nature, as the sunlight of long-past mornings is wrought
up in the soft mellowness of the apricot. (20)

The story itself is seen in these terms; at the end, with the
marriage of Dinah and Adam, Irwine asks himself 'what
better harvest from that painful seed-time could there
be?' (55)

Men and animals are close; to Mrs Poyser men are 'dumb
creatures' (24); Bartle Massey's mature students seem
'almost as if three rough animals were making humble
efforts to learn how they might become human' (21); a man
looks at Hetty 'with a slow bovine gaze' (37); Adam is seen
'chewing the cud of this new hope' (20); Bartle Massey
thinks of his pet bitch as 'the woman in the house' (21) and
his reflections on canine nature are also his reflections on
female nature. Hetty, too, is described in animal and natural
terms; she is 'like a bright cheeked apple hanging over the
orchard wall . . . a kitten' (19) and hers 'was a spring-like
beauty, it was the beauty of young frisking things' (7). But
this note changes after her seduction; in her journey to and
from Windsor she is gradually alienated from human nature
until she seeks shelter in a sheepfold; finally with the murder
of her child she is alienated from nature itself. In prison
'Hetty kept her eyes fixed on Dinah's face—at first like an
animal that gazes, and gazes, and keeps aloof' (45). Hetty
is so easily alienated because she lacks roots—another
commonplace which is given new metaphorical body in the
novel. 'There are some plants that have hardly any roots;
you may tear them from their native nook of rock or wall,
and just lay them over your ornamental flower pot, and they
blossom none the worse. Hetty could have cast all her past
life behind her, and never cared to be reminded of it again.'
(15)   She is the opposite of Mr Poyser who, when confronted with eviction, says, 'I should be loath to leave th' old
place and the parish where I was bred and born, and father
afore me. We should leave our roots behind us, I doubt, and
niver thrive again.' (32)

But the stunted quality of Hetty's moral life is not conveyed only in terms of animals; she is, after all, human, she is one child in Nature's large family. Thus the childishness of Hetty is equally insisted on, not only to point the pathos of her plight, but also to convey her moral narrowness. She is literally almost a child as Adam points out on several occasions—she is only seventeen when the action takes place. We have seen that Dinah thinks of her as a poor child, ill-equipped to deal with the demands of maturity; when she reads Arthur's letter she sees in the mirror 'a white marble face with rounded childish forms, but with something sadder than a child's pain' (31) and when pregnant she feels 'something else would happen—something *must* happen—to set her free from this dread. In young, childish, ignorant souls there is constantly this blind trust in some unshapen chance.' (35) (This, in Hetty, is a diminished parallel to Arthur's egoistic belief in the intervention of some benign Providence.) And if, at first in prison she is like an animal, later when she has repented and confessed, she obeys Dinah 'like a little child' (47). In this way, then, the central metaphor of Nature's family, at the beginning of Chapter 27, radiates throughout the book. Perhaps it is not accidental that Dinah (like Arthur and Hetty) is an only child and an orphan; of these three only she has learnt the lesson of the large family, 'not to expect that our hurts will be made much of—to be content with little nurture and caressing, and help each other the more'.

Natural imagery has one other main function in *Adam Bede* to assist in something like foreshortening, to convey the impression of a lengthy process in a short time. I am thinking particularly of the last chapter where George Eliot tries—unsuccessfully, I think—to distract our attention from the novelist's contriving hand by emphasizing Adam's courtship of Dinah as a process of nature. She insists on this; for example she speaks of:

the slight words, the timid looks, the tremulous touches,
by which two human souls approach each other gradually,

like two little quivering rain-streams, before they mingle in one. (50)

Here she does for Adam and Dinah what she has already done for Arthur and Hetty when she writes that they:

mingle as easy as two brooklets that ask for nothing but to entwine themselves and ripple with ever-interlacing curves into the leafiest hiding-places. (12)

Again, in Book VI George Eliot describes Adam's feelings:

Strange, till that moment the possibility of their ever being lovers had never crossed his mind, and yet now, all his longing suddenly went out towards that possibility; he had no more doubt or hesitation as to his own wishes than the bird that flies towards the opening through which the daylight gleams and the breath of heaven enters.

The autumnal Sunday sunshine soothed him; but not by preparing him with resignation to the disappointment if his mother—if he himself, proved to be mistaken about Dinah; it soothed him by gentle encouragement of his hopes. Her love was so like that calm sunshine that they seemed to make one presence to him, and he believed in them both alike. And Dinah was so bound up with the sad memories of his first passion, that he was not forsaking them, but rather giving them a new sacredness by loving her. Nay, his love for her had grown out of that past, it was the noon of that morning. (51)

We may well feel an element of rationalization and special pleading in Adam's meditation here; but if this attempt at foreshortening by the assimilation of human love to natural process does not quite succeed in *Adam Bede*, it does succeed, brilliantly, in *The Mill On The Floss*. I am thinking, of course, of Book VI, Chapter 13, in which Stephen and Maggie are, as the chapter heading says, 'borne along by the tide', in which Maggie's moral and emotional drift is conveyed in terms of the river until both literally and metaphorically she and Stephen pass the point of no return. We shall examine this chapter later; before we leave *Adam Bede* we should notice one other instance, not of functional imagery, but of the way in which insignificant objects may by their context be symbolically extended.

It has been often noticed that until Hetty's pregnancy is obvious, one of the few oblique signs of her seduction is the fate of her pink silk handkerchief. But this is linked up with the finery she so adores, the gimcrack jewellery she wears in her bedroom giving way to Arthur's presents as later she dresses for his birthday celebrations:

> There was something more to be done, apparently, before she put on her neckerchief and long sleeves, which she was to wear in the daytime, for now she unlocked the drawer that held her private treasures. It is more than a month now since we saw her unlock that drawer before, and now it holds new treasures, so much more precious than the old ones that these are thrust into the corner. Hetty would not care to put the large coloured glass earrings into her ears now; for see! she has got a beautiful pair of gold and pearls and garnet, lying snugly in a pretty little box lined with white satin. (22)

These jewels figure significantly later in the novel as a material index of Hetty's dwindling dreams and hopes—she has eventually to use them as security to raise the money for her homeward journey from Windsor. The hard facts of life overtake the pretty emblems of romance. But the jewellery does not, like the neckerchief, function simply as a means of hinting at that part of the story which cannot be explicitly told; it also allows, by extension, for contrasts of character. It is perhaps significant that Arthur gives Dinah no ornament but his watch and chain which he knows she will use. Again, when Adam goes to Hall Farm to court Hetty, he gives her not jewels but a rose which, he adds prudentially— it is a revealing touch—she can later put in water. But Hetty's mind is on Arthur and she can only treat Adam's gift as she would Arthur's:

> Hetty took the rose, smiling as she did so at the pleasant thought that Arthur could so soon get back if he liked.

There was a flash of hope and happiness in her mind, and with a sudden impulse of gaiety she did what she had very often done before—stuck the rose in her hair a little above the left ear. The tender admiration in Adam's face was slightly shadowed by reluctant disapproval. (20)

So far we have seen image and symbol as revealing character, as creating an enveloping natural background, as a foreshortening agent and as a device for conveying obliquely part of the plot of the novel. But image and symbol may have to carry much more of a novel's meaning than this. They may indeed be essential to the success of the whole novel in that they can persuade us to accept what we would reject if developed on a purely naturalistic plane. The clearest example of this is the function of the river in *The Mill On The Floss*. We have already seen that the end of the novel suffers, mainly for structural reasons, grave defects. George Eliot may not succeed in persuading us to overlook the designing, contriving hand of the novelist, but if we *are* persuaded it is largely because we feel that the final catastrophe has the kind of inevitability which is created by a continuous pressure of anticipation and foreboding throughout the novel. There is plenty of evidence of this pressure; Mrs Tulliver's repeatedly expressed fear, 'I thought so—wanderin' up an' down by the water, like a wild thing—she'll tumble in some day'; (I. 2); Maggie's childish view of the drowned witch; memories of previous floods; Phillip's dream which anticipates both Maggie's moral drift and the final catastrophe, 'in which he fancied Maggie was slipping down a glistening, green, slimy channel of a waterfall' (V. 8). The river is with us constantly from the very first sentence of the novel:

A wide plain, where the broadening Floss hurries on between its green banks to the sea, and the loving tide, rushing to meet it, checks its passage with an impetuous embrace.

The usual process of assimilating man and nature is here reversed; the natural is described in distinctively human terms. Normally, as we have seen, psychological or moral states are described in imagery derived from the river. Thus Wakem and Mr Tulliver are like the pike and the roach (III. 7); Stephen feels 'the stream of his recollections running rather shallow' (VI. 2); Phillip and Maggie reach 'one of those dangerous moments when speech is at once sincere and deceptive—when feeling, rising high above its average depth, leaves flood-marks which are never reached again' (V. 4); of Mr Tulliver, when sick, 'it was well that there was this interest of narrative to keep under the vague but fierce sense of triumph over Wakem, which would otherwise have been the channel his joy would have rushed into with dangerous force' (V. 6).

This kind of language is especially used to define Maggie's relations with Stephen; before the crisis she feels, 'If it were *not* wrong—if she were once convinced of that, and need no longer beat and struggle against this current, soft and yet strong as the summer stream' (VI. 11), while afterwards she recalls 'the tremulous delights of his presence with her that made existence an easy floating in a stream of joy' (VI. 14). This last phrase sums up the quality of the experience presented in the crucial Chapter 13 of Book VI, which is the exactly right metaphorical equivalent of the moral crisis through which Maggie passes and which, by its very success, throws the final scene of flood and drowning a little out of balance. In both cases one notices how the river is not only there as an actual presence but how it provides terms which can illuminate the inner life of the characters; thus at the very end is it when 'Tom had pushed off and they were on the wide water—he face to face with Maggie—that the full meaning of what had happened rushed upon his mind. It came with so overpowering a force—it was such a new revelation to his spirit, of the depths in life' (VII. 5), or again, when Maggie feels that 'there was no choice of courses, no room for hesitation and she floated into the current' (VII. 5), the two meanings—the literal course of the river and the choice of action—coalesce into the one phrase.

How far the sustained energy of this kind of language counteracts the structural defects of the novel is one of the basic critical questions confronting the reader of *The Mill On The Floss*. I do not think that George Eliot completely dispels our misgivings. But certainly there is no clash between the symbolism and the naturalistic surface such as we find when she uses the same vein of imagery in *Romola*. One must surely disagree with Mrs Hardy[1] when she lumps the two novels together with the comment that 'This solidity and ease is found . . . in the river images in *The Mill On The Floss* and *Romola*, though in these last two it has the other function of giving the story a twist into fantasy.' For one thing no actual river in the later novel has the central status of the Floss; it is the city of Florence which attracts our attention. There are, it is true, the usual subdued metaphors —'invisible currents of feeling' (6), 'undercurrent of consciousness' (20), 'the little rills of selfishness had united and made a current' (9)—and so on, and these are elaborated when George Eliot deals with the drifting apart of Romola and Tito. On Romola's part, she is 'cold and motionless as locked waters' (32), while Tito 'went on in a clear voice, under which she shuddered as if it had been a narrow cold stream coursing over a hot cheek' (32). But this is insufficient textural preparation for the crucial chapter in which Romola drifts towards a rebirth; one feels that this scene is inadequately rooted in a body of created life and that consequently its symbolism is arbitrary and externally imposed. There is a hint of this in a letter from George Eliot to Sara Hennell in which she writes:

> The various *strands* of thought I had to work out forced me into a more ideal treatment of Romola than I had foreseen at the outset—though the 'Drifting Away' and the Village with the Plague belonged to my earliest vision of the story and were by deliberate forecast adopted as romantic and symbolical elements. (*Haight*, IV, p. 104)

[1] The references to Mrs Hardy in this chapter are all from the article cited on p. 214, n 1.

One feels with 'Drifting Away' (61) that the novel has suddenly been jerked into a different mode of writing and that the trouble lies precisely in the too 'ideal treatment' of Romola herself. Romola is entirely too theoretical; her dilemma is treated in exclusively moral terms and the analysis of her does not achieve that human intimacy of which George Eliot at her best is capable.

One important aspect of George Eliot's growth to full artistic maturity is the increasingly economic way in which she uses imagery for purposes at once more precise and more complex. I do not mean that her works become more sparsely imaged; *Middlemarch* is easily the richest of them from this point of view. By economy I mean the way in which she can make one image or one pattern of images do a greater amount of work than in the early novels. Imagery located in a character's consciousness tends to grow in importance as against imagery of comment and thus, as Mrs Hardy observes, creates in yet another way 'a private ironical understanding between author and reader'. Revelation of character and implicit evaluation of a character's attitude thus tend to coalesce; the need for omniscient guidance diminishes.

We should, perhaps, distinguish between the kind of imagery which is constant in all of George Eliot's novels and the kind of imagery which is distinctive of one novel. In the first category one would place imagery drawn from nature or from music which is, especially in *The Mill On The Floss* but strongly so in all the novels, a source of metaphor conveying the emotional quality of a character's life. Stephen's enchantment of Maggie rarely lacks a musical accompaniment. An example of the distinctive kind of image which also serves to show George Eliot's increasing maturity is the vein of artistic and especially theatrical imagery in *Daniel Deronda*.

As always, we have the literal counterpart of the image pattern. There is Herr Klesmer—one of the few convincing geniuses of fiction; there is Deronda's mother in whom life and the stage are one and continuous—'I am not a loving woman. That is the truth. It is a talent to love—I lacked it. Others have loved me—and I have acted their love' (53). There is Mirah who tends to see things in terms of her experience of the theatre:

> Her peculiar life and education had produced in her an extraordinary mixture of unworldliness, with knowledge of the world's evil, and even this knowledge was a strange blending of direct observation with the effects of reading and theatrical study. Her memory was furnished with abundant passionate situation and intrigues, which she never made emotionally her own, but felt a repelled aloofness from, as she had done from the actual life around her. Some of that imaginative knowledge began now to weave itself around Mrs Grandcourt. (52)

Life overtakes the theatre for Mirah—'What I have read about and sung about and seen acted, is happening to me' (61). But we do not feel that she deserves Mordecai's pontifical warning:

> My sister, thou hast read too many plays, where the writers delight in showing the human passions as indwelling demons, unmixed with the relenting and devout elements of the soul. Thou judgest by the plays and not by thy own heart. (61)

This admonition applies more forcibly to Gwendolen than to Mirah. For if theatrical imagery helps to establish Mirah's innocence, it equally helps to establish Gwendolen's ignorance. On a naturalistic level Gwendolen is a fumbling amateur compared with Klesmer or Deronda's mother or even Mirah; the height of her achievement can only be graceful posturing in charades (which are to drama as Gwendolen is to real life). Her professional hopes are blasted by Klesmer in a scene which equals anything in *The Tragic Muse*; he tells her to 'clear your mind of these notions, which have no more resemblance to reality than a pantomime' (23). It is as a pantomime that Gwendolen's relations with Rex are defined:

The elders were not in the least alive to this agitating drama which went forward chiefly in a sort of pantomime extremely lucid in the minds thus expressing themselves, but easily missed by spectators. (7)

Later the narrowness of Gwendolen's egoistic outlook is similarly conveyed; hers was a 'consciousness which was busy with a small social drama almost as little penetrated by a feeling of wider relations as if it had been a puppet show' (14). It is essentially Gwendolen rather than Mirah who sees life as a play and her playing at life is no more accomplished and much more disastrous than her theatrical ambitions. (We are reminded of another egoistical heroine, Rosamund Vincy, who 'was by nature an actress of parts that entered into her *physique*; she even acted her own character, and so well, that she did not know it to be precisely her own'.) Playing pantomimes with the innocuous Rex is one thing; when Gwendolen attempts to practise her art on Grandcourt the results can only be catastrophic. But try she does and at first Grandcourt is prepared to accept her on her own terms:

Grandcourt preferred the drama; and Gwendolen, left at ease, found her spirits rising continually as she played at reigning. (28)

Everything seems well. 'Gwendolen was just then enjoying the scenery of her life' (29); she was 'the heroine of an admired play without the pains of art' (31). She soon realizes, however, that she had more than met her match in her husband. Grandcourt, to whom appearances are everything, turns on her with:

Oblige me in future by not showing whims like a mad woman in a play . . . you will please to behave as becomes my wife and not make a spectacle of yourself. (36)

And painfully keeping up appearances is what Gwendolen's married life amounts to.

Constantly she had to be on the scene as Mrs Grandcourt; and to feel herself watched in that part by the exacting eyes of a husband who had found a motive to exercise his tenacity—that of making his marriage answer all the ends he chose, and with the more completeness the more he discerned any opposing will in her. And she herself, whatever rebellion might be going on within her, could not have made up her mind to failure in her representation. (44)

The image of the theatre is of course a natural vehicle for expressing the favourite theme of all thematic critics, one which is to be found in well-nigh all great novels—the theme of illusion and reality. But if Gwendolen's egoism, her moral narrowness and her power of being taken in by appearances —since at the outset appearances *are* reality to her—if all these are defined and evaluated for us by theatrical imagery, so too is the capacity for education and for painful moral growth which distinguishes her from Grandcourt, the civilized mask which conceals a moral vacuum. This countermovement begins even before her marriage and it centres naturally on Deronda. Gwendolen is acutely aware of him; 'she seemed to herself to be doing nothing but notice him; everything else was automatic performance of an habitual part' (29). This growth is further indicated by the widening of her vision which enables her to see herself as something other than the heroine of a play; at the very moment when she feels just that, on her wedding day, she also feels something else:

When her husband said 'Here we are at home!' . . . it was no more than the passive acceptance of a greeting in the midst of an absorbing show. Was not all her hurrying life of the last three months a show, in which her consciousness was a wondering spectator? (31)

Deronda tells her that 'some real knowledge would give you an interest in the world beyond the small drama of personal desires' (36); that 'real knowledge' Gwendolen can only acquire by the experience of suffering and by realizing that her part in the drama of life is not the glamorous and applauded thing she took it to be.

If imagery thus simultaneously expresses and evaluates

the moral nature of one character it may also be one means of conveying the quality of moral vision which permeates and informs a whole novel. To illustrate this fully would clearly demand a disproportionate amount of space; thus I shall hope to indicate some aspects of this most complex and inclusive function of imagery by isolating one kind of image which, although it recurs throughout the whole of George Eliot's work, is particularly dominant in *Middlemarch*. I stressed in the chapter on the aesthetic bases of George Eliot's work that one of her imperatives is 'only connect' and I have tried to show how complex the modes of connection may be, not only in the relation of one part of a book to its whole, but also as a central and determining structural principle. The interweaving of concurrent stories, the emphasis on cause and effect, the placing and relationships of characters, the social analysis, the operations of the omniscient author—all these, as well as the use of imagery, reflect George Eliot's concern with the various processes of life we have labelled 'connections'. The imagery of entanglement in its various forms is the textural counterpart of the novel's structure. At least at two points in *Middlemarch* George Eliot uses one of her favourite connective images to express not just her deepest sense of what life in all its complications is like, but also her awareness of the novelist's duty to give form and significance to the flux and chaos of existence while at the same time acknowledging that the flux and the chaos will always remain. One instance I have already quoted but it is worth repeating since both the image and the concept it expresses are seminal of a large part of the novel's texture; it comes at the opening of Chapter 15— George Eliot has been commenting on Fielding's use of digressions:

> I at least have so much to do in unravelling certain human lots, and seeing how they were woven and interwoven, that all the light I can command must be concentrated on this particular web, and not dispersed over that tempting range of relevances called the universe.

Q

Again, at the opening of the Finale, when justifying her
sense of that continuum of time in which her novels are
placed, that sense of an over-arching and enveloping human
context which must transcend any one novel, she writes:

> Every limit is a beginning as well as an ending. Who
> can quit young lives after being long in company with
> them, and not desire to know what befell them in their
> after-years? For the fragment of a life, however typical, is
> not the sample of an even web; promises may not be kept,
> and an ardent outset may be followed by declension;
> latent powers may find their long-waited opportunity; a
> past error may urge a grand retrieval.

There are many different kinds of webs in *Middlemarch*;
that stretching into the past:

> Mentally surrounded with that past again, Bulstrode
> had the same pleas—indeed the years had been perpetu-
> ally spinning them into intricate thickness, like masses of
> spider-web, padding the moral sensibility. (61)

Opposed to this there is the web stretching into the future,
spun by Lydgate and Rosamund. (We are surely warned
here, if warning were needed, by George Eliot's comment
on the courtship of Dorothea and Casaubon—'Has any one
pinched into its pilulous smallness the cobweb of pre-
matrimonial acquaintanceship?' Certainly, we may reply, not
Lydgate and Rosamund.)

> Young love-making—that gossamer web! Even the
> points it clings to—the thing whence its subtle inter-
> lacings are swung—are scarcely perceptible; momentary
> touches of fingertips, meetings of rays from blue and dark
> orbs, unfinished phrases, lightest changes of cheek and
> lip, faintest tremours. The web itself is made of spon-
> taneous beliefs and indefinable joys, yearnings of one life
> towards another, visions of completeness, indefinite trust.
> And Lydgate fell to spinning that web from his inmost
> self with wonderful rapidity. . . . As for Rosamund, she
> was in the water-lily's expanding wonderment at its own

fuller life, and she too was spinning industriously at the mutual web. (36)

The web, as we know, soon turns into something else for Rosamund and Lydgate and as that relationship changes in quality so does the imagery expressing it. Indeed, the web itself is a good metaphor for the operation of George Eliot's imagery; one strand of language connects with or crosses another, so that at whatever point we start we are led, by intersections and interactions, to perceive the pattern of the whole. Thus Bulstrode's web is not far from the labyrinthine imagery attached to Casaubon; both are creatures of dark, tortuous paths in which they not only lose their way but actually seek to lose it, Bulstrode in order to free himself of his guilty past, Casaubon in order to purge himself of the suspicion that all his scholarly endeavours are futile. Similarly the web as an ensnaring thing merges naturally with other images of entanglement and enslaving relations. Dorothea feels thus when she has to face the fact that her husband's ambitions may govern her even from the grave:

> Neither law nor the world's opinion compelled her to do this—only her husband's nature and her own compassion, only the ideal and not the real yoke of marriage. She saw clearly enough the whole situation, yet she was fettered; she could not strike the stricken soul that entreated hers. (48)

Fred Vincy occasionally backslides from his efforts at reformation; he feels that 'It was a little too bad . . . that he should be kept in the traces with more severity than if he had been a clergyman' (66). But Caleb Garth speaks the truth about Fred; 'Marriage is a taming thing. Fred would want less of my bit and bridle' (68). In this, Fred Vincy is only a light and sketchy adumbration of the plight of Lydgate. In two crucial scenes Farebrother warns Lydgate that independence is necessary to his scientific integrity; he must not get entangled. And Farebrother should know; he has chosen a wrong vocation and can never be more than an amateur naturalist. He tells Lydgate:

> You must keep yourself independent. Very few men can do that. Either you slip out of service altogether, and become good for nothing, or you wear the harness and draw a good deal where your yoke-fellows pull you. (17)

What Lydgate must keep clear of is Middlemarch intrigue, getting into debt and binding himself with the wrong kind of family ties. And, of course, it is in precisely these three ways that he entangles himself. Already, by the time of Farebrother's warning, 'Lydgate was feeling the hampering threadlike pressure of small social conditions, and their frustrating complexity' (18). Already, professionally and personally, he is caught up in the gossip of Middlemarch, which is such an important factor in the interwoven strands of the novel and which is given so precise an image in the picture of 'Mrs Taft, who was always counting stitches and gathered her information in misleading fragments caught between the rows of her knitting' (26). And since Lydgate is only one stitch in the pattern of Middlemarch life, his flirtation with Rosamund cannot remain a private affair:

> It was not more possible to find social isolation in that town than elsewhere, and two people persistently flirting could by no means escape from the 'various entanglements, weights, blows, clashings, motions by which things severally go on'. (31)

We have seen in Chapter 2 how his engagement to Rosamund fits in this pattern, and the web of love they spin soon turns into something else under the pressure of married life. Marriage closes like pincers upon Lydgate; he is soon 'bowing his neck under the yoke' (58), soon afraid of sinking 'into the hideous fettering of domestic hate' (65). Like Fred he makes momentary and futile attempts to escape:

> Under the first galling pressure of foreseen difficulties, and the first perception that his marriage, if it were not to

be a yoked loneliness, must be a state of effort to go on loving without too much care about being loved, he had once or twice tried a dose of opium. (66)

But he has to learn to carry his burden as best he can, accepting Rosamund's 'dumb mastery' and the hampering, entangling pressure of the world, acquiescing finally in his trap.

This kind of language, which is only occasionally elaborated into overt metaphor and which unobtrusively but insistently expressed the twistings and turnings of the life portrayed, reflects perhaps the deepest and most inclusive function of George Eliot's imagery. It is, as Mark Schorer (who has written very cogently of the imagery of *Middlemarch*) says, 'language as used to create a certain texture and tone which in themselves state and define themes and meanings; or language, the counters of our ordinary speech, as forced, through conscious manipulation, into those larger meanings which our ordinary speech almost never intends'.[2]

Or, as George Eliot maintains at the end of Chapter 50 of *Adam Bede*:

> Those slight words and looks and touches are part of the soul's language; and the finest language, I believe, is chiefly made up of unimposing words, such as 'light', 'sound', 'stars', 'music'—words really not worth looking at, or hearing, in themselves, any more than 'chips' or 'sawdust': it is only that they happen to be the signs of something unspeakably great and beautiful. I am of your opinion that love is a great and beautiful thing too; and if you agree with me the smallest signs of it will not be chips and sawdust to you; they will rather be like those little words, 'light' and 'music', stirring the long-winding fibres of your memory, and enriching your present with your most precious past.

[2] M. Schorer, *Fiction and the Analogical Matrix* in *Critiques and Essays In Modern Fiction*, pp. 83-100. N.Y.: The Ronald Press, 1952.

Notes

CHAPTER I

*If we can admit evidence of so late a date (November 8, 1903), James makes this point himself in a letter to Howard Sturgis, returning the proofs of *Belchamber*:

> I am a bad person, really, to expose 'fictitious work' to—I, as a battered producer and 'technician' myself have long ceased inevitably to read with *naïveté*; I can only read critically, constructively, *re*constructively, writing the thing over (if I can swallow it at all) *my* way, and looking at it, so to speak, from within.

CHAPTER III

* While Mrs Bennett makes the right point, her choice of illustration is curious. She quotes this passage from Chapter 20 of *Adam Bede*:

> 'Nay, nay, mother,' said Adam gravely, and standing still while he put his arm on her shoulder, 'I'm not angered. But I wish, for thy own sake, thee'dst be more contented to let me do what I've made up my mind to do. I'll never be other than a good son to thee as long as we live. But a man has other feelings beside what he owes to's father and mother, and thee oughtna to want to rule over me body and soul. And thee must make up thy mind, as I'll not give way to thee where I've a right to do what I like. So let us have no more words about it.'

Surely we cannot call this 'gratuitous didacticism'? I read it rather as the entirely natural outburst of feeling of a grown man resenting his mother's too firm grasp of the apron-strings. It is only faintly coloured by Adam's naturally sententious cast of mind. I quote this instance of a discontinuity between a point and its illustration as an example of the way in which a valid critical point of view may covertly enlarge its scope until it encompasses irrelevant or even hostile material.

† This is a curious chapter, deserving closer analysis than I can give it. Probably it is the result of conflicting artistic impulses. On the one hand George Eliot, having put the main stress on the prison scene, does not want two climaxes so close together, while on the other hand

she cannot resist the dramatic possibilities of a last-minute reprieve. So she has made the chapter almost casual in its brevity and at the same time has tried to arouse excitement by using the historic present.

‡ If we were to trace the semantic biography of this phrase, I conjecture that one of its important ancestors would turn out to be Coleridge's 'willing suspension of disbelief for the moment, which constitutes poetic faith' (*Biographia Literaria*, Chapter 14). Coleridge was writing about a particular aspect of the *Lyrical Ballads*, but the phrase and its various descendants have been widely applied both to the drama and the novel. This extension of meaning, whereby a phrase valid in one context has been transferred without examination to a different context, has involved a good deal of confusion, one aspect of which I have barely touched on in this chapter. As an antidote and an indication of a more profitable approach to George Eliot's work, I would invoke Dr Johnson, 'Imitations produce pain or pleasure, not because they are mistaken for realities, but because they bring realities to mind' (*Preface to Shakespeare*).

§ Statistics count for little in aesthetic matters, especially when they ignore the length, placing or quality of instances; but for what it is worth, my count of omniscient intrusions in my edition of the novels gives the following ratio of instances to pages. *Adam Bede* 1:10. *The Mill On The Floss* 1:14. *Middlemarch* 1:33. This serves at least to underline the growing economy in George Eliot's use of the convention.

‖ Of course, one reason why this is a local success is that it is not entirely local. It is taken up in the same chapter (Chapter 69) when we encounter Mr Trumbull's auctioneering methods:

Six pounds—six guineas—a *Guydo* of the first order going at six guineas—it is an insult to religion, ladies; it touches us all as Christians, gentlemen, that a subject like this should go at such a low figure—six pounds ten—seven.

In a wider context still this relates to the mixture of piety and worldliness we find in the Bulstrodes. It is this mixture which distinguishes the *Middlemarch* passage from the simple humour of an earlier treatment of the point in *Mr Gilfil's Love Story*, Chapter 4:

For as for them furrin churches as Sir Cristifer is so unaccountable mad after, wi' pictures o' men an' women a-showing themselves just for all the world as God made 'em, I think, for my part, as it's almost a sin to go into 'em.'

CHAPTER V

* There is, in fact, one irregularity in the time-scheme; unimportant but curious when we bear in mind how meticulous were George Eliot's habits as a novelist, how by careful reading and enquiry she built up the background and the historical flavour of the period with which she was concerned. The point, briefly, is this: the novel begins on Tuesday, July 1799, which corresponds exactly with the real calendar day of that year. It continues correctly enough until August 18th—we are told the date but not the day, but if chronological consistency is maintained the 18th must be a Sunday. This is most improbable considering the events of that day; it is certainly represented as a normal working day. Later we are told that it is Sunday, November 2nd; this agrees neither with the calendar nor with the time-scheme as maintained within the novel itself. Finally the events of 1800 agree neither with the calendar nor with the time scheme of 1799 but are internally consistent.

CHAPTER VII

* This instance is noted by Leavis in *The Great Tradition*. I cannot, however, accept Leavis's valuation of Mary Garth without some reserve. George Eliot is not always sure in her handling of the character; there is for instance a wrongness of tone—surely unintended—in Mary's refusal to tamper with Featherstone's will.

'I cannot help that, sir. I will not let the close of your life soil the beginning of mine.' (*Middlemarch*, Chapter 29)

CHAPTER IX

* This persists in her work from the very beginning. See, for example, the very explicit instance at the end of Chapter 4 of *Janet's Repentance*.

Bibliography

I have listed only those books and articles which I have found useful in writing this study. A complete bibliography is in progress. I have not listed any editions of George Eliot since all the quotations in the text are given chapter and not page references. Place of publication is London unless otherwise stated.

(A) HENRY JAMES ON GEORGE ELIOT

For fuller details see the *Bibliography of Henry James* (ed. Edel and Laurence, London, 1957).

1. 'Felix Holt, The Radical', *The Nation*, 3, 16 Aug. 1866, pp. 127-8.
2. 'The Novels of George Eliot', *Atlantic Monthly*, 18, 1866, pp. 479-92.
3. 'Middlemarch', *Galaxy*, 15, 1873, pp. 424-8.
4. 'Daniel Deronda: A Conversation', *Atlantic Monthly*, 38, 1876, pp. 684-94.
5. 'The Life of George Eliot', *Atlantic Monthly*, 55, 1885, pp. 668-78.

Items 4 and 5 were reprinted in *Partial Portraits* (1888); Item 2 in *Views and Reviews* (Boston, 1902); Item 1 in *Notes and Reviews* (Cambridge, Mass., 1921); Item 3 in *Nineteenth Century Fiction*, 8, 1953, pp. 161-70, and in *The House of Fiction* (ed. Edel, 1957). Item 4 is most easily to be found in an appendix to *The Great Tradition* by F. R. Leavis.

(B) BOOKS AND PARTS OF BOOKS

Bennett, J., *George Eliot*, 1948.
Hardy, B., *The Novels of George Eliot*, 1959.
Holloway, J., *The Victorian Sage*, 1953.
Kettle, A., *Introduction to the English Novel*, Vol. I, 1951.
Kitchel, A. T., *George Lewes and George Eliot*, New York, 1933.
Leavis, F. R., *The Great Tradition*, 1948.

Speaight, R., *George Eliot*, 1954.
Van Ghent, D., *The English Novel: Form and Function*, New York, 1953.

(C) ARTICLES

Beatty, J., 'Visions and Revisions; Chapter 81 of *Middlemarch*', *P.M.L.A.*, 72, 1952, pp. 662-72.
Bissell, C. 'Social Analysis in the novels of George Eliot', *English Literary History*, 18, 1951, pp. 221-39.
Diekhoff, J. S., 'The happy ending of *Adam Bede*', *English Literary History*, 3, 1936, pp. 221-7.
Hough, G., 'George Eliot', *Horizon*, 17, 1948, pp. 50-62.
Hussey, M., 'Structure and Imagery in *Adam Bede*', *Nineteenth Century Fiction*, 10, 1955, pp. 115-129.
Naumann, W., 'The architecture of George Eliot's novels', *Modern Language Quarterly*, 9, 1948, pp. 37-56.
Parlett, M., 'The influence of contemporary criticism on George Eliot', *Studies in Philology*, 30, 1933, pp. 103-32.
Steiner, G., 'A Preface to *Middlemarch*', *Nineteenth Century Fiction*, 9, 1954, pp. 262-79.

Index